PRAISE FOR

Brandon Davis Jennings

"Brandon Davis Jennings inevitably positions himself as the descendant of postmodernists such as Joseph Heller and Tim O'Brien while standing alongside other twenty-first-century veteran fiction writers such as Kevin Powers and Phil Klay. What separates Jennings from these better-known authors is his unwillingness to entertain the notion that his writing might actually illuminate something about the experience of war. In comparison to the gleefully dark meaninglessness of *Battle Rattle*, the horror and absurdity of Heller's gags or the compulsive amorality of O'Brien's reiterations of events seem nearly as quaint as the moral formulations those writers sought to overturn."
—Frank Fucile, *War, Literature and the Arts*

"Jennings is an intense and masterful story-teller, and like a blood-soaked boot kick in the gut followed by a chaser of whiskey and razor wire, *Battle Rattle* delivers in spades. I couldn't put this book down."
— Brian Castner, author of *All the Ways We Kill and Die* and *The Long Walk*

"Read *Battle Rattle* and find yourself eagerly surrendering to the superior force — the mastery — of a writer telling a story that every American needs to hear."
— Jay Baron Nicorvo, author of *The Standard Grand* and Deadbeat

"*Battle Rattle* ... scrubs the varnish off of the war narrative we've come to expect, and finds the strange and oft-ignored ornaments of our stressed-out and recuperating world."
— Matthew Gavin Frank, author of *The Mad Feast* and *Preparing the Ghost*

"Reading Brandon Davis Jennings is kind of like being a camel snared in razor wire: brutal and excruciating as these stories may be, you can't stop reading any more than that camel can untangle itself and get free."
—Thisbe Nissen, author of *Out iof the Girls' Room and Into the Night* and *Osprey Island*

"The stories in Brandon Jennings's Waiting for the Enemy startle not with graphic evocations of war but with how deeply they cut to the essence of soldiers' lives and thoughts, their fears and regrets. It isn't a brutal honesty; such a characterization would imply gratuitousness and showmanship. Rather, it's a simple honesty, and, because of this, his stories—by turns funny and horrifying, familiar and disturbing—are not at all simple. It is a hard thing to tell the truth. But here it is, in all its complexity and wonder."
—Mark Brazaitis, author of *The River of Lost Voices: Stories from Guatemanla* and *The Incurables: Stories*

"Much of his prose involving the American military experience is part of the best being written today."
—Hugh J. Martin, author of *The Stick Soldiers*.

"Jennings continues to establish himself as one of our most important chroniclers of America's twenty-first century wars. In an era when the vast majority of us have no direct, personal connection to the combat and its toll, Jennings describes men so true-to-life--admirable and pitiable...there's immense artistry underpinning the book, artistry that's never showy but ever-present. Simultaneously graceful and a gut-punch."
—Adam Schiutema, author of *Freshwater Boys* and *Haymaker*

ISBN: 978-0692717103

2nd Edition

All of these stories, aside from *High Desert Rats*, were first published elsewhere."Bosnian Roulette" first appeared in *Hayden's Ferry Review*. "Boots" first appeared in *Monkeybicycle*. "Bosnian Roulette", "Boots", "Waiting for the Enemy", "The Last Story My Father Told Me", and "Another Shoddy Moonlit Apocalypse" (now chapter 2 and chapter 6 of *High Desert Rats* respectively) were published first by *Iron Horse Literary Review* as the winning chapbook of their 2012 single author chapbook competition, and that chapbook, *Waiting for the Enemy,* was re-released by Amazon as a Kindle Single. *Battle Rattle* was first released as a Kindle Single as well. Chapter 7 of *Battle Rattle* was originally published as "Spectres" in *The Baltimore Review*. And Chapter 9 of *Battle Rattle* was first published as "Deflated" in *The Ghost Town Literary Magazine*. I owe thanks to each and every one of the editors at all of those magazines and to the many, many people who helped me to get my stories into their hands.

ACKNOWLEDGMENTS

Thanks and gratitude for the help I've received while writing this book are due to many people. First I have to thank Andrew Eisenman at Kindle Singles for believing in what I'm doing, and for helping me to share the work with the world, and thanks to Tim Johnston at *Little Presque Books* for his editorial help on all those essays that *will* get out into the world soon.

I am grateful to Hugh J. Martin for his constant support (including his help with my feeble attempts at poetry) and his ability to tell me the truth even when I don't want to hear it.

I owe years of thanks to Dustin M. Hoffman, who was with me back in the MFA days at BGSU for helping me to care about my sentences as much as I care about the ideas that those sentences are designed to communicate. You kept me from going over the edge, dude; that's not an exaggeration.

Other folks who played major roles in shaping these stories (and who deserve much more thanks than a mere name mention) are: Thisbe Nissen, Theresa Williams, Wendell Mayo, Lawrence Coates, Mark Brazaitis, Dan Mancilla, Emily Stinson, Laurie Ann Cedilnik, Jon Robert Adams, David Johnson, Leslie Jill Patterson, Jeremy Wilson, Clint Monson, Andrew Wickenden, Megan Ayers, Lydia Fettig, Stuart Dybek, Jamie Gordon, and all the people in those many, many workshop who told me "nice dialogue" because they had no idea what else to say.

Tom Schaefer: BGSU was the best of times and the worst of times; I can't believe that we both have wives and daughters who love us. How is that for weight *and* merit?

I am also deeply indebted to my parents, James and Lisa Jennings, for being there each time I needed them no matter how stupid my decisions were and for helping me to land on my feet more than once; I love you both. To my brother, Ryan, for being there for me when things were ugly and for continuing to work his way through life, one day at a time, even when things aren't always going the way he'd hoped. To Ang, John, and A.J. for keeping the family growing down in the hollers of Monroe County, W.V.

Eric Smallwood: thank you for being much more than just the drummer in a band I played in a million years ago, for talking with me about things most people wouldn't care about, and for raising hell with me in Ireland. And, of course, for making such a great cover for this book; we finished something together, and it only took decade. We ought to drink a couple Scrumpy Jacks to celebrate soon, but I'm guessing we won't.

To all my friends over the years who helped me to survive, thank you. This book wouldn't have been possible without the support of so many people, some of whom bear the same names as characters in this book. Cammack, I'm sorry you died in the book; I'm glad you're alive and well in Texas. Manchin, sorry you died in the book; I'm glad you're alive too. Harris, sorry you died in the book; I have no idea where you are, but I'm imagining that you're alive and well somewhere.

Matt Reed: I owe you big for your handgun expertise and your ability to realize that you were not, in fact, having a seizure while reading the first edition of the book. We probably should just brew a new beer since the last one is almost as old Shannon now, and I still haven't tried it.

The largest amount of thanks, though, is due to my wife, Tina. If not for you, babe, there is no way I would've been able to do this. You've helped me to have the confidence and the drive to finish the countless projects I'd started and gave up on. You are the reason I continue to work at this (at anything really), and I owe you more than I can possibly repay in one lifetime. Because of you, I also get to thank Shannon, our amazing daughter, who has, without words, done so much to inspire me to keep writing stories that I believe must be told. Because of you, Tina, I have more love in my life than any man deserves. I will continue doing all that I can to honor and earn your love.

Preface

It's unlikely that most people will read this preface (I hardly ever read them myself unless guided there by someone; this habit created a very specific problem when I tried to read Nabaokov's *Pale Fire*), but here is a preface regardless: written with the hope that I may one day ask inquisitive readers, "Did you read the preface?" in order to avoid answering the same question hundreds of times.

These stories *are* all connected, and they are meant to inform one another. *Battle Rattle* is where the book begins despite being where this part of the story, the part of the story contained in this book, ends. Conversely, *High Desert Rats* is where this part of the story begins, while being where the book ends. I could spend a bunch of time justifying this decision, but I don't want to color anyone's reading beyond this; Derrick Vezchek is Derrick in every story, and that matters as much or as little as you want it to.

You can read each story individually, but if you read the book as a single artifact, the stories will be richer. I have no control over how you read the book, though. I can only present it to you in the way in which I hope it will be read. These stories were not published in the order they were written, and no better thing could've happened. Only now, after publication of the ebooks, the audiobook, and the impending publication of a physical audiobook, am I able to offer readers something close to the full story of Derrick Vezchek's life in the form of an old-fashioned print book that you can hold in your hands. Here is that book.

Thanks so much for reading (even if you never read the preface),
    BDJ

Contents

Battle Rattle
and
Other Stories

by

Brandon Davis Jennings

Cover artwork designed and illustrated by Eric Smallwood
www.ericsmallwood.com

To huddle over the coals of flickering hope? Not I.
Honor in life, or honor in death; there is no other thing.
                                            —Sophocles' Ajax

BATTLE RATTLE

Rake broke his back when he tried to sit on a chair that wasn't there. He was drinking off our last deployment and had stomped upstairs to his office when Taylor came over to pick up some of the things she'd left behind after she'd bailed in the middle of Rake's most recent bender. He'd shoved his roller chair out of the way so he could duck under his desk to unplug and reseat the mouse cable. After he plugged it in, he stood and stepped back to where he thought the chair would be and sat down hard enough to break his back; before this happened to Rake, I never thought breaking your back was so easy. Taylor found him up there: passed out, pants soaked in his piss. She called an ambulance, and as far as I know, that was the last kind thing she did for him.

I met Taylor that day at the base hospital outside Rake's room. The tips of her brown hair tickled her freckled shoulders, hid the mangled ear some pill-head boyfriend had given her a couple years before she and Rake were married. "He's all yours," she said.

"It's fucked you're leaving him when he's like this."

"You could've told him the truth about the baby."

"You could've handled it and pretended there was never anything to say about a baby."

"The baby's been *handled*." Taylor bit her bottom lip and then shook her head. "I'm not going to wait around the rest of my life wondering if my husband's coming home. I'm too old for this. We all are. But you both choose to not grow up." She folded her arms beneath her breasts so her shirt molded around them; it reminded me of how much I'd liked having them in my mouth, how much I loved pressing my face between them, how much I hated myself for having slept with her behind Rake's back. But we'd both been drunk every time, and I'm sure she wanted to hurt Rake more than she wanted to fuck me. To avoid looking at her chest, I stared at the room number: 314. Silver numbers. Fingerprints made the "4" look gold when light hit it right.

She grabbed my left hand and squeezed. "I love him." Her fingers were rough and bony. "You know that."

"You don't leave people like this when you love them."

"Take care of him." She leaned in and kissed me on the cheek, then let go of my hand and walked away. The tips of her hair swayed about the small of her back, and I followed the curls down to her jean skirt and felt sick as soon as I realized I was staring at her ass.

I wrapped my fingers around the cool doorknob for a while. Metal pressed deep into my palm. Taylor's heels clicked and echoed down the hallway. People passed, coming and going. They probably thought I was crazy: some big dumb vet who went to war and came home wondering why doors needed knobs when you could bash them down so easily. No one offered to help me turn the knob; if someone had offered to help or had asked what I was doing, I might've actually seen Rake that day. I'm not sure how long I stood there before I let go.

I WENT HOME to Kaylynn and Ariel; they were reading a book together: *Oh No! Don't Let Me Go.* I leaned against the doorframe while Kaylynn read Ariel some of the rhymes: "If I fall asleep and the water's too deep? No, baby. I will not let you go. If I'm always picked last? Wrapped in a full-body cast? No, baby. I will not let you go." They didn't notice me, so I went to the garage and pounded my canvas heavy bag with unwrapped hands until my knuckles seeped blood and my shoulders struggled to hold my arms onto my body. Then I grabbed a bottle of Jameson from the liquor cabinet and headed out back to watch the sunset through the trees in the woods behind my house. I dragged a lawn chair from the porch out onto the wet grass and then sat there drinking until long after the sun was gone.

I woke shirtless the next morning stretched out in the grass. The uncapped and half-empty bottle lay on its side near my feet. The label was peeled off and the liquid sparkled green-gold in the sunlight. My head was on the teeter-totter seat, and it would've been easy for anyone to break my neck while I slept that way: a little pressure in the right spot, and *snap!* Ariel found me, though. She tugged at a fistful of my hair and sang, "Silly daddy lost his shirt. Silly daddy's in the dirt."

I smiled and tried not to exhale while she was close enough to smell my breath. "Silly Daddy was a jerk."

"Wanna teeter?" she asked and then skipped to the other side. Her yellow dress billowed in the light breeze. She was barefoot, and I didn't like that she was out there shoeless. We had a chestnut tree, and there were probably burrs I'd missed when I raked the yard before I deployed last; it was impossible to get them all. I wasn't in any position to question Kaylynn's mothering without bringing a lot of hell on myself, though; that song Ariel had sung was probably Kaylynn's invention. She knew it pissed me off when Ariel saw me hungover, so I figured this was her way of making me endure the non-physical repercussions of my stupidity.

I mounted the seat that had been wedged into the back of my neck all night and lifted my end so Ariel could climb onto her side. My head didn't hurt, but each descent wrenched my guts. I thought Ariel would be more excited to spend time with me, but she only smiled when I smiled at her first. Before long, Kaylynn came outside to get Ariel ready for ballet. Kaylynn didn't ask what had happened, and I didn't offer to talk about it. When they were gone, I leaned over the fence and vomited onto my neighbor's too-green grass.

HEAVY DRINKING WASN'T a new thing for Rake and me, but after Manchin drowned in a training exercise off the California coast a few months before our last deployment, Rake and I made drinking an essential post-PT ritual. I'd drink with Rake until he passed out, and then I'd drive home to sleep it off and show Kaylynn that I was still alive and still stupid enough to think the biggest danger with driving drunk was that I might get a DUI. The next day when I'd roll back to Rake's place, he'd be at it again: filthy and silent. Living like that was hard on our bodies, and being with someone who was living that way wasn't easy. Lucky for me Kaylynn had the endurance to deal with it for as long as it went on. Rake wasn't as fortunate. Taylor ditched him after we deployed, and the next time Rake heard from her was the day before we were set to call an air strike in on some desert village. She emailed to tell him that she'd had an abortion; she didn't want the baby because she wouldn't waste her life raising a kid for a man who was never home.

Kaylynn never said ugly shit like that to me. Rake emailed back and called Taylor a cold bitch. She filed divorce papers before we made it home.

Ariel was two the first time we went to the desert. I didn't like leaving her and Kaylynn, but Ariel was too young to really understand where I had gone back then. Kaylynn seemed to have adjusted to living life in segments; six months home and six months away wasn't uncommon. But there were a lot of shorter deployments that popped up; those she hated most because there was rarely any warning before I was packing my bags and heading out the door. I always told her there was nothing I could do about it. Whenever it was time to re-up, she'd tell me that I didn't have to sign the paper, that I could do something else. Each time, I said, "I don't know how to do anything else." Then I signed the paper, committed us to another four years of bulletproof excuses for why I had to leave whenever I was ordered to.

On our first desert deployment, we demoed a Soviet-era anti-air cannon. The wreckage smoldered on a hill a hundred yards or so from where we'd parked the Humvee to watch the results of our handiwork. I'd learned to admire explosions, the way the dirt and dust rippled, surfing the blast's shockwave. I felt most alive when something was exploding and I was the reason it had gone up.

Rake leaned against the Humvee. Firelight flickered and illuminated the scar that traced his jawline, the stubble that had sprouted on his face and throat over the last two days. "When me and Taylor have a son, I'm gonna tell him not to do any of this dumb shit."

Sergeant Harris said, "It's just another thing you're going to miss while you're out here. Women. Kids. Trucks. I dreamt about clean socks last night."

"No one cares about your dreams," Rake said. "At least it'll give me something to miss. And when my son grows up, I'll tell him all the things my dad never told me." Rake tossed his helmet onto the Humvee's hood and a small dust cloud punctuated the thud and the clacking chinstrap. He pulled his Leatherman out of its holster. "I know what a boy needs to know to keep safe in this world." He clipped his fingernails as we talked.

"What's that?"

"Don't join the military." Rake smiled. "Somebody's gotta do this. But not my kid."

"I hear you," I said. "I never thought I'd be so glad to have a daughter."

"Fuck that," Rake said. "You know what you want to do to women."

"Ariel doesn't have to let some asshole like us take advantage of her."

Harris had climbed into the Humvee by then. He set his helmet on the dashboard and scratched his shaved head. "You guys think your kids are going to be special? My wife caught my son in his closet getting a blowjob from the neighbor's daughter a few weeks back."

"So?" Rake said. "Like you didn't get terrible blowjobs when you were a teenager."

"My son's five," he said. "The girl is six."

Rake bit at a nail he'd misclipped and then spat. "Does that make them both pedophiles?"

"Shut up," I said.

"It's going to be my fault too. *You're never home. You're a bad father.* Because I'm over here hunting bastards that want to take away my five-year-old son's right to get head before he learns the alphabet. That's the shit we're fighting for." Harris said. "That's what Cammack died trying to protect."

"Cammack's boots." Rake whistled slow and quiet. "Could you believe those boots?" He closed his Leatherman, slid it back in its holster.

"Not the boots again," I said.

RAKE HAD CRACKED a couple vertebrae, and the doctors said it was possible he'd never walk again. It's corny, but I knew that if anyone had a 100 percent chance of recovery, it was him. And Rake did recover, but he never jumped from a C-130 again, and he never carried the same weight he once had. He was thirty-two years old, and the only job he'd ever wanted to do was taken from him: all because he was too drunk to look before he sat.

Rake had something with Manchin that I never had with any of the guys. Both Rake and I are the bastard sons of military fathers who died fighting wars that few people have ever heard about. Dad died somewhere near Alaska, and Rake never learned where his father died. Both our fathers had serious medals, not just Purple Hearts but Bronze Stars. Neither me or Rake ever earned medals like that. Or maybe we earned them. We weren't awarded them, though; so what difference does it make? But Manchin and Rake were like shields for one another. Somehow I never walked into a situation where I had a close call that someone could've saved me from. Rake: he shot guys that might've killed Manchin, and Manchin shot guys that might've killed Rake.

Once we raided a house in a desert village, and a dark-colored blanket nailed above a doorway rippled in the breeze whipped up by each man thumping past. The first man who got to that door should've cleared the room, but I won't lie and try to fool anyone into thinking anybody's infallible; Rake wouldn't want me glamorizing any of this because kids might read it. Rake was point man and never even tilted his weapon in the direction of that blanket-covered doorway; maybe he was tired because we hadn't slept in two days; maybe he was lazy because we'd done the same thing so many times without incident; maybe he was thinking about how Taylor was back home and surely fucking around on him. No matter what the reason was, as he peered around the corner at the end of the hall, doing exactly what he should have done at the door he missed, a man with a pistol stepped through the blanket-covered doorway and aimed at Rake. Before the man could squeeze the trigger, Manchin capped him in the head. Rake didn't turn around, didn't acknowledge what had happened. Manchin never said anything either. We all just stepped over the corpse and cleared the rest of the house. We found the ordnance that had been stashed there, in a hole that was hidden beneath a box spring in one of the bedrooms, and then we blew the place into shards. The night breeze smelled like coriander as that house burned. I remember the coriander because that house was one of the rare ones that actually had what we were searching for inside.

That's shit that happened in the desert, though. This is about

Rake missing a damn chair and breaking his back like he was already some kind of invalid before he swallowed a whole bottle of Klonopin and his muscles relaxed him to death. I've gone into his office and looked at the desk. I've seen the plastic mat where the roller chair was supposed to sit. I've kicked the chair away from the desk, heard the wheels scratch across the floor, go silent as they rolled onto the mat, and then thump back onto the hardwood. I've thought about drinking my ass off to see if anyone could drink himself deaf enough to manage this feat of stupidity on purpose. But I don't know who lives there now, and I imagine they wouldn't like it if I broke into their house to get drunk and try to paralyze myself. Kaylynn would beat the hell out of the parts of me that could still feel pain if she found out I'd paralyzed myself on purpose. Then Ariel would have a disabled dad, and I like to think the use of my legs has something to do with her happiness; her ability to walk and run and jump and dance definitely has something to do with mine.

Rake is the one who told me how it happened, and I wonder how he could remember what he was doing if he was so drunk that he couldn't hear the chair rolling away. I've been there—so drunk that I'm stumbling around pissing myself, aware of my disgusting behavior, but also fine with it because I know it's mostly a result of all the drinking, though I can't blame the alcohol alone. I'd ask Rake if he lied to me, but he's dead now, and he wouldn't have talked to anyone: the Little Bitch Fairy's orbiting us, sprinkling her "Don't be a pussy" dust all over the place while we tuck and roll to avoid it. Or we're all strong enough to carry our own shit no matter how heavy it gets. We jump out of airplanes and destroy buildings, towns, and anything that's in the way of our goals—even goals we're unaware of.

I never believed in PTSD before Rake killed himself. He was the last guy I thought would do a thing like that. It's easy to convince yourself that something is real when someone you know might've died because of that *something* you didn't believe in. Anyway: he's dead, and I'm not, and I know I'd never kill myself. Kaylynn has something to do with that. She's never left me, no matter how stupid I've been. No matter how long I've been gone, she's been there when I came home. Sometimes she seems so good that I wish she'd take Ariel and leave before I ruin them both. But what the fuck does that have to do with Rake?

Manchin might've told this better, but he drowned during a training exercise. He dropped over the side of a boat with his scuba gear and never resurfaced. His last breath of air was some stale shit out of a tank. Manchin died in a way that was sort of respectable, though. Cammack was an idiot for walking into that house with the naval mine propped against it, trying to help some old man, but at least he died in a war zone. Harris was murdered on his lawn by a white supremacist, so you could argue that he was a casualty of a war here at home that never ended. Rake's the biggest asshole of us all because he just swallowed a bottle of pills and died in his garage because of a war he was fighting inside himself.

RAKE MADE GOOD choices most of the time. He followed Cammack out to that naval mine but was smart enough not to follow Cammack over to the house where the naval mine rested. Rake saw Cammack splattered all over some town between where we picked up our Humvee and where we were headed. Rake told me, "Stay here. If this is a setup, you, Manchin, and Harris can get the hell on. I'll get Cammack to the target."

Aside from a cut on his face, nothing serious happened to Rake that day—physically. But he couldn't stop talking about Cammack's boots. "How did he get them to shine like that?"

"We should roll," Harris said. He thumbed his safety on and spit a stream of tobacco juice between the gap in his front teeth. "Manchin's waiting."

"His boots are still shining," Rake said. "That's gotta mean something."

"Like what?" Meaning was the last thing I wanted to discuss while I looked at the pieces of a guy who I'd just spent the last two days telling your-mom jokes with.

"I don't know," he said. "Something, Vez. Maybe you'll get it. You're smart."

Harris said, "It means he spent too much time shining his boots and not enough time studying the common-sense handbook." He dragged his freckled black cheek across his collar to wipe the wet away. "Let's move."

Rake laughed. It was abrupt, high-pitched, like there was a smaller version of Rake inside of this large one. He peeled a clump of mud from his face. His jawline had a cut that ran from the back of his jaw and slipped underneath his chin. Dirty blood trickled over his sharp Adam's apple and down his neck, soaking his undershirt collar.

"Rake," I said. "Your face is bleeding."

He plucked one of the boots from the mud and looked at his reflection in the toe. "That's some shit."

"Are you all right?" I said.

Rake snorted. "I'm just hurt. Not injured."

"Okay," Harris said. "Let's go."

"Hey!" Rake shouted. The boot flopped in his hand as he talked. "We'll see you back at the Humvee when you pull yourself together."

"This isn't funny." Harris scooped the hunk of dip out from behind his lip and flung it to the ground. He wiped his fingers against his pants and then looked at me like I was supposed to know what to do.

Rake dropped the boot back into the mud. "I'm fucking embarrassed. What did Pig Nose Rose say in basic, Vez?"

"What?"

"About our boots."

" 'Did you polish those with peanut butter?' "

"Yeah." Rake laughed. "What would Pig Nose say about our boots compared to Cammack's right now? Your boots are an embarrassment to the history of our training squadron: the finest training squadron in the world."

"He'd say we need to get your face looked at," I said. "It's gonna get infected."

"Do you think there's any Cammack in my cut?"

"This isn't a joke," I said.

Rake kicked Cammack's weapon out of a mud puddle. "I'm fine. That's the joke."

"You're bleeding." Harris tried to put his arm around Rake's shoulders and Rake shoved him so hard that Harris slipped in a bloody mud puddle and landed on his ass. "Mother fuck. Get him, Vezchek."

Rake gestured erratically with his weapon, and then he grabbed Cammack's weapon from the mud. "Cammack' fucked up. Not me." Rake rested each weapon on a shoulder. "That's right," I said.

"What was that old song?" Rake sang, " 'Oh well. What the hell?' "

"Yeah," I said. "*That's* it." I helped Harris to his feet. Some unidentifiable chunk of flesh was stuck to his web belt. Rake laughed when he noticed it. "Good idea. We can mail a piece of Cammack to each of his family members."

Harris scowled and then searched for what Rake had meant. He slapped the flesh-and-gore chunk off his mud-caked web belt, and then we all went back to the Humvee.

Manchin wrapped his big fingers around the wheel so tight that his knuckles cracked. "Where's Cammack?"

"Cammack fell apart," Rake said.

Manchin adjusted the rearview mirror. "What the fuck's he talking about?"

"Just drive," Harris said. And Manchin did.

I handed Rake some gauze, and he mashed it against his cheek. But he kept reopening the cut because he couldn't stop laughing, and he wouldn't shut up about Cammack's boots. "Boot-tastic." That was what he kept saying until he passed out, his dirty head rattling against the Humvee's door.

After Rake had been quiet for half an hour or so, Harris said, "I don't know how you can hang out with this moron off duty."

"Who else am I supposed to spend time with?"

"Get a girlfriend and fuck your brains out."

"Life's real simple for you, isn't it, Harris?"

"I never should've reenlisted."

I said, "Nothing made you." But I knew better: even back then.

WE SPENT A lot of hours polishing boots after Cammack died, and if we hadn't switched to the tan fleshouts in preparation for desert deployments, Rake might never have gotten over whatever it was about Cammack's death that fucked with him so much. We might still be sitting on his back porch, swirling tube socks over boot toes and watching the sunset. If we were still polishing our jungle boots, maybe Taylor wouldn't have divorced him.

It pissed me off to spend so much time talking about and polishing boots, but Rake had saved me from seeing Cammack go from a skinny FNG to a thousand shards of flesh and bone that littered the mud. I saw the shards, but there wasn't anything human enough left to feel sorry for or to get fucked up over. It was just a bunch of bone debris, flesh-shrapnel, those boots and their mirror-shine that Rake kept talking about. "Boot-tastic, Vez. Can you believe it?"

RAKE WAS AN animal sometimes. When we took that airfield on our second trip to the desert, he shot a camel's front left knee off and then shot it in the belly. We'd been stuck there for two days with no orders before the camel tumbled to the sand and rolled into the razor wire that lined the fence; it tried to stand, but the razor wire had wrapped it in all the wrong places and standing was impossible. So Rake shot it. I didn't realize until he'd shot it in the belly that he was hurting it on purpose.

When the camel moaned, I felt sick. "Aren't you going to finish it?"

"It is finished," Rake said. "Just a matter of time."

So I said, "Goddamn it." And I walked over to the fence and prepared to stick the barrel of my weapon through the diamond of links and press it against the camel's head. At the time I remember thinking I would *end the camel's suffering*: a phrase that makes me laugh now. The camel breathed heavy. Its nostrils sucked sand grains in and then blasted them back out. Blood-caked sand clung about the leg wounds. Each inhalation and exhalation made me feel like something was trying to twist my stomach in two. Before I pulled the trigger, I heard a shot and the top of the camel's head exploded. The head became a jagged, white-and-red hole connected to a cleft muzzle; it made me think of a blooming violet chiseled out of white marble.

Sergeant Harris said, "Go bury that camel, or I'll shoot *your* knee off."

Rake said, "Go ahead."

Harris pulled his nine from its holster and aimed at Rake's leg. Rake laughed. "I'll bury the camel because I want to. It'll be an homage to Cammack. Since you made us leave his pieces behind."

Harris holstered the nine and said, "We're not here to solve our own problems, Rake. We have a job to do."

"What the fuck is it?" Rake asked. "We just fell out of the sky, and all of a sudden we have a damned airfield in the middle of the desert. How do we fight an enemy that isn't here?"

"You know what you need to know."

"I know you're a dipshit."

"Bury the camel, Rake. That's an order."

Rake laughed and said, "Yes, sir."

Rake and I clipped a hole in the fence that we then squeezed through. We cut the dead camel free from the razor wire. We dug a grave deep enough to barely cover the camel, grabbed the carcass by its blood-caked legs, and dragged it into the hole. Rake picked up the severed shin-and-hoof and tossed it onto the camel's flank. Then we kicked sand over the mess.

"How about that?" Rake said. "I finally got to bury something."

TAYLOR CALLED THE day after she'd found Rake dead. She said he was in his garage, facedown on an oil pan and surrounded by tattered rags. He'd been out there planing wood. He never used the wood he planed for anything useful that I'd seen. He'd just buy wood and plane it. Maybe he liked the sound of the planer, the hum of the motor. The planer was still running when Taylor found him. He'd planed a stack of boards, and then glued seven of them together: one stacked on top of another. C-clamps on both ends to ensure the glue set perfectly; it didn't resemble anything I'd ever seen. Could've been a table for a small dog, I guess. No matter what its function was supposed to be, it was seven boards, each board two inches thick, glued on top of one another, and that seven-board-thing sat next to a full, red plastic gas jug and a box of strike-anywhere matches.

I never saw Rake's body because Taylor handled the funeral, and she made it closed-casket; seeing his corpse wouldn't have brought him back, so I didn't care. A few days after the funeral, she asked me to come over and look through his shit. "In case there are any memories," she'd said. Like, what the fuck did she mean? I couldn't pick up a memory and hold it if I wanted to.

But I can't look or not-look at my own face, at her tits, at the goddamn night sky without *having* memories, so why did I need some random crap that me and Rake had a bonding moment over to help me remember anything? And I doubted there'd be anything like that anyway; we didn't spend much time looking for souvenirs in any of the places we traveled. Still I went over to see where he'd died, to try to make sense of it: a stupid idea. I took the planer home with me "because of the memories" and I took that glued stack of planks too.

Taylor was wearing a short orange skirt and some absurdly high heels that looked painful to stand in: the straps dug into her ankles. She was squeezed into a blue tube top, and Kaylynn says tube tops are ridiculous, but when one is wrapped around a tight waist and big tits, it's hard for me to care about fashion. Out of respect for Rake, I tried to avoid looking; it was impossible. She was there, and she was showing off, and I liked being shown off to.

"We were getting back together," she said. "That's why I was here."

I was dragging the boards to my truck bed. They were heavier than I'd expected and scratched loudly against the concrete. "Yeah," I said. "No wonder he killed himself."

She pushed some of her hair behind her good ear. "You think that's a joke, but it's true."

I dropped the boards. They smacked the concrete, didn't even vibrate because of how heavy they were. "What does that mean?"

"I told him." She massaged her left elbow nervously.

"*Told* him. That the kid was ours?"

"I feel horrible about this, Vez."

"Awesome. That fixes everything."

"Stop." Anger wrinkles cracked between her nose and forehead.

"Why would you tell him? What fucking good did it do?"

"How could we really be together with a lie that big eating a hole inside me?"

"He's dead because of that. Are you fucking crazy?"

She started toward me. "You know I'm not." And each step that brought her closer made me want to smash her more violently. Her hair, the way it cascaded over her shoulders, the way her shirt hugged her waist and chest, the way her skirt let me see high up on her pale thighs that brushed past one another. Each of the things that made me want to fall on top of her made me want to squeeze my hands into fists and wreck everything about her that I found beautiful. But I didn't: not when she wrapped her arms around me, not when she kissed me, and not when she pulled me onto the oil-stained, rag-littered floor where Rake had died.

CHAPTER 2

Kaylynn and I met after I came home from my third deployment. She worked at Last Chance, this bar just outside the East Gate. Rake and I drank there between deployments when we got bored with the E-Club. When I was a kid Mom had warned me that it was bad luck to drink alone, but my experience drinking with Rake made me think she had it backward. Last Chance was a bar where I never expected to start a relationship that didn't end the same night or early the next morning. That's why it made me feel safe.

Rake and I had just beaten the hell out of each other because Taylor left him again. I was sick of her leaving him when we came home and angry at him because he always took her back before we deployed. Every time we rotated back home and she wasn't at his place, he'd roll around in his own filth for a couple weeks, trying to forget whatever we'd just done and trying to forget that he loved and missed Taylor. This particular time I'd found him in his living room at noon with the shades drawn. Depeche Mode's "Personal Jesus" was blasting so loud that the bass rattled my chest. He was stretched out on his gray carpet, and a small fire burned in a ceramic ashtray shaped like an elephant's foot. He splashed Bacardi 151 into the ashtray to feed the flame. I had to shout so loud to get his attention that it hurt my head. "You're going to burn your house down."

"I hope my house burns down," he shouted.

"Don't be an idiot."

"Go fuck yourself." He swigged from the bottle, and rum spilled out his mouth and slid down his chin. Droplets clung to his red-brown, post-deployment beard and sparkled in the firelight.

I gave up on talking and tried to drag him to the shower to see if cold water might smack him back into reality, but he punched me in the mouth before I could get a hold on him. We wrestled for a while, and when I was too tired to fight on, I left. I knew we'd repeat this stupid cycle every couple days until Taylor came home, so there was no point going all-in on it this time. When Taylor did come back, Rake would just pretend he hadn't missed her, and I'd pretend we'd never punched each other in the face, and life would go on.

The truth about why I was so concerned about Rake's well-being, though, is that I knew Taylor was capable of fucking with his head so much that it could've got me killed. I didn't want to die because Rake wasn't paying attention.

I drove straight to Last Chance. My face was tight and bruised up pretty good; so were my knuckles. No broken bones or anything, but I'm sure anybody who saw me at the bar that night thought twice before talking to me. Not that I cared; what would I have said to a stranger? I pounded a couple shots of Jameson and then switched to St. Finn's Warhound Ale, this Belgian-style beer they had in bottles. It had coriander in it, and each drink tasted like the explosion that happened the night Manchin shot a guy in the head to save Rake's life. I drank them slow to smell and taste that violence without the fear of hurting anyone; it felt good to be home and safe enough to fearlessly drink until I couldn't stand.

Kaylynn had served me the whole night. Her hair was pulled up in pigtails, and she wore red jeans and a blue T-shirt with Cookie Monster on the chest. I had trouble deciding if it was her tits or the blue fur ball holding a half-eaten cookie that kept my attention. When she leaned against the mirrored wall behind the bar, her pelvic bones pushed hard against her pale skin, and I thought about pressing up against her to fold those bones back, to protect her skin from the sharpness beneath it. I glanced at the TV to avoid getting caught. It was football season; some bald guy was talking to a fat guy about a bunch of grown men chasing a ball around. I remembered a touchdown pass I'd thrown to my friend Sean in high school. He'd beaten up his girlfriend, a girl I liked more than I should have because she wasn't mine to like, the day before a game. So when he crossed over the middle, I threw the ball high to let the linebackers and the safety light him up. They hit him so hard his helmet flew off, but he held the ball. That was one of the few touchdown passes I ever threw. But like Dad said, I was too small for professional sports anyway, so too many touchdowns would've just increased the disappointment I would feel when I didn't make it as a pro. Dad wasn't around long enough to tell me if I was or wasn't big enough for war; I had to figure that out on my own.

Kaylynn walked over and leaned forward across the bar top, rested her chin in her hands. Her nails weren't painted and were clipped short. "Did an elephant sit on your face?"

"I've looked worse."

"Gee." She licked her lips, the bottom lip plumper and shinier than the top. "Aren't you a badass?"

"Yeah." I laughed. "What's with the Cookie Monster shirt?"

She aimed a thumb at her chest. "You weren't staring at my tits."

I drank and thought about fuses and C4, about Cammack's boots, about a boy impaled on an iron rod. "That shirt makes your chest look like one of those magic eye things."

"What the hell are you talking about?"

"I don't know," I said. "Nice tits. I guess is what I'm trying to say."

A guy in a John Deere cap called her over and ordered some drinks. She poured a few shots of vodka and set them on the bar. The guy paid and she thanked him. Her narrow hips didn't shake much when she walked, and there was something sexy about that: like she wasn't interested in trying that hard. The silver button on her jeans, despite how thin she was, seemed strained. She came back over and set a short glass in front of me. "Buy me a drink?"

"I guess."

"Good." She scooped ice into the glass and poured a heavy-handed gin and tonic. "You've bought me drinks the last five times you've been here."

"What?"

"I thought you'd notice the charges on your receipts and then come in and complain when you sobered up. Since that didn't work, I'm trying this."

"Who put you up to this?"

"Look at your face," she said. "You need someone to take care of you."

"Are you joking?"

She drank half the gin and tonic and set it down. She wiped her mouth with the back of her hand. "I don't joke around much."

"But you wear Cookie Monster T-shirts." I scooted forward, and she backed away from the bar, smiling. I peered over the bar top to see her shoes. "And Converse All-Stars? How old are you?" The stool scratched against the floor as I readjusted it.

"Old enough to know you need help."

"Did Harris set this up?"

"I don't know any Harris." She shook her head. "You're ruined already. Aren't you?"

"Ruined?" I'd never thought of it like that. "Yeah. Probably."

She stuck out her bottom lip. "What's the longest you've gone without hating yourself?"

My face started hurting then. My right cheek pulsed. "Did I fuck your sister?"

"I don't have a sister."

"Okay." I finished my beer. Heartburn rumbled up my throat. "My heartbeat's trying to smash through my face. This is too much right now."

"You just get back from a deployment?"

"Why do you care?" My knuckles were swelling. My fingers didn't want to extend all the way. The first fight Rake and I had after our second deployment, I got a boxer's fracture on my right hand because he'd ducked and I hit him in the forehead with my outside knuckles. I bought a heavy bag after that, so that when my hand healed, I could better prepare myself for the next time I needed to punch a friend in the face.

She grabbed another beer, cracked it open and set it in front of me. "Tell me what happened." Then she filled a plastic bag with ice, wrapped a towel around it and said, "Put this on your hollow head."

I held the towel against my temple and coolness crept from the towel to my face. "I got in a fight with my best friend." It sounded ridiculous. "My friend, I mean."

"Did he do something stupid while you were deployed?"

"He didn't," I said. "He does his stupid shit at home. But forget it. It doesn't matter."

"I'm not gonna tug it out of your throat."

"Sorry," I said. "I'm half drunk. My face hurts. My knuckles hurt. I'm probably going to piss blood for two days."

"Poor baby." She finished her drink and poured another. "You need a babysitter."

"A babysitter? Look. I'm happy to pay for those drinks. You're nice. Close me out. I need to sleep this off." I set the towel on the bar; it unfurled, and a few ice cubes tumbled free and skated across the glistening bar top.

"You're going home alone after all this?" Her jaw dropped and revealed a blue tipped barbell in her tongue; she rattled it against her front bottom teeth.

"All what?"

"Are you retarded?" She grabbed a pen and a napkin and scribbled her name and number on it. "I get off in twenty minutes, Derrick *Vezchek*? I'm not calling you that. Wait for me, or you can sober up and hope you don't lose that napkin. I work tomorrow. But I'll never try this hard to get you to come home with me again. You'd think I was missing an eye or something."

"I don't get it."

"I want to fix you up. Call it payment for all the drinks if you need a reason."

She put her hand on my shoulder. The warmth made me close my eyes for a moment; I felt like I could sleep forever. The feeling was familiar, but I couldn't remember where it was from. "Okay. All right." I said. "Fix me up."

I stayed in her apartment for a couple days. She cleaned my cuts, iced my knuckles and face. I figured she'd be one of those lunatics who just wanted to fuck all the time, but she didn't even try while I was healing. At first I was disappointed, but I wouldn't have been any good while I was in so much pain anyway. My dick respected me less, but I respected her more: one of the dumbass dualities of man we all seem aware of and are still unable to conquer.

WE SAT AT folding chairs and a foldout card table in her kitchen to eat the meals she cooked: eggs, grilled cheese, pan-fried chicken. She barely ate, and I thought to ask if she was fattening me up for some kind of witches' banquet, but she'd said she didn't joke around much, and I didn't want to risk losing the ease of this temporary new life to a shitty joke that I didn't even get myself.

Rake and I only had a month of leave before we'd be training, if not deploying, again. So I wanted to soak up as much of this as I could. Her bed was a mattress on the bedroom floor, and that's where I spent most of the time, sleeping or half asleep. It was a twin, and when we slept together, my legs dangled off the edge. She'd back herself as far into my chest and stomach as she could, and I'd squeeze her closer when I felt her rolling away. I fell asleep easiest when her warm, smooth stomach expanded against my open palm.

The whole time I was there I couldn't stop thinking about Elizabeth, this girl I'd known in first grade—as well as anyone can know someone at that age. We were in choir together and she'd asked me to her birthday party. We'd sung "Anything you can do, I can do better" boys versus girls in a school concert a few days before her party, and in the parking lot after the concert we'd stared at each other dumbly while our mothers blabbed about how cute we were. The only thing I remember from the party is that Elizabeth grabbed my hand a short while before it was time to go home, pulled me into her bedroom, and then she kissed me before running out of the room. She and her family moved to France the next week, and there were a lot of years that I hated the French for stealing her from me: like she was mine to steal, like anyone is ever anyone else's. And then France became this mystical place that I planned to run away to. That was all before my friend's uncle fucked me up by asking if I'd ever seen a cock squirt. If I just would've pretended to be asleep that night, who knows what my life might have been?

Regardless of what happened to me in the past, I was in bed with a woman who, for some reason I'll never understand, wanted desperately to help me. And she did. She healed me, fed me, kept me warm. She didn't ask questions about anything I didn't want to talk about. And sure, some of that is pure chance. But so much of life is pure chance that, a lot of the time, I wonder how random chance really is.

A COUPLE DAYS of lying around had brought me back to mint. So after breakfast on the third morning I said, "I think it's time to roll."

Kaylynn stood at the sink; she'd washed all the dishes and now swirled a towel over them, one at a time, and stacked them in the cabinet. "Where are we going?"

"We?"

She set the last dish and the towel on the counter, and then turned around and leaned against it. Her pelvic bones pressed out like they had that night at the bar: sharp. I knew that if I could get her to wrap her legs around me, those bones would disappear like knives resheathed. "I'm not staying here anymore if you're not." We hadn't talked much, even though we'd been in almost constant contact except for when she went to work every night. It seemed to me that she'd wanted to say whatever she was about to say for a while now. She'd been more distant than I'd grown used to, which seems absurd because we'd just met. But I figured she had something on her mind, and I was too thick to realize it might be that the thing that bothered her was that I wasn't talking.

"Where are you going?"

"With you," she said.

"Why?"

"I don't know, Vez." She shook her head. "If I could explain it, I would."

"I'm probably going to get killed. I'm gone all the time. I can barely keep my dick in my pants. I'm a fucking idiot. I—"

"Shut up," she said. "What do you think of me?"

"Should I shut up or answer?"

"Fuck off." She bit her cheek and sighed through her nose. "What do you think of me?"

"I like you."

"Why?"

"You took care of me."

"Fuck you."

"I owe you a lot for what you did for me."

"For you?" She nodded. "If that's all, then go on."

I didn't know what she wanted me to say, but I wanted to say the right thing because I hadn't felt this safe around anyone for as long as I could remember. And I felt like such an idiot because I couldn't understand why. So I said, "When you touched my shoulder at the bar, it made me feel like I could sleep."

"What?"

"That's so stupid."

"No it's not." She laughed. "I'm the Sandwoman."

"Maybe."

"So marry me."

"Are you crazy?"

"If I can help you sleep, then you should marry me."

"Do you imagine me doing exciting shit and coming home to tell you about it? Most of the time nothing happens. Most of the time it's boring."

"I'm bored. You're bored. Let's fuck already."

"Is this some kind of game?"

"Come on." She pulled her shirt over her head, tossed it at my face, and ran into the bedroom too fast for me to see her tits. The mattress creaked when she flopped onto it. "Get in or get out."

"Are you trying to confuse me?"

"I'm trying to fuck you."

"You are crazy."

"Who isn't?" she said. "Now get in here and show me that all my kindness was worth it."

I grabbed her shirt off my lap and set it on the table. "What makes you think I'm any good in bed?"

"Jesus Christ," she said. "Stop. Talking."

CHAPTER 3

I dropped Ariel off at ballet because Kaylynn had spin class: another one of the things she did while I wasn't deployed that annoyed me, but I'd have been more annoyed if she just drank Diet Coke and ate Cheetos all day while complaining about being fat; she wasn't fat, but I know as well as anyone that separating how we see ourselves from how we actually are is rarely as easy as we'd like. I opened the studio door for Ariel, told her goodbye, and then headed back to my truck. A man with a patchy black mustache and thinning, side-parted hair stood next to a blonde girl in the parking lot. I gave a half nod as I reached them.

After I'd walked by, the man said, "How's your wife?"

I stopped and pivoted to face him. I said, "She's good." But I meant *Why the fuck are you asking that?*

"Bobbie," he said. "Go on in, baby." He patted the girl on her head, between her pigtails, and she sprinted to the door. Once there, she struggled to pull it open. "She'll get it," he said. She'd leaned so far back that I was sure she'd fall, but the door opened and the hydraulics caught it so that she could slip inside the building. She disappeared into the studio, and over the low hiss of hydraulics the man said, "Kaylynn said you'd be back from the desert soon."

"Who are you?"

"Ed McCabe." He extended his hand, and I had to force myself to shake it without squeezing hard enough to mash his knuckles together. "Thank you for your service."

I smiled; that phrase seemed so ridiculous. "We all do our part, Ed. What do you do?"

"My wife's a doctor," he said. "I stay home."

"Is that right?"

"I wanted to join up, but I have screws in my ankle." He pointed to his foot as if I could see the screws through his shoes and socks and skin. "I always thought it would be cool to fly an A-10." His eyebrows shifted up. "The Flying Tigers. Right?"

"Warthogs," I told him. "Tigers is the name of a squadron."

"Oh," he said.

"If everybody knew everything, then we wouldn't have any reason to talk to one another." The statement was automatic, but I couldn't remember where I'd heard it: Dad? Rake? Harris? "Forgive me for bailing, man. But I've got shit to do while Ariel flails around in there."

"Sorry." He scratched the back of his neck and nodded. "Didn't mean to hold you up. I just wanted to meet you in case Kaylynn ever mentioned me and Bobbie." He shoved his hands deep into his pants pockets. "You know? So it wouldn't be weird."

"This is weird now, Ed."

"Damn." He snorted. "Better weird than shocking, right?"

"I'm just fucking with you. You can tell me all about what you did to mess up your ankle over a few beers sometime."

"Yeah. It'd be nice to get to know the guy Kaylynn's always talking about."

Always talking about? "Sounds great." I flashed him a Cub Scout salute and headed to my truck.

On the drive home, I stopped at a four-way intersection where a guy wearing a field jacket stood holding a sign: Homeless and disabled vet need food God bless. I figured he forgot to pluralize *need* on purpose, to seem more pathetic. His short, trimmed beard and the way he held his head high, staring right through all the cars that approached, made me wonder if he was full of shit. He wore one of those unit hats that NCOs often pushed on young enlisted men— as if guys wanted to advertise their unit when they were out of uniform. The insignia and letters on his hat were too dirty to read from my truck: from too many nights sleeping in the dirt or maybe because he found it in a ditch. He never looked at me, but I never carried cash anyway. It was easier to not feel guilty about not helping if I had an honest excuse.

When I got home, I went straight to the garage. I wasn't happy about my heavy-bag setup, but I didn't know how long we'd be in that house, so I used the least destructive setup I could. It was a metal stand with a chain that the bag dangled from. I couldn't circle the bag because of the steel legs on either side and the speed-bag platform on the back. I never used the speed bag because I wasn't trying to improve any skills. I wasn't a boxer, and I never wanted to be one.

Forty-five-pound plates were stacked on the three prongs molded to the feet of the stand so it didn't fall over when I hit the bag, and those plates never moved from the stand because I didn't have a gym at home. On the rare occasions that Rake and I did barbell training, we did it at the gym on base.

For the first couple years I'd hit the bag without wrapping my hands. I liked to watch blood seep from my knuckles, to experience the numbness that eventually took hold of my hands after I'd rocked the bag a while. Waiting for my hands to heal became a problem, though. Kaylynn hated looking at the scabs and sores that spread over them. "Why hurt yourself on purpose?" she'd say, and then she'd roll her eyes regardless of the reason I gave. Every time I washed my hands while the cuts were still fresh, soap would creep into the wounds and burn like hell. I couldn't peel oranges or lemons or limes or chop onions, and once while peeling potatoes, I discovered that even the juice of that bland vegetable made the cuts sting. All of those little annoyances bothered me, but what ultimately made me change my approach was Ariel.

One day while I was hunched over on my metal folding chair after beating the bag for a while, Ariel ran into the garage. She was five years old, and I was already beginning to forget what it had been like when she couldn't stand on her own. I had vague memories of her latching onto my jeans with her tiny fists as she wobbled in front of me, staring up with her wide blue eyes, pushing my hands away when I tried to steady her. She'd stood just as tall as my knee when she was barely a year old. Four years had morphed her from a sure-to-tumble baby into a girl with better balance than me.

"Daddy," she said, "Mommy wanted me to ask you if I could have a Rocket Pop."

My breathing had slowed enough that I was able to speak without too much extra effort between words. "Sure, babe."

The freezer door opened and closed, then its motor kicked on and hummed. The heavy bag creaked as it swung gently at the end of its chain.

"What happened to your hands, Daddy?"

Ariel stood right in front of me, a foot away, and her peanut butter breath wafted over my face, made my stomach growl. Sweat rolled from my forehead into my right eye as I raised my head to look at her. It was hard to tell whose eyes she had because both Kaylynn and I have blue eyes, and funny as it is to think about, Kaylynn's eyes remind me of my own. Ariel had my nose, though. Two tiny humps on the bridge that would probably bother her one day because she'd see women in magazines with noses unlike her own and decide that her nose was wrong or else *it* would be in a magazine.

"My hands are bleeding because I hit the heavy bag too much."

"Then why did you hit it?"

"It's good exercise."

"Good exercise is supposed to make you bleed?"

"Well, no."

"Then why does it hurt you?"

She grasped the plastic-wrapped Rocket Pop by the stick with both hands like it was a broadsword. The red, white, and blue Popsicle was ridiculous: were we so jingoistic that we couldn't have Klondike bars or Drumsticks? Her bare feet were pale and small, and I remembered how she'd kicked me in the balls all those times Kaylynn had brought her into our bed in the middle of the night to feed her or soothe her crying. I'd wake ready to hit someone every time those tiny, flailing feet smashed into my nuts, and then I'd laugh myself to sleep after realizing I'd been hurt by this baby girl who had no idea what she was doing. Kicked in the balls by a baby: a life between deployments.

"I don't wrap my hands, and the bag is nylon. So it rubs against my skin and makes my knuckles bleed."

"Oh," she said. "Maybe you should wrap your hands, then."

"Yeah," I said. "Maybe I should."

She walked a few steps toward the door, and then turned and asked me if I wanted a Popsicle too.

"No thanks, sweetheart," I said. And then she went back into the house and shut the door behind her.

After that day, I wrapped my hands with the yellow Everlast wraps that came with the bag and stand when I'd bought them.

It became a ritual. Over the knuckles, under the palm, and then down and around the wrist. Over the knuckles and under the palm, then down and around the wrist. Between two fingers and around the wrist. Around the wrist and across the knuckles and down around the wrist until the wrap ran out. I didn't have a coach, so who knows how good a job I did. All that mattered to me was that my knuckles no longer bled; that way neither Ariel nor Kaylynn could come out there and tell me I was stupid for hurting myself in a way that was so easy to prevent.

Motivating myself to hit the bag that day after meeting Ed was tough. Why hadn't Kaylynn talked about him before? I was there, and he was there, and Kaylynn wasn't, so his meeting me before Kaylynn mentioned him was just pure chance. Maybe Kaylynn was going to tell me about this guy and his wife later that day. Maybe she hadn't told me because she was worried that I would do exactly what I was doing right at this moment: overanalyzing a normal situation. If that were true, though, wouldn't she have wanted to tell me that she knew this guy before I bumped into him at Ariel's practice? She had to know I would meet him when I dropped Ariel off. She talked to him *all the time*, apparently. So that must have meant she and he chatted it up while the girls practiced—unless they talked someplace else. And why did he know so much about our lives? It was none of his business if I was deploying or if I'd been deployed. Could Kaylynn not find a woman to talk to? She had to talk to this fucking stay-at-home dad while I was off risking my ass.

I headed over to the corrugated shelf on the back wall and grabbed the yellow wraps from their bin. The smell was awful. I never let them air-dry before I rolled them up after a workout, and the funk that emanated from them was the same as the smell that always hung over the air of the locker room back in high school: jock straps and undershirts marinating in decades' worth of sweat and grime.

Better weird than shocking, right? Yeah, Ed. Way fucking better. I wrapped my right hand first and then wrapped my left. The one thing I knew I did right was to make sure my wrists were tight. I didn't want to break my wrists, and even though the original intent was to keep my knuckles from bleeding, the main goal of the wraps was to protect the wrists. There are no wrists in boxing. I read that somewhere. Or someone said it. I don't think I made it up.

There wasn't really a routine that I followed. I didn't spend time working on my jab and my hook. I wasn't interested in developing a world-class uppercut. I just hit the bag until I couldn't hit the bag anymore. If I hit the bag and it didn't crumple enough or make a deep enough thud, then I hit it harder. I drove my hips with my punches. My fists were the tips of whips and I snapped my body as hard as I could to rattle the bag and send it twisting left and right. I aimed for the Everlast logo as the bag wiggled and twirled back and forth. I punched at the bag seams when the letters faced away. I exhaled hard with each punch, and once I'd hit the bag long enough that I couldn't hit it with force anymore, I sat on my metal folding chair and listened to the creaking chain and felt the deep pulses of my heart, thumping in my chest, my head, and my feet.

This was the first time I'd taken Ariel to ballet, and it was the first time I'd left her alone at a place with people I didn't know. It was difficult to motivate myself to punch the bag, but I needed to. I couldn't go back there and make small talk with Ed if I didn't punch out some of this irrational anger. He was probably a decent guy. Why wouldn't he be? And even if he was a total piece of shit, that didn't mean he'd done anything to hurt Kaylynn, Ariel, or me; it didn't mean that he would or that he even intended to.

I hit the bag a few times. It felt heavier than usual. My arms felt weighted. My shoulders felt tight, like sand-seized gears. My hips popped when I followed my punches through. There was no one to see any of it, but I was embarrassed for myself. I might've hit the bag for two minutes before I was on my chair, breathing heavy. But I'd done nothing. There I was, a man too concerned with imaginary shit to effectively live in the world he'd been born into. I tried to concentrate on what I was doing, to focus on punching the bag and getting as much out of the moment as I could, and before I threw another punch, my phone alarm buzzed. I unwrapped my hands, rolled up the sweaty wraps, and then stuffed them back into their bin.

I drove back to the ballet studio and felt anxious about having to see that homeless vet at the intersection again. It made me sick thinking that he may have been a guy like me at one time and then, somehow, despite all he'd done, he still wound up a beggar.

I told myself over and over that he was full of shit, that he wasn't a veteran, that he was just using people's guilt. And when I got to the intersection, he wasn't even there. All that preparation was just wasted energy. I hoped I'd never see that man or another man like him again.

ED WAS TALKING to the instructor when I walked through the door. Mirrors lined the walls, and reflections of her, Ed, Ariel, and Bobbie surrounded me. The instructor was tall and thin, with long black hair that she'd pulled over her left shoulder and twisted absently while listening to Ed. Ariel and Bobbie were playing a game in which one of them did a dance move in front of a mirror and the other tried to imitate it. They clapped for each other no matter how poorly the move was matched.

The instructor flipped her hair back over her shoulder and waved at me as I approached. Ed smiled, and I tried my best not to appear anxious to leave, but I felt my palms sweating. "Daddy," Ariel called from across the room, "Miss Joanna said we danced wonderfully today."

"That's great, babe," I said.

"Hello, Mr. Vezchek," the instructor said. "I'm Joanna."

"Nice to meet you," I said. "And 'Vez' is fine." Ed stood there with his hands behind his back, rocking on his heels like a stiff-jointed dipping bird. "Same to you, Ed."

"Thanks," he said.

For a couple moments, Ariel and Bobbie's clapping was the only sound other than my breathing. "So," I said. "Better get Ariel home so Kaylynn doesn't worry. Her spin class ends soon, and we were hoping to do something special tonight."

Joanna said, "Ed was telling me you just came home from the desert."

What the fuck did these people care for? "Yeah. It's not a big deal. People are there all the time anymore."

Joanna nodded. "Well, thank you for your service all the same." She extended her hand, and I shook it. Her thin fingers were strong, and my sweaty hand slipped against her rough palm. Her hand clamped around my fingers, and she laughed at our botched shake.

I slid my hand out of her grasp and said, "Nice grip."

"Pull-ups," she said. "But I'm sure you know all about that."

"What?" I rubbed my hands on my pants leg to dry them.

"The calluses are from pull-ups. You guys do a lot of those, I guess." Her eyebrows shifted up a bit to turn the statement into a question.

"Yeah," I said. "My calluses are mostly from deadlifts, though. I'm surprised you do pull-ups for ballet. Ariel can do pull-ups?"

Joanna laughed. "She's not started that yet. That comes later."

"Oh," I said. "Well, thanks for making Ariel stay interested in something. It's gotta be hard when they're so little."

"Ariel's very good, you know?"

"How can you tell?"

Ed said, "They have to be able to tell which of the girls are skilled when they're young. They only have so many years of dancing in their bodies before they'll lose their balance. Among other things."

"You're an expert too, then?" I asked.

"No." Ed laughed. "I'm no expert."

"Ed's right," Joanna said. "Ariel has a chance to be something really special."

"Listen," I said. "Am I missing something?"

They both looked at me with furrowed brows.

"Did she do something wrong?" I asked. "Or did Kaylynn not tell me something that I should know about? This all feels a little familiar to me."

Joanna said, "No." Her smile revealed a small gap between her top front teeth that reminded me of a bunny. "I just thought you might like to hear it from me that your daughter is one of the best students I've ever had. It's been a treat to see this kind of talent. It lets me daydream about what might be if we can help her reach her potential. I know that you don't know me and this is all new to you because you're gone all the time. But I thought it might make it easier on you when you're away to know that your daughter is doing so well at something."

Ariel and Bobbie played; their reflections seemed to be everywhere, attempting somersaults that resulted in them saying *ouch* when they made it halfway and then fell onto their sides laughing. "I assume you make them do more than roll around like drunk pill bugs to determine their potential."

"They're just playing," she said, and then she crossed her arms across her flat chest. "Based on those smiles, it seems to me that there's a great deal of potential for their friendship to be a good one. But, yes, Vez. I make them do much more than applaud one another for failed somersaults and twirling their hair around their fingers. This is serious to me, and I make it serious for my students. Practice ended before you got here. So now they're free to do as they please."

"You should stay for a practice sometime," Ed said. "Then you'd see."

"Not sure if that's going to work out anytime soon."

"Back to the desert again?" Ed asked.

"Does that excite you?"

"Of course not," he said. "Why would it?"

"Why would it excite anyone?"

"Girls!" Joanna snapped so loudly I might have thought an M80 had exploded if I hadn't seen her do it. "Come over here so your fathers can take you home to recover. You have a big day coming up next weekend."

They both ran over, waving their arms. Ariel slammed into me and locked her arms and legs around my thigh. I'd had enough of this conversation, so I said, "Nice meeting you, Joanna." Then I walked away with Ariel latched onto my leg. She giggled and said, "Oh no. Don't let me go," over and over.

We made it outside the studio and into the parking lot before I heard Bobbie say, "Daddy. I want a ride like that."

"I can't, honey," Ed said. And that's when I remembered his stupid fucking ankle.

I stopped and said, "Ariel. Let go, sweetheart."

"Why?"

"Just do it, please."

"This is stupid." She let go and flopped onto the ground. Then she crossed her legs and folded her arms like Joanna had. I looked at Ed, and he nodded as if to say thank you. I wanted to rip his gimpy ankle off his leg.

"Why did I have to let go?" Ariel asked.

"Because it hurt me."

"It never did before."

"Maybe I just never told you that it did."

"Hmm." She considered this for a little bit by placing her index finger on her lips and tapping. When she came to a conclusion, she stood. "I don't want to hurt you."

"That's very nice of you," I said. "Let's go home and see Mommy."

I opened the truck door and hoisted her into her car seat. "Mom," she said. And I buckled her in. "I'm not a baby."

"Okay." Another car door opened and closed. "Whatever."

A window behind me squeaked as it rolled down. I turned to see Ed stick his head out the window and raise his chin at me. "Really, Vez. Let's do get a drink before you go back again."

"I'll talk to the boss."

"Awesome," he said, and then he drove out of the lot.

After I'd buckled in and started the engine, I asked Ariel, "What's your mom say about Ed?"

"Ed." Ariel laughed like I'd said the funniest thing she'd ever heard. Her laughter was almost enough to make me forget I was angry. Her curls bounced, and she made little fists that she pounded against her thighs. "Ed. That's hi-*lar*-ious, Daddy."

"Pay attention, sweetheart. Ed. What does your mom say about him?"

"Who's Ed?" Ariel asked. She laughed again, so I just ruffled her curls and drove home while she sang her own words to the songs that came on the radio. After I was gone, there'd be nothing I could do to stop her or her mother from doing anything they wanted to do. That was one thing that I knew for sure.

CHAPTER 4

Sergeant Harris died a few weeks before we went to the desert the third time. He was watching his boys roll Tonka trucks over the front lawn and fight with battery-powered lightsabers. A guy I now know as Detmer sped through the neighborhood in his cobalt blue, raised F-150, and Harris yelled for him to slow down. Detmer stopped, hopped out of his truck, and jogged toward Harris's house.

"Get inside, boys," Harris said. I know this because his wife told me she heard him say it. I also know Detmer shouted, "What did you say to me, nigger?" because Harris's wife had heard that too. I don't know why she decided to tell me these things. Maybe because I'd never talked to her before the funeral, and maybe Harris had talked about me like I was an okay guy; she never told me that, though. I don't know if Detmer has a family, but because of him, I want to believe there is a heaven and a hell, so that when he dies, he'll burn for eternity.

Detmer shot Harris three times with an M1911: chest, face, and right shoulder. That's why Harris had a closed-casket funeral. Detmer was arrested, and he's in prison for life. Harris is dead, and his boys have no father; they saw his bloody corpse on their front lawn. Harris died splayed out between a Tonka dump truck and a flickering, red plastic lightsaber.

Rake and I handled Harris's death the way we handled most things that were supposed to depress us. We drove out to the woods and shotgun-blasted empty wine bottles, blew bowling pins into oblivion and destroyed an acoustic guitar that Taylor had bought him a couple Christmases before. Rake said he never played the guitar so there was no reason to keep it; that was a lie I didn't discover until after he died. It was a lie that didn't hurt anyone, but it was hard to believe he kept a secret like that from me. He was the closest thing to a best friend I ever had, and I'd kept a secret from him that may have killed him, so I probably knew him a lot less well than I believed I did—an uncertainty that'll haunt me forever.

After we'd blasted holes into everything we'd brought to shoot, we drove back to his place and started small fires in his backyard.

We sloshed gasoline on a pile of dried leaves, and they burned so fast that the sporadic breezes that swept through the yard didn't have a chance to snatch a flaming leaf and send it into someone else's yard and set the whole neighborhood on fire, one leaf and one yard at a time.

"I want to set this whole neighborhood on fire," Rake said. "One leaf and one yard at a time."

"No you don't."

"I wish I could at least watch the guy who shot Harris burn alive."

"His name was Detmer."

Rake splashed gas onto another pile of leaves. "The only good Detmer is a charred Detmer." He lit a match and tossed it on the pile. Leaves flared, and the heat swelled, shoving the cold away for a moment before the leaves were ashes. Soon we were left with nothing to burn that wouldn't potentially get us in serious trouble, and I invited Rake over to my place. It was better to get out of there before the neighbors called the cops or came over to confront Rake about how stupid it was to do something like that in the middle of a residential area; a discussion like that with someone Rake didn't know was unlikely to be settled with words alone.

We sat on my back porch. Gold and red rays beamed through the branches of the leafless trees and lit up the pink hopscotch squares Ariel had scratched onto the concrete with chalk. Kaylynn and Ariel bounced on the teeter-totter while Rake and I talked. Kaylynn had offered us food, but Rake and I were in a bad spot from drinking by then. Food was only going to knock me down, and Rake didn't like eating food he didn't pay for himself. So I'd grabbed a half-empty case of Bud heavy from the refrigerator and set it between a couple folding chairs.

Rake said, "Harris could've got me booted."

"For killing that camel?"

Rake shook his head. "No. He understood that."

"You shouldn't have done it."

Ariel and Kaylynn both laughed as the teeter-totter squeaked and rattled. Rake stared off into the woods beyond the fence.

Most of the leaves had fallen, so the view was mostly branches crisscrossing until you looked hard enough in one spot, and then all of those branches seemed to clasp together and slash out swaths of the blue-gray sky: made it look like the world was caught in a net weaved from shadows.

"Last year I shot a urinal off the wall down at the range."

"What?"

He scratched the scar along his chin. "I know."

"Were you pissed at Taylor?"

He clenched his right hand and the knuckles popped. "When am I not pissed at her?"

The breeze was cold. Kaylynn and Ariel seemed to be winding down, and I wasn't sure if their being outside was making this harder for Rake.

He reached down, shuffled the box for a few seconds and said, "You remember when you shot that dead kid?" I knew he'd made all the noise to ensure that Kaylynn and Ariel couldn't hear him.

"Yeah." I shot a dead boy in the head on our first deployment —back when deployment wasn't synonymous with desert. We'd seen a boy impaled on an iron rod on a hill outside a town where there was supposed to be an abandoned weapons site. Later we learned that killing someone in that way was a game for those people. They'd jam the rod up the person's ass, and the object of the game was to hit as few vital organs as possible: to try to keep the person alive and in pain. I saw a boy like this, a game piece, on top of a hill when Rake and I were on an Op that resulted in a lot of wasted time in the present and a lot of wasted days trying to forget what we'd seen afterward.

"Sometimes I think we shouldn't have just left him there. Like we left Cammack."

"There was nothing we could do for Cammack," I said.

He grunted and shook his head.

Kaylynn and Ariel dismounted the teeter-totter and walked over, hand in hand. When they made it to us, Kaylynn said, "Can we get you boys anything?"

"No, babe," I said. "We're good."

She nodded.

Ariel looked at Rake and said, "What's wrong, Uncle Rake?"

He laughed. "Give me a hug, sweetheart, and I'll forget everything that's ever bothered me." He leaned forward in his chair and hugged her.

She kissed him on his scar and said, "Your face hurts my lips."

"If I'd have known I was gonna get a kiss from you, I'd have shaved."

"Okay, Ariel," Kaylynn said. "Let's go watch some TV."

"There's never anything good on."

"Do you want to read a book?"

"I don't know," Ariel said. "I guess TV's okay."

Kaylynn said, "I wonder where she picked up this desire to create conflicts for no reason." She eyed me but didn't seem to mean it maliciously.

"Why don't you and your mom read a book together?" I said.

"Fine," Ariel said. "It better be amazing." Then she walked into the house.

Kaylynn said, "I'm so sorry about Harris, babe. He was a good guy." She squeezed my shoulder. Warmth was there, but I had to tell myself I felt it. She left us to talk, and I grabbed a beer from the case and cracked it open. Rake grabbed a second.

"We keep saying there was nothing we could do." He sighed. "There was something. We just didn't."

"I did something." I reached behind my head and yanked the sliding door closed. "I shot a dead kid in the head because I'd convinced myself I saw him breathing."

Rake said, "We should've buried him."

"You wanted to bury Cammack, too. What fucking difference does it make?"

"It just seems wrong, leaving them in the open like that for someone else to find. What if Harris had been shot, and then they just left his body out there so kids headed to school or out playing two-hand touch had to watch him rot and be eaten by bugs and buzzards?"

"That's one thing that makes America great. We don't let people rot on our front lawns."

"Yeah. We fought for that. We fought for the right to get so drunk that we can get in our cars and crash into a school bus and walk away with no memory of killing sixty kids. We fought to get shitty service from anyone who doesn't find us attractive."

"What?"

"Just some dumb shit I read a while ago."

"When did you learn to read?"

"Fuck you." He smiled.

"Come on. What's up with the urinal?"

"I was sitting in a stall at first. I didn't even have the balls to put the barrel in my mouth. I just ran my thumb along the metal, reminding myself how metal can stop motion. How a steel wall could just be there and stop something from moving because it's real. Thinking about how a projectile is kind of like a wall compressed. You aim, pull a trigger, and then, instantly, a wall stops the thing you want to stop." He sipped his beer. "I know it's not the best analogy."

"I'm glad you didn't do it."

He nodded. "After I bitched out, I stood in the bathroom and stared at the urinals for a while. There were seven. I couldn't stop thinking that it was stupid that there were seven. There were only four stalls but seven urinals. Why not eight? Why not six? I didn't think for a second about why there were four stalls. I couldn't let the number of urinals go."

I scratched my beer can lightly across the concrete, back and forth.

"So I shot one of the urinals and the porcelain cracked and dropped onto the floor and water gushed onto the tiles: clean water. I stood there watching water slide across the floor. It slapped against my boots. And I thought, for a minute, that the bathroom might seal itself up, and then the water would rise until I drowned. Then I wouldn't have to shoot myself. The water could swallow me and I wouldn't ever have to make another choice about anything."

"So what happened?"

"Harris came in. Took my weapon and told me to get the fuck out of there. So I left, and then he never talked to me about it again."

"He got it. I'm sure."

"I shouldn't have shot that camel, Vez. I shouldn't have been such a dick to Harris. He kept my head on straight."

"Just because Harris is dead doesn't mean you need to feel bad about all that shit you did. I mean, yeah. The camel. That was fucked up. But how much of this isn't fucked up?"

Rake finished his beer and grabbed another. "Taylor left again."

"Oh, God. Can you wait a week before you start acting like an asshole?"

"I know where she is this time."

"Don't do anything stupid."

"He cut part of her ear off."

"And she went back to him?"

"I'm going over there. I'm going to peel his face off and pour salt all over him. Then I'm going to talk to him for a while: about baseball or football." He nodded as if it made sense. "After that, I'm not sure."

"That's a terrible plan."

"What would you do if someone cut Kaylynn?"

"I don't know."

"Or Ariel."

"I don't know, man. I don't sit around trying to come up with hypothetical sick shit to worry about when there's already enough real problems to deal with."

"Think about it now, then. What would you do?"

I crushed my empty beer can, tossed it onto my lawn, and then we went after Taylor.

CHAPTER 5

We lost a guy in training because he broke his foot on a ruck march and then ran fifteen miles on the broken bones. Guys do that all the time and are fine, but this guy fucked his foot up so bad he was discharged; I don't even remember his name. Cammack joined us about halfway through our specialized training, and even though he was with us during most of the tough shit, he hadn't been there in the beginning. This isn't about training, though. This is about our first deployment.

While we were still en route to the drop zone, strapped into our jump seats, Cammack kept talking about how proud his dad would be to see him doing this. He had to shout over the C-130's rumbling engines: "Making a difference in something that matters." Cammack said this over and over and nodded his head in agreement with himself.

After a few minutes, Rake pulled his helmet over his eyes.

"That's what my dad says about stuff like this. Making a difference in something that matters."

"Ka-doosh!" Manchin pantomimed a mushroom cloud that started by his balls and then bloomed up beside his smiling, freckled face.

After the third or fourth time, I said, "Your mom is like a Howitzer."

"What?" Cammack leaned closer to me. His teeth showed a little, like he expected me to say something funny, like he believed we all felt exactly the same as he did, and that an unbreakable bond had formed between us just because we were on the same plane and headed to the same destination.

"Your mom. Is like. A Howitzer."

Rake pushed his helmet back and sneered. His jaw was smooth and sharp back then.

Cammack laughed and then said, "Why?"

"Cause fuck you," I said. Then Manchin said, "Ka-doosh!" and Rake laughed so hard his helmet fell off and *thunked* between his boots.

A Humvee was waiting when we landed, and we wasted no time admiring the scenery. It rained almost constantly except for that day; that was the only day the sun broke through the gray and black cloud cover, the only day the mud had a chance to dry up enough to hold tracks.

While we rolled over soggy dirt roads, Cammack talked about how his family was all veterans: "All the way back to the Revolution. Dad flew Tomcats. Grandpa was a Comm guy," and so on. He kept adjusting his chinstrap, pulling it tighter, trying the helmet on, and then loosening the chinstrap and trying the helmet on again. "Even my grandma was a nurse. She met my grandpa in the hospital after he got shot in the ass while trying to drag a Comm line across no-man's-land. Dad was conceived in a military hospital bed while a bunch of wounded guys watched my grandparents fuck."

"Are you sure that wasn't a porno?" Manchin asked.

"I don't watch porn."

"What the fuck do you mean you don't watch porn?" Rake said. "You think you're better than me?"

Manchin said, "That escalated quickly."

"I just don't like it," Cammack said. "It's so fake."

Rake snorted. "Sex is sex."

I didn't ask Cammack, but I was pretty sure he was talking about something that happened in an old story. Most of his stories sounded like they belonged to someone else. It didn't matter to me if what he said was true or not, though. He could give himself whatever history he wanted as long as he did his job and didn't get me killed.

There were a few reasons we might've given Cammack the most shit: he was FNG; he was from a city; he'd gone to college for a couple semesters trying to get a degree in anthropology, whatever the fuck the point of that is. But there were at least as many reasons that we could've just accepted him right away. He wasn't much smaller than any of us; he was bigger than Harris: we all were bigger than Harris. Cammack qualified as a marksman, and he was no stupider than the rest of us; we were all doing the same fucking job no matter how smart any of us believed we were. The thing that bothered me most about Cammack was that he seemed excited to be where we were.

I wasn't angry about the deployment; we'd been training for this for so long that I was glad we were finally doing something with our training. It felt good to be useful. I didn't see it as an amusement park, though. Cammack's excitement made me think that he thought war was, and would continue to be, fun.

"I can't wait to use my weapon," he said.

Rake said, "Use it on yourself then."

Harris said, "Enough of that bullshit."

"Who says something like that, Harris?" Rake asked. "We don't need this hard-on running around ready to spurt at the first sign of enemy ankles."

"Hey, Cammack," Manchin said. "Your mom is like an illumination round."

Cammack tightened his chinstrap and then put his helmet on. He snapped the buckle. It was too tight, made creases in his chin. "Why?" he mumbled.

Everyone but Harris said, "Cause fuck you."

CAMMACK'S BOOTS WERE shined so well it was hard to see scuffs unless someone shoved them in your face. "I've been shining boots since I was six." He unsnapped his chinstrap; it dangled from the left snap. "That was one of the things I did every day with my dad."

"Yeah?" Rake said. "You need to get a girlfriend."

"I have a girlfriend," he said.

"What's his name?" Manchin asked.

Cammack laughed. "You guys are such dicks."

"Oh?" Manchin said. "Your mom's like an MRE."

"How many of these do I have to listen to?" Cammack asked.

Rake shrugged. "Harris. How many hours till we get where we're going?"

"A lot," Harris said. "So pare it back."

"Are we there yet, mommy?" Rake smiled at me.

"I'll turn this car around, you little fucks," Manchin said.

"Your mom is like an MRE," Rake said.

"No she isn't," Cammack said.

Rake raised his eyebrows. "That's not what I heard."

"Your mom is like a flak vest," Cammack said.

Rake said, "Why's that?"

"Cause fuck you." Cammack smiled.

Rake said, "Somehow it's less funny when we aren't talking about your mom."

"Shit," Manchin said. "Look at this guy."

Rake peeked around the passenger-side headrest and said, "Some old dude's standing in a mud puddle waving his arms around. He's gonna give himself a heart attack doing that fucked-up Tai Chi."

"This isn't good," Manchin said.

"Driveon," Harris said.

"Maybe we can help him," Cammack said.

"Maybe it's a trap," Rake said.

"Stop, Manchin." Cammack opened his door. "Or I'll jump."

"Oh no. It's like two feet down. Don't do it."

"Fucking stop," Cammack said.

Manchin sighed and mashed the brakes. The Humvee squealed to a stop. Cammack hopped out and walked over to the man. I couldn't understand what the man said, but he sounded excited. Soon Cammack came back. "I need to go see what this guy's freaked out about."

"Peace," Manchin said. "We'll see your dumb ass back in the States."

Cammack scanned each of us, and his face went slack. "None of you are coming?"

"I'm not," I said. "I'm not here to help random old men."

"Neither are you," Harris said. "Get back in."

Cammack shook his head. "I'll be back." Then he ran over to the old man, and they jogged into an alley between a couple houses and out of sight.

Rake set his helmet on his head, thumbed his weapon to fire and said, "Fuck it. You guys go ahead. I'll get Cammack to the target." He stepped into the mud and ran after them.

Manchin said, "Is this shit really happening?"

I didn't know what else to do, so I said, "Your mom's like a patriot missile."

"For fuck's sake, Vezchek," Harris said. "Fuck you. Fuck. You."

We sat there for a while. Clouds coasted across the gray sky, and I tried to make out shapes: a bear, a fish, a scorpion's stinger. But I couldn't concentrate on that distraction for long.

I felt like an asshole for letting Rake go alone; I was an asshole. Ugly what-ifs circled around and around my head until we heard an explosion. Smoke billowed from behind the buildings where Rake, Cammack, and the old man had disappeared, so I grabbed my weapon and headed after them before anyone could talk me out of it.

I made it through the alleyway and saw Rake on his back in the mud. His flak helmet was twenty feet behind him, beside my boots, two feet from the alleyway's end or entrance, depending on how you approached it. There was no old man. There was no Cammack. There was just smoke, flames, body parts, and Rake's laughter. I picked up his helmet. The chinstrap was severed, but the buckles were snapped. The halved strap swayed in the breeze that shoved the smoke rising from the rubble into oblivion. I didn't see Cammack's helmet anywhere. I wondered if he'd adjusted it perfectly before all that remained of him was gore and boots. And I wondered what Cammack's dad would've said about the way that his son had died.

CHAPTER 6

After I brought Rake's creation to my house, I spent a few hours each day in my garage staring at the seven planed boards that Rake had pressed flush and glued together. On the top board, he'd carved "Oh well. What the hell?" into the center. He'd left no explanation for why he'd done it, and I don't know if he'd finished the thing a long time before he killed himself, or if he'd just finished working on it a few minutes before the muscle relaxers he swallowed killed him.

Taylor didn't know what it was for either. After we'd fucked that day, the day I went over to get the planer, I asked her if she had any idea what he was working on.

She groaned and then said, "Shut up so I can pretend this is real for one minute."

I counted twelve breaths before I asked her again and she said, "Oh my God. Who cares about a bunch of wood that some dead asshole glued together? 'Oh well, what the hell?' What the hell do I care?"

"You don't mean that."

"Damn it." She stood, pulled her skirt down to hide her ass and upper thighs. "Who cares about any of this anymore?" And then she went into the house and locked the door behind her.

I cared—which was why I'd spent so much time in my garage staring at the wood. At different times that week, Kaylynn and Ariel had both found me out in the garage, slumped in my metal folding chair; they'd let it go on three days before Kaylynn came out and asked me, "Has that thing moved yet?"

To which I replied, "Har har, babe."

Later that same day Ariel came out and asked what I was doing.

"Looking at this wood," I told her.

"That's so boring, Dad." Her shoes scratched dirt over the concrete. "Mom said to ask if you want chili or lasagna."

"What do you want?"

"I don't care."

"Lasagna, I guess."

"Great." She opened the freezer and pulled out a tube of ground beef. Then she went back into the house.

I couldn't stop thinking about the phrase on the top board: "Oh well. What the hell?" Rake had sung that the day Cammack died; it was such a long time ago. But when I saw that phrase on the board, I felt like we'd just been there, on a mission to destroy some weapons that weren't there or that never existed. Before I knew it, I was hearing Rake say that Cammack's boots were "Boot-tastic. Can you believe it?"

Where had Rake heard that song? What was that song? That's what he said. "Do you remember that old song?" And then he sang it while blood ran from the gash on his face. I stood and then squatted beside the boards. My knees cracked to remind me how beat up they were, how beat up I was. I ran my fingers over the words. He'd sanded the boards down after he planed them. The chiseled-out words were smooth. Each letter was perfect as far as I could tell. But I'm no carpenter, so who really knows how well done it was? All I know is I didn't get any splinters, and that has to be an indication of some level of skill.

"Oh well," I sang. "What the hell?" It echoed in the near-empty garage. All that I kept in there was the planer, Rake's boards, the corrugated shelves on the back wall, the freezer, an electric chain saw, the lawnmower, the gas can, the folding chair, and my heavy bag and its stand. My truck was too tall to fit in the garage, and Kaylynn liked to park on the street in front of the house, which pissed me off for a long time. It's ridiculous that something like that had ever irritated me. *What's the deal? Are you too good to park in our garage?* If she'd parked in the garage, I'd have just been annoyed every time I needed to move her car so that I could hit the heavy bag or so I could sit in there like a dope, staring at this stack of boards that my dead friend had glued together.

I stretched out over the cool concrete on my back beside the wood; the thing was as long as I am tall. Maybe Rake was making an effigy of me to burn because he found out I fucked his wife, and because he'd mourned the loss of a child that wasn't his to mourn because I had been too scared to tell him the truth. Of course that's not what it was, because the whole world didn't revolve around me.

But this thing, this pointless stack of connected boards, did involve me, whether Rake intended it or not: because of that fucking phrase, because he'd sung that song, because I'd heard him sing it. Because he was my friend and I'd hurt him and now there was no way for me to ever receive or even ask for his forgiveness.

The fluorescent light hanging from the ceiling hummed. I ran my fingers along the boards' edge and felt carvings I'd not noticed before. I rolled over and pushed myself to my feet and walked around the boards looking for clues. Along the top edge of each board was a roman numeral: I through VII. The top board, with the phrase on it, was VII. The board on the floor was I. "Oh well," I sang, "What the hell?" There was a pattern. My phone alarm pulsed, and the phone vibrated itself off the chair arm and crashed onto the concrete floor. It continued to pulse, making an irritating buzz that drowned out the fluorescent light's hum and reminded me how much I hated phones. It reminded me of Rake forgetting to charge the sat phone near the end of what could've been a completely unremarkable deployment. As far as I know, nothing was hurt except for the village the Spectre had pounded into ashes and dust, and it wasn't my job to do anything more than call in the air strike. Rake had fucked that up; the guilt of what might have happened on that mission could've died with Rake if I'd let it go. How hard could it be to just forget what had happened and focus on living the best life I was capable of? How hard is it to just forget about what-ifs and live?

CHAPTER 7

Two days before the end of our second desert deployment, Rake and I sat in the shade cast by a rusted-out deuce-and-a-half that was buried to its wheel wells in hard-packed sand. That truck was a relic from a war we had nothing to do with, but we were glad it was there to lean on. Rake ejected his clip into his palm and slapped it back into the magazine well over and over while we waited for the Spectre. We'd called in an air strike on a village a couple hundred yards from where we sat because weapons were in the houses, or there were terrorists; it didn't really matter. We were short, and Kaylynn and Ariel were my first priorities—which is another way of saying staying alive was my first priority. So Rake and I had said, "Yes, sir," to our orders and rushed over the sand and fields dotted by scorched poppies. We couldn't have swept the houses if we wanted to, though. We never got closer than the truck we leaned against.

If the Spectre would've come right away, then the kids in those houses might've been blasted into nothing without us ever knowing they were there. But kids had swarmed out the doors not long after Rake had made the call. Rake tried to call the strike off right away, but the sat phone was dead. He hadn't charged the battery the night before and didn't turn the phone off before shoving it into his cargo pocket after making the call. I don't know exactly how long we waited there; what I do know is that it was long enough to kill the phone's battery and give us plenty of time to think about what was headed our way.

"It's probably not even coming." Rake kicked out a shallow trench with his boot heel.

"It's coming," I said. "It always does."

I could've shouted for those kids to run, but they might've been there to draw us out, and I wasn't interested in bleeding to death in the sand beside a fallow poppy field a few days before I left the desert. There were other options. I could've fired rounds at the sky to try to scatter the children. I could've run the seven miles back to the FOB and used the fixed Comm to call the strike off. I could have done a lot of things. What I did was press my back harder against the rusty metal of the truck; then I spat and watched frothy bubbles pop until there was nothing left but dark sand. That darkness faded quickly; the sun's heat sucked moisture from the shaded ground as fiercely as it drew sweat from my armpits and chest. Sweat beads slipped down the backs of my knees and rolled across my calves. I wanted the sun to evaporate *me* so that the wind might shove me out of the desert.

Rake slapped the clip into his weapon and said, "My dad saw the Spectre cut up some jungle in Nam once." He laughed. "He called it the fucking Spooky."

I said, "Who cares what he called it?" because I didn't want to talk. I had this stupid idea that if I was silent, I might be able to think this situation into something less awful. But there was little else for us to do but talk or watch those kids throw rocks at one another, and I didn't want to think about what might happen if they ran back into their homes before the Spectre showed: not that the result of that had many facets to consider; they'd be charred bone chips and soggy ashes splattered around the cracked cinder blocks and dirt-caked stones their homes were made up of.

Rake unsnapped his chinstrap and scratched the dark scar that ran along his cheek and wrapped underneath his blocky jaw. He ejected his clip, popped out the top round, and then mashed the rest of the rounds down with his thumb. The spring creaked. "Does this sound like mice fucking to you?"

"It sounds like you're an asshole."

Through my binoculars, I watched the frayed bottoms of blankets suspended from brown-gray, rock-and-mortar doorways sway like pendulums. A boy in blue trotted away from the group, sat on the ground, and stared toward his village. Rocks bounced off kids' shoulders and chests. Some children tossed fistfuls of sand, others covered their faces with elbows and loose shirt collars to keep the grains out of their eyes. The boy's blue shirt flapped as the wind rushed over him. Sand grains carried on a windburst rapped against my forehead, nose, and cheeks, so I blinked hard and shielded my face with my forearm. When I opened my eyes, the boy in blue was gone. I scanned the kids who tossed rocks. Brown. Green. Orange. No blue. Then I let my binoculars hang around my neck. Dust had settled on my rifle barrel. So I slid my thumb along the metal, and awhorl of finger grease and sweat sparkled where dust had been. I buffed it away on the thigh of my DCU pants. Rake squeaked the clip spring at varying speeds, gauging my reaction with each tempo change. I told him to stop that bullshit and tell me his dad's story.

"The old man wakes up in the middle of the night to take a piss that came on so hard he thought his dick might crack. And he hears this sound—'like a giant washing machine,' he said."

"What cycle?"

"What the hell are you talking about?"

"Spin? Rinse? Washing machines make a bunch of different sounds."

Rake rolled the stray round between his grimy thumb and forefinger. "Do you want to hear this or not, knucklefucker?"

I heeled out a small trench and rested my leg in it. The cool sand in the hole felt good against my sweaty calf—even through my pants. "Go on."

"You finished building your sand castle?"

I gripped my M4 by the barrel and pounded the butt into the sand. "Tell the goddamn story."

"Out past the perimeter this giant laser beamed down into the jungle. Flames rose from the ground and lit up the smoke the fires made. Dad said it looked like someone was pouring black clouds into the sky. Like he'd walked into God's cloud forge. He forgot why he'd left the tent because he pissed his pants while he watched the fire and smoke rising." Rake thumbed the stray round into his clip. "Didn't even notice his pants were wet till he sat on his cot and the piss cooled enough to give him goose bumps."

"Why would your dad tell you that he pissed himself?"

"The old bastard made birdhouses out of old Clorox bottles. I don't think he had reasons for most of the things he did."

"What about the Spectre then? What was it there for?"

"He said it was like a flying washing machine that shot lasers. Why does it matter?"

"What was the target, Rake? Weapons cache? Water buffaloes? Ugly leaves?"

"Make it whatever you want."

"Jesus."

"What did you expect?"

"Something else," I said. "Try the sat phone again."

Rake yanked it from his cargo pocket and mashed the on button a few times. "Guess it's not one of those self-charging batteries." He tossed the phone into the trench between his boots and kicked sand over it.

"Those kids must have something better to do," I said.

"Like what? Hide-and-go-landmine?"

I didn't think about it much at the time, but since then I've wondered why the kids played that particular game. Maybe they wanted to feel the sting of rocks so they could understand pain at manageable levels before they were forced to deal with wounds that couldn't be cleaned, sutured, or cauterized; maybe it was a game of necessity. Not one of them dropped to the ground crying; no parents rushed across the craggy sand shouting for the children to stop, to tell them someone might get hurt. I don't even know if there were any parents around. Maybe the only people who could've said a word were Rake and me. But we just waited. Sunlight oozed over the brown earth, and our shadows stretched farther from us. It seemed like a lifetime passed before the Spectre arrived, and when it did, Rake slapped his clip into his weapon one last time and said, "Thank. Fucking. God."

Seconds after the Spectre's engines growled overhead, a barrage of shells ripped up the village just beyond where the children played. I didn't need my binoculars to see that. In the purple light of dusk, tracer rounds were fired so soon after one another that they slashed the ground like a red-orange laser. There was no slow buildup. The Spectre had always been there, had always been firing. Shells pounded the earth with such force that the ground trembled, and smoke plumes billowed behind the silhouettes of those children. Their reds, greens, and yellows faded into dusty shadows. Cinder blocks and rocks burst into roiling gray clouds that disintegrated and revealed hunks of flaming shards and singed stone. I expected to see flesh and bone and blood when the explosions stopped. If there was any of that, we weren't close enough to see it, and we didn't stick around and search for it.

All that remains of that village is my memory: small flames flickering on jagged stones; a few half-burned books with pages spread open, covered in letters I can't read; and some dark fabric that the wind catches and lifts above the smoke and flames.

Once the dust from the explosions had sprinkled over us, the children were gone, like they'd never been there, like the Spectre hadn't been, like nothing ever had.

"I hoped one day I'd have a story like my dad's to tell my son." Rake stood and slapped the dust off his pants. "Sorry, son. Your uncle Vez and me went looking for the cloud forge your grandpa saw in Vietnam. But all we ever found was a big ball of dust."

"Dust clouds are clouds."

"Not all bullshit shines the same." He snapped his chinstrap and rested his rifle on his shoulder. The dust had mostly settled. Small fires burned and illuminated smoke plumes that the wind bent into gray-black Ls. "The more I polish this, the duller it's gonna get."

"No one asked you to make the Spectre into a nursery rhyme."

Rake spat. "I wonder why Dad called it the Spooky."

"Some guys still do."

"You think that suits it better? Or is it too corny?"

"I don't know what difference it makes."

Rake thumbed his weapon to fire and said, "I guess I don't have to call it anything."

"No. You don't," I said. "We never saw it anyway."

CHAPTER 8

Rake pointed to Taylor's red Civic parked along the curb near the house that Rake had followed her to earlier that day. I hadn't meant to make such a grand entrance to the scene, but I was so distracted by the thought of Taylor going back to be with a man who'd sliced off part of her ear that I slammed into the curb and the truck hopped onto the lawn. The shocks were still creaking when Rake kicked his door open and jumped out. A weeping willow's leaves scratched the hood of my truck, and Rake backhanded limp branches in his path as he crunched over the yellowed grass. Tinfoil lined the windows. Cracks spiderwebbed the driveway. A tattered and twisted American flag drooped from a straining pole above the front door. Branches dragged across my face and shoulders as I headed after Rake. The rusty screen door had fallen off its hinges or been removed, and it rested against the house's mossy brick exterior. The moss was yellow-brown, dead; it crumbled to dust when I ran my fingers over it. I yanked the flag from its holder and dropped it into one of the leafless bushes that lined the house front.

Before I even entered the house, I saw the guy's pants around his ankles. Taylor was passed out on a brown couch. Her clothes were tossed on the floor, breasts flattened by gravity, ribs rising and falling calmly. Rake had the guy by the shirt collar and was pulling him across the room. The guy's limp dick flopped against his pale, hairless thighs as Rake dragged him into the kitchen. "Oh no," the guy said. "Let me go."

"Shut the fucking door, Vez."

I did, and Taylor groaned. Come had dried on her pale stomach, just below her belly button. A pipe, the bowl of which was covered in tinfoil, lay on an end table. A huge painting of a highway in the middle of the desert hung on the wall behind the couch. Someone had painted "A Man Apart" in red letters onto the starless night sky. All the other walls were bare.

"Come on, Vez."

I thumped across the creaky hardwood and into the kitchen. Rake's knuckles were bleeding and so was the guy's face.

A molar had fallen into a small puddle of blood and spit between the man's knees. Rake pulled the guy up by his hair and then smashed his bloody knuckles against the guy's face.

"Oh no. Let me go," the man gargled.

"What do you want me to do?" I asked.

"I want this piece of shit to tell me why this is happening to him."

Snot and blood oozed out of the man's broad nose. When he opened his mouth, strings of blood and spit stretched between his lips like rubber bands. "I hurt Taylor."

"Yeah," Rake said. "You cut her ear, you sick fuck."

"I didn't mean to."

"How do you accidentally do that?" I asked.

"I'm sorry," the guy said. "I'm sorry."

"That's the appropriate response." Rake dropped the man, and he slumped onto the floor. "I'm gonna cut his face off."

I said, "You don't need to do that."

"I don't *need* to do anything."

"Let's just get Taylor and get out of here."

"Please," the guy said. "Let me go."

Rake said, "Did you see her in there?"

I nodded.

"What the fuck did you give her?"

"Pills. She likes pills."

"So you drug her, and then you rape her?"

"No," he said. "She likes it."

Rake spit in the guy's face. Froth and bubbles slipped down his greasy forehead. "Fuck you, 'She likes it.' She's passed out. How could she like it?"

"This is how it is with us, man. It's been like this for months." The guy wiped the spit from his face with the back of his hand.

Rake walked over to the counter, and he banged his head against a cabinet door lightly for a couple seconds. "We're out killing terrorists, and she's back here fucking around on me with this piece of shit."

"Rake," I said. "We just need to get Taylor and roll out."

Rake nodded. "Right."

"We'll take her to Manchin's so Traci can look at her."

"I don't want Manchin to see this."

"Rake," I said. "She needs help we can't give her."

The guy spit another tooth onto his floor. Then he tried to stand.

"Stay down." Rake ripped drawers out and dropped them onto the linoleum. They thudded hollowly. "I'm gonna cut him a little before we go. I want him to remember this every time he looks in the mirror."

"Oh no," the guy said. "Let me go."

Rake found the knife drawer and pulled out a chef's knife that was in a cardboard sheath. "This is going to hurt." Rake drew the knife from the sheath; the green ceramic blade glowed dully in the ugly yellow kitchen light. "I bet you wish you were high right now."

The guy scooted back toward the refrigerator, and without thinking, I grabbed him by his greasy hair and yanked him to the ground. Rake froze. I let go of the man's hair, stood and tore the refrigerator from the wall; it slammed down on top of the guy, and he made a sound like air mashed out of a wet balloon. His arm curled around the Frigidaire, and his foot and shin shot out like he was popping to attention; his limbs relaxed immediately.

"Ding dong, the witch is dead," Rake said.

"Let's get Taylor."

Rake dropped the knife on the floor; it clanged, then settled near the guy's blue-socked foot. "I wasn't really going to cut him."

"I don't believe you."

"Did you kill him?" Rake thumbed the guy's wrist. "He's got a pulse."

"Let's go."

"It's like you crushed a beetle or something."

"All right," I said. "Let's go."

Rake snorted. "Yes, sir." He gathered Taylor's clothes and then slid her skirt up onto her hips. Then he pulled her shirt over her head and shoulders. "This is so fucked." He bit his cheek.

"You should ride in the bed with her," I said. "There's no way we'll all fit in the cab."

"I don't want Manchin to see this."

"Manchin is supposed to go to California for training. He might already be gone."

"If he's home, we are not taking Taylor there."

"Fine," I said.

He picked her up and draped her over his shoulder. Then he carried her outside, laid her in the bed, and crawled in with her. He threw his arm across her and spooned her. He was whispering into her good ear when I shut the tailgate. It sounded like he was saying *I forgive you*, over and over. I hoped to God that the guy under the refrigerator wasn't dead. And if he wasn't, I hoped none of this would ever come back to haunt me.

CHAPTER 9

Dad was still alive when I was twelve. We'd just moved to the desert, and because he wanted me out of the house after school, he signed me up for football. I didn't like football. I didn't like violence or pain. But I didn't say any of those things to him. I had no idea how to talk to him or Mom about anything.

Dad left work early to watch my first practice, and he saw me tossed aside and knocked over by boy after boy. He yelled from the sidelines at first, but when the yelling stopped, I looked over at him, hands in his BDU pockets, staring at his boots. The next play I was thinking so much about making him proud that I was slow to react to the snap. A hole in the line opened up in front of me, and the fullback ran me over, stomping on my chest with a cleat. When my back hit the ground, Dad yelled, "Jesus Christ." By the time I stood and jogged back to the huddle, he was gone.

I'd ridden my bike, so I had to ride it home. My arms were black and blue, elbows and knees covered in dried blood streaks. I imagined pedaling into the dry lakebed until I was swallowed by a mirage or riding onto the firing range to be blown apart by an A-10's Gatling gun. I knew if I didn't go straight home I'd make things worse, though. So I rode home, hung my bike on the yellow hooks in the garage and reluctantly opened the door to see Dad on the couch watching college football.

"Come here and sit down," he said. A vein in his forehead looked swollen enough to pop. "Watch these guys. See how they do it." His boots were shined, but they'd been worn so much that deep creases had formed in spots that made the shiniest parts look too glassy, almost fake. He sat forward on the couch, elbows on knees. His big shoulders stretched the seams on his starched blouse; the sharp creases in his sleeves reminded me of razors.

The guys on TV were huge, and even at that age I understood that no matter what my technique was, I'd never be able to compete with men that size. I was too heavy for the junior league, so I had to move up to senior league—which meant that instead of being the biggest and the oldest, I was the smallest and the youngest.

It seemed hopeless, but I sat and watched because disobeying Dad wasn't something I'd ever done without immediate regret.

A giant defensive tackle wrapped up the quarterback and slammed him to the turf. "See?" he said. "He used the rip move." Dad stood. His boots thumped on the hardwood. "Rip your arm up underneath the other guy's and then shove him out of the damn way." He demonstrated on the air. The crinkling of his blouse punctuated his movements. "It's that simple."

"Yes, sir," I said.

"Bullshit," he said. "Stand up and show me."

"Do I have to?"

"What the fuck did I just say?"

I stood.

"I'm on offense," he said. "I can't use my hands. Rip up underneath my arm. Then shove me out of the way."

He was a foot taller than me, so he crouched. "I'll call 'hut' and then you get past me." It seemed insane that we were doing this in the living room, so close to the television, to the lamps, the pictures and all the other shit that decorated it. Mom was crazy about the pictures and the vases even though I'd never met half the people in the pictures, and the flowers in the vases were most often brown and limp or without petals.

Before we had a chance to destroy anything, the door opened and Mom walked in. A paper grocery bag rumpled, and then her keys rattled and clanked when she dropped them into the ceramic dish on the table by the door. "What are you boys doing?"

"Headed out back," he said. "Derrick's gonna learn a few techniques."

"Techniques?" Mom shifted the bag up onto her big hip. "We're eating before long. So don't get too technical."

"You're an infinite well of puns, babe."

"Make sure he has enough time to shower and wash his hands before he sits at the table."

Dad said, "You got it."

We went out back and into the middle of the yard, away from the concrete-slab porch. Hard patches of dry earth and tumbleweed fragments dotted the backyard.

We had the worst lawn on the block, but the grass out front was green enough and trimmed enough to keep the housing inspectors off our backs. *Fucking jokers*, Dad always called them when Mom brought them up in order to motivate him to water the lawn or fertilize it.

"All right," Dad said. He unbuttoned his BDU blouse, peeled it off, and then tossed it onto the ground; it half-stood there—a corpse that wanted to push itself up but lacked the limbs to do so. "Like I said before. 'Hut,' then get past me. We're gonna stay out here till you beat me. Understood?"

"Yes, sir." I didn't want to do it, but Dad got these ideas in his head, that somehow I would grow into a man right in the middle of a lesson like this. He'd get angrier with each of my successive failures until he couldn't stand it anymore. That was what I feared most— what he would do when he realized I wouldn't immediately become what he'd hoped I would.

He got into a three-point stance, and I dropped my helmet on the ground and got into position across from him. "Put your god- damn helmet on," he said. "What do you think it's for?"

I stood, squeezed my helmet onto my head and buckled the chinstrap. The helmet pressed into my forehead, and I rocked it back and forth until the pain numbed enough so that it became secondary to my fear of what Dad would do to me after I'd failed to beat him.

We both lined up and stared at one another. I saw my ridiculous helmeted face reflected in his pupils. Black hairs curled out of his nostrils, and he ran his tongue along the bottom of his bushy mus- tache. "Hut," he said.

Before I had moved, he smashed his elbow into my helmet, and I was on my face in the dusty grass. "For God's sake," he said. "Use the rip move. I just taught it to you. Don't look in my eyes. Watch my chest. I can't go anywhere without my chest."

I pushed up to my knees, then stood. "Yes, sir." Tumbleweed thorns stabbed my palms; I pulled a couple free and dropped them on the crackly grass.

We lined up again. He said, "Rip your arm up under mine. Get your elbow into my armpit and then knock me out of the fucking way." He cleared his throat. "Got it?"

"Yes, sir," I said.

"Hut."

I took one step and moved my arm toward his, but he slapped it out of the way and then elbowed me in the helmet again. I dropped to the ground, and a tumbleweed thorn bit into my knee. Grass blades scratched my shins and ankles. Blood ran down Dad's forearm. "Are you even trying?"

"Yes, sir."

He sighed, ran his finger along the stream of blood. Then he looked at me and licked the blood off his fingers and spat. "Son," he said, in this tone he always used to indicate how important what followed would be. "You have to live *in this world*. I don't know what's going on in that head of yours. But it doesn't matter. You are *here*. Be here. Let's go again."

I stood and lined up once more. My body weight rested on my fingers, toes, and my thighs. My head thumped. Dad chewed his cheek. His jawline was so sharp and mine was so round. I couldn't see myself in him, and I think in that moment that he couldn't see himself in me, and that it made him sick. He stopped breathing. "Hut."

I didn't make it one step. He grabbed me underneath the shoulder pads and lifted me off the ground. There was an instant then, when I wasn't going up or going down; I just was. But then Dad drove me into the grass, and I couldn't breathe. There was nothing other than the need for air and the inability to capture it until Dad ripped me from the ground by the facemask and said, "Breathe, you fucking idiot." And when I sucked a breath in, he dropped me. I lay on the ground, gasping. "That's what it feels like to have the wind knocked out of you."

Between heaves, I said, "Yes, sir." I coughed and spat. Soreness spread across my back. Fire burned in my throat, and tears welled in my eyes, but they weren't from sadness.

"It's no big deal," he said. "Don't whine about it."

"No, sir."

"Now you'll be ready when it happens in a game." He slapped dust from his knees. "Or whenever."

"Yes, sir."

Dad rubbed the drying blood from his forearm. He snatched his BDU blouse from the ground and pulled it on, and then rolled the sleeves to his elbows, staring at me while he did it. There was a look on his face, a blankness that I didn't understand for a long time. "I love you, boy," he said. "You have to understand that."

"Yes, sir."

"Get cleaned up for dinner."

I ran inside, showered quickly to get away from the water that stung all the nicks and scratches on my arms and legs, and then met them at the table. Dad didn't look at me during dinner. He just smothered his well-done steak in A.1. sauce and chewed and cut and chewed and cut until there was nothing left. Dad left the table and turned on the TV while Mom and I still ate. When I finished, Mom said, "Put the dishes in the sink and get ready for bed."

"Yes, ma'am."

I did as I was told, and that night while I stared at my bedroom ceiling I decided to join the military, to show Dad I was strong, to become stronger than he ever was. It was easy to choose that then, six years before I'd be old enough to actually do anything about it. But Dad died somewhere near Alaska a few years later, and we never learned how he died. You know we weren't even at war back then? Does anyone remember what that was like?

CHAPTER 10

The only other time we went looking for Taylor, Rake and I went back to that guy's house where we'd found her. No one was home or the house was abandoned. The street lamp shone through the bay window and dimly lit the living room; we passed through it, and when we entered the kitchen, Rake flipped the light switch. No light shone down from the ceiling, and Rake pointed up. All that was in the ceiling was an empty socket. The refrigerator I'd pulled onto that guy was still in the kitchen; it had been righted and pushed back where it belonged; the cord was plugged in, but it wasn't running. Rake went deeper into the house. I headed back to the living room to wait for him. I knew we wouldn't find anyone there.

The couch we'd found Taylor passed out on was in the living room; some of the fabric had been torn, and white stuffing puffed out of the armrests. But that painting, what had been a desert scene with a road that ran from the bottom middle all the way to some point beyond sight in its center, was still on the living room wall. And as we were leaving, I grabbed it.

I brought it home and hung it in my bedroom so I could look at it before I fell asleep.

Kaylynn saw it the first night and said, "What is that crap?"

"Art."

"According to who?"

"Me."

"Take it someplace where you can appreciate it on your own, then."

The next morning I hung it on my office wall. I'd stare at it until my eyes relaxed, and it all blurred together. I'd think about that guy's arm curled around the refrigerator, about the noise he made as he was crushed. To avoid thinking about that, I shoved the painting in my closet, buried it beneath some old BDUs, and after that, I only pulled it out when I couldn't get those thoughts out of my head anyway.

"A Man Apart" in red letters was still visible. The gray road was diluted and smeared.

The desert sand was clearly desert sand at the edges, but less than an inch from the border, the sand melted into the road and the road melted into the sand: a mixture of gray and yellow. A single white line visible at the bottom center of the painting showed where the road had originated. Silhouettes of trees still sprouted from various spots, but I'm sure there'd been many more at one time. The darkness of the sky had mellowed except for a shaky oval around the red letters. Whatever was done to the painting had been done with the intention of keeping that phrase intact. I'm no painter, so I have no idea how this could've happened or why.

When I first saw it, it didn't really seem like that great of a painting. I was focused more on Taylor's nakedness, though. I'd always been distracted by her tits, even before we'd ever really talked. And she was wounded; part of her ear was cut off and Rake was threatening to cut that guy's face. The painting wasn't my first priority. On top of all that, a road that stretched through the desert didn't seem that complicated to paint. Those were the kinds of "landscapes" I'd drawn in art class when I was in grade school; we had to draw something, and a couple lines to make a road with a bunch of black dots in the white space outside the road to represent sand was easy. I'd also dismissed the painting because it was hung on some junkie's wall. And even now it isn't the painting that I see first when I look at it; I see Taylor's tits, flattened, spread wide over her chest as she lay there, passed out, ribs rising and falling, the bloody bandage on her right ear, dried come crusted into the blonde hairs above her belly button. Her pelvic bones pressed against her soft, pale skin. Then I think about the spit and blood and the tooth on the floor between the guy's naked knees, as he cowered, begging Rake to let him go, begging us to let him go. Then I think about Rake ripping drawers out of their slots, searching for knives. About how I decided to save the guy by pulling a refrigerator on top of him. After I shove all that out of the way, there is the painting. A road that goes to nowhere, a road no one drives on; a road and a night sky and Joshua trees; sand that is sliced by that pointless road; that phrase: A Man Apart.

But *that* painting is a memory. I have this painting: everything that was crisp and clear is smeared or cloudy except at the very edges.

Maybe there's some artsy word to describe what's happened to it. Muddling? Muddying? I don't know. And who gives a fuck what the technique is called anyway? What matters is the effect it has.

When Rake saw the painting in my truck bed on the night I stole it, he said, "We should burn that piece of shit and do a rain dance."

"I'm hanging it in my bedroom," I told him.

"Kaylynn's gonna hate it."

"Are you some kind of authority on what Kaylynn likes?"

"No," he said. "But if I know anything, I know what women hate."

And Kaylynn did hate it. She climbed into bed, seven months pregnant. Tired all the time from chasing after Ariel, from the baby growing inside her, tired of me coming home beat up or drunk or sad. And then I'd tacked this painting on the wall.

"You don't like it?"

"Not even a little."

She wasn't about to let the house turn into a representation of the shit inside my head; that's what I tell myself, anyway. I took it down the next morning.

I tried to figure the painting out for a while; this was after Cammack had died. So the phrase became a pun. "A Man Apart." I told Rake, and he started in on the boots immediately. I mentioned it to Harris and he just said, "Sounds like a personal problem." So I stopped talking about it and just stuffed it in my closet; if I couldn't talk to anyone about it, then I didn't want to sit around staring at it and thinking about it all day.

A few days before Kaylynn lost the baby, what would've been our boy, I'd pulled the painting out of my closet again. I was on leave and there wasn't much going on at home aside from waiting—which was a lot like what we did when we were deployed. Sitting around, telling yourself you have a good idea of what's coming, but knowing that no matter what you do to explain to yourself that you're prepared, you just aren't prepared because it's impossible to know what will happen until it has already happened. And then, if you weren't prepared, it was too late. But I had the painting on the floor, was running my fingertips over it. The paint was thicker in spots, and the colors were like waves when I looked really close.

The biggest dip in the painting was the darkness around "A Man Apart," and I ran my fingers up and down that ridge from both sides, traced the ridge all the way around a few times. The floor creaked behind me; I didn't turn because I knew it had to be Kaylynn. Rake would've said something, and Taylor had gone back to him by then anyway, so he was at home pretending everything was fine until we left again in a couple weeks. Taylor loved Rake when he was leaving. She hated him when he was home.

"What are you doing, Vez?" Kaylynn was breathing heavy just from standing. Sometimes I laughed about how the pregnancy affected her. It made me happy to know that she was constantly working so hard to make something we would both be able to love without ever having to justify that love to anyone.

"Just looking at this painting."

"Why are you on the floor?"

"A Man Apart, babe. What do you think that means?"

She took a deep breath, exhaled. I turned and saw her leaning against the doorframe. She had sleepy eyes, and her hair was short because she didn't want to spend as much time washing and blow-drying it. I didn't care. I liked it; it was hers.

"Where did you get that, anyway?"

"At a friend's house," I said. "He was throwing it away and said I could have it."

"Our baby's going to be able to paint something better than that after a couple years. Ariel could paint something better than that right now."

"Yeah. But what about the phrase?"

She walked over and put her hands on my shoulders. Her weight compressed me into the carpet. "A Man Apart," she said. "Is that supposed to be the desert?"

"Yeah." I pointed to the sand at the border and the white line in the bottom center. "It was a road that ran through the middle of the desert."

"Do you think you might like it because it's so bad?"

I shrugged and she squeezed my shoulders. Her thumbs dug into my neck, sent warm vibrations up to the base of my skull.

"You look like a little boy right now. Down on the floor, finger painting. It makes me love you more."

"Yeah?" I said. "Well, I'll love you more if you tell me what that phrase means."

"Jesus, Vez."

"Sorry."

"Sometimes words are just there. Sometimes they aren't meant to be understood."

"Then why write them? Why write anything if you don't want to be understood?"

"I don't know." She made a clicking sound and sighed. "Come rub some cocoa butter on my stretch marks. You'll like my stomach better if it's not stretched out and weird."

"I wouldn't care," I said. "You're perfect to me no matter what you look like. No matter what you do." I looked up at her.

She rolled her eyes. "You *want* to be that good."

NOW WHEN I look at this painting, after everyone's dead, I still don't know what the hell to think. Ariel doesn't like it: "It's an ugly mess, Dad." Kaylynn hates it, hates that I ever take the thing out of the closet. She's asked me to throw it away a few times. But I can't. I want to. I want to take it out of the closet, walk it to the trash bin and toss it in. I've started to, but I only get about two steps before I'm on the floor, looking at it, running my fingers over the ridges, reading the stupid fucking phrase. And then I'm thinking about Rake, and Taylor, and Manchin, and Harris, and Cammack: a son I'll never have: two sons I'll never have. I'm thinking about how I got this painting. About why I'm stuck here trying to decipher something that probably was never written to be deciphered. And maybe I'm doing it because no one else will, because everyone else thinks it's a waste of time. Throwing the damn thing away isn't going to make a difference now. There's only one potential way I know of to *un*-see things; and even that is surrounded by uncertainty. I couldn't leave Ariel without a father. I don't want to leave Kaylynn after all she's done for Ariel and me. But Rake's gone now and Taylor's alone because she told him the truth. Because Rake couldn't deal with the truth. Because I can't see any way to get to a place where all of this is solved and where no one gets hurt.

CHAPTER 11

Rake and I stood on the downslope of a clear-cut hill a few hundred yards outside a village. One of the buildings was supposed to be an abandoned weapons storage site that was disguised as a Red Cross clinic. Despite being briefed that the village was deserted, we weren't about to just stomp into town. It had only been two days since Cammack had died, and the vivid memory of his death made me more cautious and aware of my mortality than probably anything else that had ever happened in my life.

Rake scanned the area with his binoculars, and I dropped my pack and searched for the C4 and the det box. It would've been too late to do anything about it if we'd forgotten the explosives, but they were there. We had everything we needed.

Rain had fallen on us the whole time we were in-country (this is the phrase commonly used); it still fell. My socks were soaked through and my feet were numb. My left heel had rubbed raw and each step was painful. I kept telling myself that the guys who'd lived in trenches during "the great war" for years on end had it worse, but knowing that didn't make me feel any better about my situation: not until I was fortunate enough to be looking back on it. And there was hope because we knew the plan: do the demo and get out of there in a couple days. So even if the extra socks in my pack were soaked through, it was easy to picture myself barefoot back home, drinking beer and grilling steaks while my feet healed in the sun. I guess that's one reason so many men died in the wars we weren't yet around to fight in: to make it easier on the guys who fought the next wars. Which was why so many of us would die: progress. So things got easier and easier, generation after generation, until everyone could live forever without having to do a single thing he didn't want to do.

"There's some fucked-up shit on that hill."

I grabbed the C4 and shoved it in my right cargo pocket, dropped the det box in my left and then buttoned them. "What?"

"Just," Rake said. "Man." He handed me the binoculars.

I peered through the binos at a hill on the far side of the village: rods were stabbed into the ground helter-skelter, and those rods alongside dark green patches of uprooted turf that littered the hill made the whole place resemble a mangy porcupine from a Dr. Seuss nightmare. As odd as all that was, it was near the hilltop where I saw what Rake meant: a naked boy impaled on one of those rods. I shoved the binoculars into Rake's chest, and he snatched them away. "We have to get him down," I said.

"No." Rake shook his head. "It might be bait."

"We can't leave him like that."

Rake shouldered his pack. "I'm not going over there and getting shot for a kid who's already dead. This isn't some dumb fucking movie." He pointed to the black and red skin on his jaw that Harris had sutured. "There are no do-overs, Vez."

"You're right," I said. "I know."

"There are four buildings that might have the Red Cross symbol on the roof. But the only place we're gonna get a clear look at the roofs is from that hill. Unless we climb to the roof of each of those buildings individually." Rake sighed. "Which would mean risking getting captured by the fucks who did that to the kid on the hill."

"I'll go to the hill," I said. "I'm faster than you."

"Sometimes." Rake snatched my pack from the mud and then handed it to me. "Spot the cross and get off the hill. Let's wreck this shit and go home."

RAKE TOLD ME a million times that the boy was dead already. He was dead, and I believe that he was dead; that matters. When you see a boy impaled on an iron rod and you shoot him in the head because you want to put him out of his misery, it *is* better if he was already dead before you shot him because then it wasn't really you who killed him—even if there was nothing you could have done to save him had he still been alive. One thing I could do was cut a suffering person's pain short; suffering is a thing I could've ended. I could have stopped his pain if he were alive. But put a boy out of his misery when he's already dead?

That was impossible—unless the boy who's being put out of his misery is actually a boy inside the man who shot the dead boy. And as romantic as that sounds, the metaphors we choose for ourselves are rarely the metaphors that truly surround us.

There was nothing other than iron rods and that impaled boy on top of that hill. I could clearly see the roofs of all the buildings, and there was no Red Cross symbol. Down in the village, a yellow dog sniffed through some trash at the side of a building. Something distant crashed and shattered, and that dog tucked his tail and bolted into an alley. Rake was somewhere waiting for me to come back and tell him which building we needed to demo. But there was no Red Cross building, so there was no target. We'd come all that way for no reason, and we'd go home with one fewer man than we'd left with.

I stood on top of that hill next to the dead boy, trying to figure out what I should do. His eyes were closed, and his lips were blue. Congealed blood formed a static river over his right thigh and shin. The blood river forked and stopped at his big toe. There might have been a pool of blood beneath him at some point, but the rain could've washed it away or diluted it, or the soft earth could've swallowed it. His blue lips were parted and the tips of his upper teeth sunk into his swollen tongue. His black hair was matted to his forehead. It was parted on the right side, halfway back on his scalp. Rain started falling again: slow fat drops. They landed on his forehead and then slid over his high cheekbones. There was no thunder or lightning, and at the time I was still unsure about God and what our relationship was, so I prayed in my own stupid way. I promised to be a better man if God would strike this boy with lightning and bring him back to life. I'd sneak the boy out of there, bring him to America and raise him as my own. I'd give this boy the life he'd never had a chance at.

A hand squeezed my shoulder. "Which building is it?"

"None of them," I said.

"What?"

"There is no Red Cross building."

Rake grabbed the binos from me and scanned the rooftops. He cleared his throat. "Were you gonna come tell me or just chill up here until someone gave you one of these rod enemas?"

"I was trying to figure out what to do with this kid."

"*Do* with him?"

"I thought I saw him breathe."

Rake shoved the kid's forehead, but the neck didn't bend. "He's been dead a while. Long enough to set. Snap out of it."

"What do we do?"

"Head to the extract." Rake knelt beside a puddle and washed his hands in it. He dried them on his pants as best he could and stood.

"With the kid, I mean."

Rake ran his tongue along his bottom lip. "We leave him here and get off this damn hill before someone sees us." Rake started downhill. His steps were heavy, and the leafless trees in the forest before him stretched as far as the rain and creeping fog let me see. A mountain was on the other side of the forest; black clouds swallowed its peak. Mist ascended from the earth like souls taking flight to escape this ugliness, and just when I was ready to follow Rake, just when I'd decided he was right and that I was being crazy, I thought I saw the boy exhale.

Rake stopped near the base of the hill and turned. "Move your ass, Vezchek."

"Give me a minute."

Rake shook his head and mumbled as he headed into the forest.

I prayed for lightning one more time, and after a short while, after no lightning came, I put the barrel of my M4 to the boy's head, closed my eyes, and pulled the trigger. I didn't look at the damage the shot caused. I turned away from the boy and jogged to the bottom of the hill, met Rake. "I pray we don't need that bullet you wasted," he said. Then we made our way toward the mountain. And still, for a long time after that, I was foolish enough to hope that one day I might have a son, and that I might be able to give him a better world than the one my father had given me.

CHAPTER 12

Ariel and I were on a park bench by the river the day before I left for the desert the third time. She was telling me stories about everything that passed us. A goose had married a blue jay and they were going to open a purple napkin store.

"Just purple napkins, babe?"

"Just purple, Daddy."

Women with strollers were on the way to birthday parties for animal kings or queens. Old men were often late for a haircut. One man and his dachshund passed by and he waved.

"What about them?"

Ariel said, "I have no idea what they're up to."

My favorite story of the day, though, was about a log floating on the river. It was an alligator named George who napped and drifted along until he bumped into someone who needed help. And then he'd wake up to help them. Once they'd been helped, he'd go back to sleep until he bumped into someone who needed help again. Today George had helped a duck who'd lost his house keys.

Kaylynn was at spin class again, and that meant I had time to do whatever I wanted with Ariel, and then, later, we'd do something as a family. Kaylynn hadn't told me what she'd planned for our last night together, and I was dreading a surprise party or something else that would require me to talk to a bunch of people whom I'd have gladly died without saying goodbye to. She always seemed to find a way to make me feel bad because of how kind she was to me: which was just another reminder of how selfish I was.

Ariel pointed at a group of flowers growing around the base of a concrete trash can just off the path and above the riverbank. "Look at the pretty blue violence, Daddy."

"How did you learn what those were called?"

"Mom. She said, 'I got violence coming out of my ears.' "

"It's *violets*, sweetheart," I said.

"I *said* violence, Daddy."

"Pardon," I said. "I guess I misheard you."

"You have to go away again?"

"I do."

"Ugh." She kicked her legs. Her red shoes reminded me of *The Wizard of Oz*, and that reminded me of the guy I'd crushed with a refrigerator.

"Do you know who the Wicked Witch of the West is?"

"A pumpkin," Ariel said.

"Why do you think she's a pumpkin?"

"Because Halloween."

"Are you going to miss me?"

"Of course." She pushed some blonde hair behind her ear. "Who's going to help me run away from Mom when she gets mad?"

"What does Mom get mad about?"

Ariel shrugged. "Dirt. Bills. Old apples. Having to do everything."

"Is that the only reason you're going to miss me?"

"No."

"I'm going to miss you."

"I *know*," she said. "When are we going home?"

"Soon," I said. "Should we bring her a violet?"

"They're coming out of her ears nowadays." She tugged at her dress. "Mom says blue violence are the prettiest. But those are gross. They're by the garbage."

"We don't have to tell her where we got them."

"I don't want to lie."

"If she never asks where we got them, then we won't have to lie." I stood. "Wanna risk it?"

Ariel slumped on the bench so that her feet almost touched the ground. "Fine, Dad."

I walked over, plucked a few of the flowers, and then met Ariel back at the bench. She hopped off, and I took her hand. She smiled and bit her lip the way that Kaylynn did when I first told her that I loved her. I squeezed the violet stems tightly, crushing wetness and green from them that seeped onto my palm. I tried to remember the last time I brought Kaylynn flowers. It had been years.

WHEN WE GOT home, Rake and Taylor were there. Ed McCabe was too. Kaylynn had everyone gathered around the kitchen island. All of them but Rake drank red wine from these big glasses I hadn't even known we owned. Taylor had half as much wine in her glass as everybody else.

Kaylynn hugged me and said, "We wanted to give you a surprise send-off."

"Surprise," Rake said. "There's no beer."

"We can get some," I said.

"Bobbie," Ed said. "Come in here and say hello to Vez."

A sick feeling twisted in my stomach about the last time we'd met. "Where's your wife?"

"Layne had to deliver a baby. She might be here later if everything goes well."

"She's an OB," Kaylynn said. "Maybe the only job in the world with less predictable hours than you two."

"Funny." I smiled.

"Beer," Rake said. "We don't have all day."

Bobbie came into the room carrying a blonde-haired doll dressed in a nurse's uniform. She said, "Hi. Ooh. Violets."

I'd almost forgotten. "Yeah. I sort of crushed them."

Kaylynn said, "Where'd you get those?"

"By the river," I said.

"Next to that trash can?" Kaylynn raised her eyebrow dramatically. "I'll put them in a glass and set them on the table. I love them, babe. Really. It's sweet."

She kissed me, grabbed the flimsy violets, and took them to the sink. She leaned over the counter to get a glass from the cabinet. Ed swirled wine around in his glass while he stared at her ass; it looked good in those jeans, so I didn't blame him. But I thought about punching him in the nose, to see blood run down over his ridiculous mustache. That would've ruined the party, and it wasn't like I was going to be able to do anything about what happened back here after I left anyway. *Go ahead and fuck my wife, buddy. That's what I'm fighting for.*

"Ed," I said. "How's ballet going?"

"Ariel keeps getting better."

Kaylynn said, "They're going to camp in a couple weeks."

"There's ballet camp?" "There's a camp for everything now," Ed said.

"Dude." Rake held his hands and made a drinking motion. "How many times do I have to say something?"

Kaylynn said, "I'll go get the beer before Rake crumbles into dust." She dropped the flowers in a half-full glass of water and set the glass on the table. Flowers drooped over the side. One fell out of the glass and flopped onto a magazine with a running woman on the cover.

Taylor held her wine glass in front of her mouth like she was afraid it would disappear if she didn't watch it closely. Her stomach was bare, tits pressed hard against her blue top. I was still mad at her for letting me fuck her that night a couple months ago when Rake had passed out. It wasn't the first time, but each time it happened, I believed it would be the last. Somehow it always happened again—even after I'd convinced myself I was better than that and that Kaylynn and Ariel deserved better than that.

Kaylynn said, "You want to come, Taylor?"

"I'll stay and watch the girls. Can't trust these nitwits to do it."

Kaylynn shrugged. "Suit yourself." She scooped her keys from the ceramic dish on the hutch by the door and left.

Rake said, "Let's go out back. Kitchens make me anxious."

We headed to the backyard. Taylor said, "Why don't you girls swing for a while?" Ariel and Bobbie sprinted to the swing set. Taylor said, "I'll be over there so you men can talk about manly things and compare chest hair."

Rake said, "I've got my eye on you."

She shook her head. "Not much to watch."

"I never know with you," he said.

"You just never *know*," she said. It sounded like a joke, but her face was serious. And I thought she made eye contact with me for too long. My stomach churned. Ed leaned against the house's stucco wall. His pants didn't reach down to the top of his shoes, and his low socks didn't cover the ball of his ankle. I thought about kicking him in his messed-up ankle to make sure he was healing the whole time I was deployed so he would think twice about making a move on Kaylynn. That would've been a disaster, though. Kaylynn would come home to me standing over this gimp who couldn't defend himself; she'd think I'd lost my mind.

"So, guys," Ed said as Taylor walked away. "How many times have you been to the desert?"

"This will be our third time," I said.

"Can't they send someone else?"

"You can go," Rake said.

"I've got pins in my ankle."

"How'd that happen?" Rake asked.

"It's stupid."

"Now I really want to hear it."

The swing chains creaked as the girls hit the peak of their up-swings and then again at the peak of their backswings. Ariel leaned back hard and stuck her feet out. Bobbie wasn't as animated, but she seemed to be having fun. Taylor leaned against the pole, had her eyes closed the way she did when I'd been inside her, imagining she was somewhere else; that's what she told me when I was dumb enough to ask.

"I was playing basketball against some eighth-graders."

"Fuck off," Rake said.

Ed nodded, pushed his thin hair back off his forehead. "I used to teach junior high."

"What subject?" I asked.

"English."

"Why'd you quit?"

"We had Bobbie and didn't need the money after Layne finished residency. So I just stayed home once my ankle healed. I don't miss it."

"What did you do to hurt it?"

"They were eight-foot rims. The kids wanted me to dunk. I dunked on this boy who was just standing under the rim. I landed on his foot and broke my ankle. The bone tore right through the skin. It was pretty serious."

Rake laughed. "What kind of asshole dunks on a little kid?"

"This kind," Ed thumbed himself in the chest. "Never again, though."

"He wanted to fly an A-10," I said.

Rake nodded. "Tanks of the sky, man. The avenger fires three thousand and nine hundred thirty-millimeter rounds a minute. Those rounds are *almost* as big as my dick."

"Come on," I said. "Ariel's right over there."

Rake didn't say anything, but I knew he was sorry. He was doing this because of what would be waiting for us when we came back home. Taylor would be gone, and this guy would be here and Rake probably could tell that I didn't like Ed. He didn't seem like a bad guy—which had a lot to do with why I didn't trust him.

Ed smiled as he watched the girls swing. They'd slowed down some and giggled every few seconds. It was good to see Ariel happy, made me think she'd be all right while I was away. Taylor was running her fingers across her soft stomach. Her wine glass was empty; sunlight hit the swill that had slid to the bottom of the glass, made it look like blood. I thought to ask if Taylor wanted more, but I knew it was best to leave that up to Rake. If he didn't ask her, then Kaylynn would when she got home. It wasn't my job to keep her glass full.

"Dick jokes aside," Ed said. "What are you guys going over there to do?"

"Don't know," I said.

"Classified?"

"No," I said. "I mean. Probably. But we don't know. We suit up and drop in and hit the ground running. Whatever we have to do, we do. Then if we don't die from something stupid, we come home and watch little girls on the swing set until we have to go back to the desert again."

"Doesn't that get scary? The not-knowing?"

"How do you want me to answer that?" I said.

"Honestly."

"Do you ever think about what it would be like to not be able to do anything to help people you want to help because you were too busy helping everybody else? And then coming home and walking around the mall or sitting in a bar where no one has any idea what it took to make it so that they're able to do the stupid shit they do. To buy shit they don't need." My face was hot. Ariel had stopped swinging, was looking at me. Taylor and Bobbie looked at me too.

"Only an idiot would think it's not scary. But the scary part is before and after. It is for me, anyway. I don't know when it is for Rake. We don't talk about this stuff much."

Ed nodded. "I didn't mean to piss you off."

"Don't sweat it," I said. "I'm just tired. I want to spend time with Kaylynn but she's off getting beer because of this dick." I raised my chin at Rake and he smiled.

After a few awkward seconds of silence, Ed said, "How'd you get that scar?"

"What scar?" Rake tilted his head to the side to show the full length of it, ear to chin.

"Don't be a jerk," I said.

"I forgot I had it." Rake smiled. "Which version do you want?"

"The real one."

"My friend exploded, and the blast knocked me on my ass. When I stood up and wiped the mud off my face, I had this thing." Rake ran his index finger along the dark ridge. "My friend's scalp was on top of a rock. The rock had little, gelled blonde spikes on it. His scalp was the biggest piece of him left over that I saw."

"What killed him?" Ed asked.

"He exploded." Rake put his hands up. "Ka-doosh, bro. What's in that wine?"

"I know he exploded."

"There's nothing else to know." Rake punched me lightly in the chest. "Where the fuck's the beer?"

"Kaylynn should be back soon," I said. "The store's just up the road."

Taylor and the girls sifted past us and went inside. Taylor brushed her shoulder against Rake, and he ran his tongue along his teeth under his lip; it made a little flesh and stubble wave.

"So you just sit at home now?" Rake asked Ed.

"I do a lot of things. Take care of the maintenance and cleaning. Take care of Bobbie. Help Joanna out at the ballet studio. I'll drive the girls to camp."

Rake nodded. I knew what he was thinking; I was thinking it too. Ed was not a man. But what difference did it make? We'd be gone and Ed would be here. He was what was around, and if his wife spent as much time with him as I suspected, he was lonely. His glass was empty, so I told him I'd fill it up.

"Thanks," Ed said.

"It's the least I can do." I went into the kitchen to talk to Taylor.

She was leaned against the living room doorframe, watching Ariel and Bobbie strip their dolls and then discuss what the best outfits for them to wear were. She twirled her wine glass back and forth by the stem.

"Taylor," I said.

She looked back over her shoulder. Pushed her hair behind her good ear. "What?"

"Do you want to tell me something?"

She laughed. "Like what? You're an asshole?"

It was awkward to talk to her like this, but I didn't want the girls to see us talking, to get any ideas. Not that they would. They were so young. Still I stayed behind Taylor, staring at her hips and her tight waist. One of her brown eyes. Her left ear was red; they always glowed red when she was drinking; I noticed this because Kaylynn had told me mine did the same thing.

"What's the deal?" I filled Ed's glass from the open bottle on the counter. There was a penguin on it. The penguin wore a yellow sombrero. I laughed at the thought of an artist walking into a room with that logo and then everyone shouting, *Perfecto!*

"There is no deal," she said.

"Do you want some more wine?"

"You want to fuck me again? You never talk to me otherwise."

I set the bottle on the counter. "What is wrong with you?"

"Nothing," she said. "Fill me up." She turned around and held out the glass.

I grabbed the bottle again and emptied it into her glass.

"Thanks." She smiled in a way that made me feel like she was saying, *fuck off.*

"All right," I said. "I'll leave you alone."

"That's what all of you are best at," she said.

I walked outside and handed Ed his glass.

He nodded to thank me. "Does all this redeployment remind you guys of *Catch-22*? I know it's not the same. Yossarian was there and couldn't leave. But isn't it funny that the war just never ends? I don't mean like, ha-ha funny. I just mean, do you ever wonder what the point is?"

"Who the hell's Yossarian?" Rake asked.

"From *Catch-22*," Ed said. "You know. The guy who is trying to get out of the war because he flew all the missions he was supposed to fly, but the commander keeps raising the required number of missions? Haven't you read it?"

"Is that fiction?"

"Yeah," Ed said.

"Fiction's a bunch of bullshit," Rake said. "Fiction's for kids."

Ed nodded at Rake and said, "Maybe you're right."

"You're too easy to fuck with," Rake said. "That's one of the things that's wrong with you."

"So you have read it?"

Rake sighed. "I'm gonna check on Taylor." He left Ed and me standing on the porch together, not talking.

Not much later, Kaylynn showed up with the beer and we all went into the living room. Rake drank a couple in quick succession to get primed, and then we all settled around the couch. Ed sat on the love seat across from us. Kaylynn sat on my lap, and I could see Ed sweating it. His anger or jealousy mixed with the way her ass felt against me made me hard, so I tried to make sure Kaylynn could feel it. She squeezed my wrist to say, *I get it.* Rake sat on the far end of the couch and Taylor sat on the couch arm beside him.

"So your wife delivers a lot of babies?" I asked.

"Yeah. She's on call almost all the time. It's good money. And she likes it."

Rake burped quietly and blew the odor out the side of his mouth. "You know," Rake said as he took a drink and then rested the can on his knee. "Maybe she can deliver Taylor and my's kid. Hopefully she's pregnant. If not already, I'll try and get it done tonight. That way we'll have something to look forward to when I come home."

"Buying diapers and onesies?" Kaylynn joked.

Taylor smiled, barely cracked her lips to show her wine-blue teeth, and then took another drink. "I can't wait. It'll be so much fun."

Kaylynn squeezed my thigh. "It will be. You'll see. It sounds horrible because"—Kaylynn looked to make sure Ariel and Bobbie were paying attention to their dolls—"it seems like you won't be yourself anymore. It's not like that. It's different. But it isn't dooms-day."

"What is doomsday?" Rake said.

"What?" Kaylynn laughed.

"Nothing," Rake said. "It's getting late. We should go."

Ed said, "I wish Layne could've made it. She really wanted to meet you all."

"Yeah," Rake said. "There's always next time." He stood. "As long as we don't die."

No one laughed but me. The girls didn't say anything, but I wasn't surprised. Their attention was focused on the dolls sitting in a big circle between them. Ariel said, "And this is where they go to wait on the army guys."

Kaylynn said, "What are you girls playing?"

"The waiting game." Ariel bent the legs of a dark-haired doll in an American-flag bikini into a sitting position, and then set her on a tiny blue couch. Taylor stood, put her empty wine glass on the coffee table. She headed to the screen door and shoved it out of her way. The door rattled each time it smacked against the frame.

"Well," Rake said. "The rest of this evening should be a blast. Too much red wine again. She can't drink for"—Rake caught himself and smiled at me. "She shouldn't drink."

"See you in the morning," I said. "Try to get some rest."

"Nice to meet you, Ed," Rake said. "I hope you pilot A-10s in your dreams."

"See you when you get back." Ed waved.

"If you're lucky," Rake said.

"Well, Bobbie," Ed said. "Should we go home so everyone can get some sleep? We've got practice tomorrow."

Bobbie pretended not to hear. She moved the nurse doll next to a doll dressed in a billowy blue dress and a police officer's cap. Then she said, "Do you think she should wait here or should she wait somewhere else? Do you think nurses and police princesses play together?"

"Okay," Ed said. "Let's move it."

Bobbie said, "Sorry, Ariel. Make sure they wait till I come back." She stood.

"I'll let you know what happens," Ariel said.

"Say bye to Ed, Ariel," Kaylynn said. "It's polite."

Ariel dropped a red-haired doll dressed in a police uniform. "Bye, Ed."

"See you tomorrow, Kaylynn," Ed said. And then he and Bobbie left.

We put Ariel to bed. She'd asked me to read her *Oh No! Don't Let Me Go*; I agreed to do it even though she seemed too old for a book like that. She fell asleep while I was searching her bookshelf anyway. Before I left her room, I kissed her on the forehead and whispered that I loved her; that way, if she was pretending to sleep, I know she heard me say the words.

Later when Kaylynn and I lay in bed, after we'd had the last sex we would until I came home, she rested her cheek on my shoulder. "Are you sad that I'm broken?" Her breath was warm on my throat, and I wanted to squeeze her so hard that she would somehow suck that question out of me and devour it so that it never existed.

"We lost a baby. That happens to a lot of people. I know people say that all the time, but it's still true."

But it was a boy. I know you wanted a boy."

"I love Ariel," I said. "I don't need a boy."

Tears slipped from her eyes and landed wet and hot on my shoulder. "Good," she said. "Because there's nothing I can do about it."

"There's nothing we can do about a lot of things. But we can try again."

She nodded, and then she turned over and backed herself as far into me as she could manage. I fell asleep with my palm resting on her expanding and contracting belly.

In the morning I grabbed my bags and left Kaylynn in bed. I didn't kiss her goodbye even though I *knew* she was pretending to sleep because she didn't want me to see her crying before I left. She wanted the last image of her I had to be one of calmness, and I loved her even more for that. I kissed Ariel on her forehead, and she whined a little before rolling away from me. I watched her shoulders swell and fall a few times, hoping I'd get to watch her sleep calmly many more times.

Then I drove to base, boarded the plane, and Rake and I went to the desert for the final time together. I still can't tell you if I was more afraid of what could've happened to me while I was in the desert or what might've happened to my family while I was away. But I can tell you that I was scared. And I'm not afraid to say it.

The End

OTHER STORIES

BOSNIAN ROULETTE

A naval mine sat in the mud beside a crumbling house. The giant orb was almost as tall as the building it sat next to, and rust-colored prongs jutted from the red-gray metal. Deep tire tracks led away from the mine and, one by one, children in tattered clothes hopped those tracks, slapped the mine, and then sprinted to the back of the line. If we had stayed in the Humvee until we got where we were headed, we never would've seen any of it.

It was the third day of our first tour and all of the country we'd seen by then was mud and rubble, seemed like luck that it stopped raining long enough for tire tracks to set. We followed the tracks of vehicles that had preceded us and hoped they'd lead us to a paved road, but before we found pavement, we rumbled into the center of a shelled-out town where an old man stood ankle deep in a mud puddle and waved his arms to flag us down

Cammack asked Sergeant Harris to hold up, and the Humvee rocked to a stop. Cammack kicked his door open, hopped out, and slogged over to the old man. The man pointed his bony finger: north, south, east, west. Since I wasn't driving, directions didn't matter to me. And when Cammack came back he said, "I don't know what the guy's saying, but he sounds upset." Black clouds stretched across the sky that morning, but no rain had fallen yet, so I told Cammack, "The old man should be happy. It hasn't rained in minutes." And Cammack told me, "Never mind," that he'd handle it himself, and then he walked back to the old man.

I don't know if it was boredom, guilt, or what, but I told Sergeant Harris, "I'd better watch Cammack's back," and I followed him out there, each step mashing a deep reminder of my size-twelve jungle boots into the mushy earth. The old man talked fast and clasped his chapped hands to his chest. He pointed again, and we nodded and took off in that direction. Sergeant Harris shouted, "You know we've got some place to be?" But we waved him off and trudged toward whatever the old man wanted us to see.

Beyond a couple three-wall building husks was the house with a naval mine resting against it. I'd never seen one on land before. And all I could think to say as I watched those children skip the tire tracks and slap the rusty orb was, "What the fuck is this? Bosnian roulette," because sometimes you just say the first the dumb thing that comes to mind. That's when a dark-haired girl with a green scarf knotted around her throat smiled at me and tossed a baseball-sized chunk of concrete that plunked off the mine. Just before it hit, the old man covered his eyes and bit his lip so hard that blood trickled down his stubble-covered chin. Neither me nor Cammack flinched when that rock hit the mine, and the kids kept hopping the deep ruts and laughing as they tugged at each others' frayed shirt tails and caused one another to slip in the drying mud.

We might have just turned around and walked away if the old man hadn't shoved a picture in Cammack's face and said, "Please, help." The only English I heard the man speak. Cammack nodded at the man, said, "Fuck," and shoved his weapon at me. "I think his wife's in that house," he said. The old man flashed the picture in front of my face, but I shook my head and told him to put the damn thing away. He stuffed it in his breast pocket whether he understood my words or not.

We should have been in the Humvee headed wherever our orders said we were headed, but I didn't say anything. I just shouldered both our weapons like a dumbass comic-book hero as Cammack jogged across the yellow-brown earth and then went through the house's doorless entry. Children tossed more rocks, the old man shielded his eyes with his liver-spotted hands, and I'd like to say that in that moment I wondered where those children's parents were; I didn't think about their parents until long after my enlistment was over, and I had a daughter of my own.

I've never worked with that kind of ordnance, so I can't say what it takes to set off a mine like that. It could have been a dud dumped there by some soldiers not unlike us. They might have hauled it from the Adriatic and left it there because it was no longer a threat to anyone on land or sea. Maybe I could have fired fifty-cal rounds into the side of it for hours or hooked it to a crane and used it as a makeshift wrecking ball without ever being in danger. None of that really matters, though, because Cammack came back unharmed.

I handed Cammack his weapon, and the old man dropped to the ground. His knees splashed into the mud and then his face did. He rocked backward and looked up at us; sludge dripped from his forehead and saggy cheeks onto his button-down shirt. "There was nothing I could do," Cammack told me. "She was already dead." And then we left the old man in the mud, and we left those kids to their game, and we hustled back to the Humvee.

Talk was all we had to pass the time as we rode on, and soon Sergeant Harris wanted to know what happened. So Cammack told him about the picture of the old man's wife and about the kids smacking the naval mine, that green-scarfed girl pelting it with rocks. He told him how he ran into the house and saw the woman's dead body on her bed, long black hair matted to a pale forehead slashed with decades of wrinkles. "She was dead before I got there," he said. And that was how his story ended.

Sergeant Harris told him, "You tried to help. You should feel good about that." And Cammack un-Velcroed his flak-vest and rested his shaved head against the door. Then he asked me, "Should I feel good?" And I told him that I didn't know how he should feel. What I didn't tell him was that walking toward that mine on purpose was the dumbest thing I'd ever seen a grown man do.

Soon the mud we traveled over became paved roads and, though no one mentioned it, we never heard an explosion. If we had, we wouldn't have stopped because we had a job to do somewhere else, and when we got somewhere else, we did our job. And for the rest of our tour Cammack didn't leave the Humvee unless we were pissing, making camp, or had reached our destination.

Some people ask what happened to those children, and I tell them that a month later, on our way back, we rolled through that same town, and I asked Sergeant Harris to stop so I could take a piss. The rain had washed my boot prints away, but I didn't need those to find my way beyond the crumbling buildings that had hidden the children and the naval mine from us before. The mine was still there, leaned up against the old man's house. I didn't see the old man, though. And I didn't see the kids.

It would have been romantic if that little girl's green scarf was tied to a lamp post or the picture of the old man's wife was half-buried in the mud. I could've brought one of those things home and shoved it in a drawer as a reminder of what could have been Cammack's last day, and what could have been my last day had the mine's blast radius been great enough to send shrapnel or a shockwave tearing through me while I helplessly pointed two M16s at the black-clouded sky. But there was no scarf and no picture. If there had been, I still wouldn't know what happened to those kids. Maybe some good people showed up and carted them off to a safer place. Maybe they're all dead. It's nice to think they could be all right, though. Because I never got a scratch, didn't stub a toe, or stay hungry for longer than it took to heat up an M.R.E.

Some nights my whole body feels like it's turning in on itself: fingers pressing into knuckles, toes pressing into feet, heart contracting too tight, and wet lungs deflating to squeeze out more air than I could've sucked in. All I can do to fight that is drink until I knock myself out. Sometimes that's enough. Other times, though, the booze makes me grab the phone and start to dial Cammack's number so we can talk about that day when he ran into the old man's home. But I never finish dialing. It's been ten years since we left that place behind, and he might not remember any of this. I'd forget it all if I could, and I'm not going to be the jackass who makes Cammack remember things that could've happened when there are enough things that did happen to deal with. What matters is that we were all fine when we made it home. All of us. And if I'd kept my mouth shut, you could have stared at us forever and never known we'd been to war.

BOOTS

Each day after P.T., Rake and I polish boots. We sit on my back porch, open our tins of kiwi and pour cool water into the lids. We stuff our right hands into white tube socks, dip the socks in polish and then water. We shove our left hands into the bottom of the boots and rest the boots on our left thighs. We swirl small circles on the toes until the sun's reflection becomes a few stars that burst off the boots, and then we grab our brushes and sweep until those few stars become two—one star for each of us. Then we polish the heels, and then the next boots. And when the polishing is finished, we pass the time talking about the day that Cammack died.

FRAYED CLOTH FRAGMENTS, red-wet flesh ribbons that stream from arms and legs, cracked shingles, hunks of jagged concrete, and shattered bits of stone. Black smoke billows from a hole in the earth, and the heat of a fire beneath the smoke presses out into the cool spring air. Rake tells Sergeant Harris, "Cammack had a smile on his face when he walked out the door." And Sergeant Harris spits a stream of tobacco juice into a yellow-brown mud puddle and says, "Dumb fucker." Sergeant Harris stuffs a pinch of wintergreen Skoal behind his bottom lip. He leans against the Humvee's hood for a short while and then shakes his head. He spits again, nods a couple times, and then tells us to get in the Humvee.

"We're leaving him?" Rake asks.

"Pick up as much of him as you want," Harris says.

A blond-haired scalp is draped over a chunk of stone, a split jawbone rests in a mud puddle inches from a cracked glass bottle. The mud has absorbed most of the blood but isn't deep enough to swallow the body parts. A jump boot stands erect, a shin sticks out the top; just below where the knee should be is a bit of BDU fabric; the blousing strap still clings to the boot despite the fact that the explosion sent the rest of the boot's owner somewhere else. "There's some of him," Sergeant Harris says. The other boot lies on its side twenty yards away. Sergeant Harris points at the other boot. "There's some, too."

Rake wraps his fingers around the barrel of his M16 and squeezes a layer of mud away then flips it at the ground.

"We're lucky he didn't get anyone else killed," Harris says.

Rake snorts. "Are all these body parts invisible to you?"

Harris squats over Cammack's weapon and says, "I meant one of us."

Rake straddles the shin-filled boot. A breeze sweeps through and the frayed cloth of the BDU pants flutters. Black clouds drag across the sky, and a few side-swept rain drops hit my cheeks. Rake grabs the boot, most of which is covered in mud, but the toe is clean enough for Rake to see the reflection of his stubble-covered jaw. He strokes his chin and says, "That motherfucker could polish a boot."

"Drop that," Harris says. "Unless you plan on stacking the whole man on top." Then he peels Cammack's weapon from the mud.

Rake drops the boot between his feet. He is surrounded. A thumb, ring finger, and middle finger connected to a bit of hand rest beside a copper soup pot; a child's arm blown off at the shoulder extended as if reaching for something: a rib cage half-covered in flesh, tangled bowels that leak from a charred torso, unnamable white and pink bits. Singed pieces of paper soak up red mud and the fire that rages in the center of the mine crater wisps into view as the smoke begins to thin out. "Senior Airman Cammack," Rake says. "A real American hero."

RAKE SOMETIMES SAYS we should have grabbed all the pieces and tossed them into the fire that raged in that crater because "it would've been the closest thing to a respectful ceremony we could get done." But we didn't burn anything. We dropped Cammack's boots in the mud and hopped back in the Humvee and drove North, away from it all like it never happened, because even though we'd lost Cammack, it was his fault for being dumb enough to think he was going to make a difference in the lives of children who spent their time tossing rocks at naval mines.

RAKE SAW SOME things I did not. He saw Cammack die, saw him step out of that house with a smile on his face. His flak helmet tilted slightly forward, almost covering his blue eyes. Children tossed hunks of rock at the naval mine and each thump of rock on metal should have been a reminder of how dumb it was for Cammack to go into that house. But Cammack was already in. An old man had flashed a photograph of a woman in Cammack's face, and Cammack had said, "The old guy's wife is in that house," and he went in after a woman he wasn't even sure was real. A girl with a green scarf knotted around her throat heaved a rock at the mine, and Rake watched it float toward that naval mine, while Cammack took his first step out of the house. His lips moved, and he said something Rake couldn't hear. All Rake saw were thin lips forming the last words Cammack would ever say.

The old man knelt on the wet ground and covered his face, twenty children tossed rocks, and Rake held a weapon in each hand. Rake had enough ammunition to kill each of those children. He could have dropped the weapons from his shoulders and fired round after round into each of the kids until they dropped lifelessly into the mud. They all died anyway, and if they were all dead, none of them would be able to throw rocks at the mine; Cammack could've walked the rest of the way over to Rake, and said something like, "She was already dead," and then we could've left the dead children and the old man behind and got on with the mission.

But Rake didn't shoot the children. And he didn't aim at each of the rocks those kids tossed at the naval mine and blast them out of the sky so that they burst like flak and became shards and dust that flittered to the soggy ground. The only thing I'm sure Rake did while I wasn't there was that he did not die. I imagine all the rest.

WHEN SERGEANT HARRIS and I got to the blast site, body parts were everywhere. A shin was sticking out of Cammack's boot; the boot was a couple steps away from the smoldering ruins of the house he'd walked out of. The crease in the boot made it look like he was taking a step when the mine went off. His shin was there, like a skin-and-bone flower with camo petals that drooped haphazard around its red, white, and black center. His scalp clung to a rock, short blond hairs still gelled into tiny spikes. The other boot had been blown twenty yards away. It was tipped over and looked empty. Rake and Harris talked about what had happened. "What an idiot," and so on. I walked over to the boot that rested on its side and picked it up. There was nothing in it, nylon laces slashed in half. I wiped gore and mud from the toe with my thumb and saw the reflection of my hairless chin in the glassy blackness. Rake had picked up the other boot by then. He'd asked about what we were supposed to do. Harris said, "Get in the Humvee." And we dropped the boots, got in the Humvee, and rode on.

THIS ISN'T FASCINATION. We don't want to remember children's body parts splattered all over a muddy town center. It's not an obsession with understanding why these things happened, it's not camaraderie or love for a man who's seen the same horrible things you've seen. Rake and I don't pause when we finish polishing one boot and look each other in the eye and just *know* something. If we did, I'd say it was coincidence.

The closest thing I have to an explanation is that once we were polishing our boots and Rake said, "I've polished these bastards for three years now and they still don't shine the way Cammack's did." He didn't say that because he misses Cammack. We don't polish our boots because we miss Cammack. We don't tell Cammack's story over and over because we want to remember Cammack. Rake's talking about boots; he's pissed that he can't shine his boots as well as a man who was dumb enough to walk into a house that had a naval mine propped against it.

And maybe Rake thinks he needs to polish his boots better than Cammack did or he'll die in a stupid way—a thought that hinges on whether or not there are ways to die that aren't stupid. I polish my boots because I love dipping the sock in polish and water, making tiny circles, and beating the brush across the leather. I love the way the smell of polish fights bonfire smoke in fall and smothers honeysuckle in summer. I love that I can step into my boots because Cammack died and I did not. I love that I barely knew him, and most of all, I love that I can still say I don't miss Cammack at all.

WAITING FOR THE ENEMY

We tumbled from the C-130's open tailgate and slashed through the night clouds that had hidden us from the desert airfield below. The plane's engines thrummed and drowned us in sound until we'd fallen so far that those thick rumblings were swallowed by the air that rushed past our ears and the rippling and popping of our D.C.U. fabric. We dropped farther still, and our chutes spilled open and bloomed, the nylon cords snapped taut, and we glided to the sand—the same way we'd done on training jumps, the same way we'd done on earlier missions, and the same way we did when we dropped into the desert many times after.

That night Rake and I landed first. Our boot heels plowed into the loose sand until we skidded stopped, and we ditched our packs and slipped over the sandy, cracked asphalt, weapons pressed into our shoulders, ready to fire at whatever resistance waited. Rake and I peeled from the group and took the control tower; the rest of the guys took everything else. No one fired a shot because there was no one there to stop us from doing what we'd been sent to do. After we cleared the tower, Rake and I stomped down the stairwell, and our footfalls reverberated like mammoth springs because when there is no enemy, there is no need for stealth. We made it back into the desert night and leaned against the tower's painted cinderblocks. With the tower under our control, all that was left to do was watch the fence line and wait.

Strapped into the jump seat earlier that night I'd imagined descending on an enemy that screamed and blasted rounds into the sky, shouting about Allah and infidels, about oil and blood, about something worth defending. I hadn't considered being confronted with nothing because I wanted, and still want, to believe someone would stick around to fight if my home was invaded. But no one was there to challenge us, and soon our backs grinded down the tower wall and we sat on the rough concrete, rested our weapons across our knees, and joked that we'd fight this war against a soldier-less army on our asses. To pass time we invented a firing position: the Lazy Ranger. Raise the barrel of your weapon just above dick level and fire indiscriminately. If you hit anything, good. If not, there'd be nothing to feel bad about because you hadn't tried that hard. No enemies came, though. So our firing position went untested. And I doubt a round would've been fired at all if that camel hadn't tumbled down a sand dune that was in our line of sight.

WE SHIFTED OUR resting spots with the shade as it wrapped around the tower, the first day just staring at things: our tan, fleshout leather boots that we didn't have to polish, fly swarms that hovered in the distance like frozen smoke, razor wire that spiraled along the base of the fence, weaving in and out of rusty tank tacks. We didn't talk much because there was little to say about the not-fighting that surrounded us. So I lived inside my head not talking about how Rake had recently stomped the shit out of the new guy who'd fucked our dead friend's wife. This was the first time the new guy had dropped in with our stick, and I wondered if Rake might be worried that the new guy would try to get revenge on a deployment, in this place where it was possible to shoot a man in the back and maybe never be questioned. I worried that Rake might try and frag the new guy in order to make sure the new guy didn't frag Rake first. But it never came to that. Those thoughts were probably in my head because of too many movies—*Platoon*, *Full Metal Jacket*, *Apocalypse Now*. We needed everyone who was there—even the guys we hated. If we made it back home, then we'd name the new guy and he'd earn the right to get back at Rake. The new guy might've had a harder time blowing Rake's teeth through the back of his skull and getting away with it at home, but the fear of repercussions might've made him search for a more civilized path to justice, a path that wouldn't cause permanent damage to Rake—maybe even revenge we'd all laugh about once we'd grown too old and tired to fear one another physically.

I thought about those things because of the silence and the waiting. Until the ground pounders showed up with their tanks and trucks, we were stuck to that control tower like it was a womb. Once they arrived, we'd climb onto a transport and ride on to the next FOB. And if there weren't a FOB where we were headed, we'd fill and stack sandbags until a FOB sprouted around us. Then we'd get our orders from a satphone and handle whatever came next, and no matter what the plan was, it would change. Soldiers would die, go missing, get captured, be stupider than they were trained to be. And that's fine. In the moment, I deal with mistakes. Motion of the body is easier for me to handle than motion of the mind. And if I have to have a reason, that's why I'm forcing these thoughts out. I want to say them well enough so that they'll take on bodies of their own and hopefully be kind enough to walk out of my head and leave some space for the memories I want to spend my time with.

THE SUN WAS still up on the second day when that camel clopped over the dune. It looked goofy, kind of drunk in the way its shoulders shuffled and its head bobbed with its steps. Rake laughed and said, "Never thought I'd see one of those outside a zoo."

"This feels like a zoo to me," I said. "All we're doing is sitting around and hoping someone shows up to carry us away."

Rake dropped his flak helmet between his legs and scratched it over the concrete toward his crotch. "But we're inside the fence."

"Yeah," I said. "So the camel's here to see us."

"You and the goddamn camel are confused."

"Help me see clearly then."

"What pisses Kahlua and has tits that squirt grape vodka?"

"I don't know. What?"

"Doesn't matter. We're in Sandghanistan, and there'll be all kinds of shit for us to shoot at soon enough."

The camel was forty yards away, but nothing else moved out there. So in my memory, in the unending emptiness of that desert, the flatness of the airfield surrounded by sand that crests and tumbles into more sand, yellow-gray and infinite, that camel stands a hundred feet tall. Its shadow creeps black and long across the dune it bumbles down, and it seems a miracle that any of the world's light escapes the gravity of that shadow. I've seen a child's headless body smashed against the spidered windshield of a rust-pocked car, a mother and father bound to chairs in a roofless, three-walled building staring at their dead son—his pale throat draped in caked blood, and an old woman angrily stabbing a charred soldier's corpse with a hoe, shouting, "Before you, there was no danger here." Not one of those things are as dark in my remembrance of them as the silhouette that camel cast over the side of the sand dune as it lumbered toward the fence. But that's no mystery. I saw the camel before it reached the bottom of the dune, before it stumbled and rolled into the razor wire. I never had a chance to change what happened to the headless child, to the boy and his family, or to the soldier or the woman who wanted to hurt him after he was already dead.

When that camel rolled down the dune and into the razor wire, Rake laughed and said, "That humpy bastard reminds me of the new guy."

I laughed because that comment was the beginning of something more than silent waiting, something we could hold on to even after we'd made it home. But when the camel tried to stand, it caught its front left leg on the razor wire, and when it stepped forward, one of the blades dug in. I remember saying, "Jesus," and looking to Rake. He'd un-Velcroed his flak-vest and was scratching his chest through his sweat-stained undershirt. The camel grunted and tugged harder than it had the first time and then fell onto the glinting wire. It flopped onto its side, kicking sand and bashing its head against the ground. Eventually it rolled to its belly and then bellowed as it tried to stand, but the wire had cut too deep into the ankle, or it was wrapped around the foot in such a way that the camel could not push itself up to standing. When the camel toppled again, Rake pulled his vest snug, set his flak helmet over his face. All I saw were his stubble-covered lips and chin and he said, "Wake me up when this bullshit's over."

A CHAIN-LINK FENCE stood between us and the sand where the camel struggled to free itself. One of the few things I'd learned from my father before he died was that it isn't smart to get close to wounded animals—especially large ones. Instinct makes animals fear those who near them when they're injured, and they don't have the ability to know if you're trying to help or hurt them. So I wouldn't have tried to step out there and cut the razor wire to free the thing even if I could have; I didn't live through firefights and nights of mortar shells hammering the earth all around me to parachute into the desert and get my face smashed in by a camel hoof. And I shouldn't have been surprised that the thing strained against the wire and cut itself deeper, wrapped itself tighter with every grunt and roll. But each time the camel kicked in the sand and the wire tore deeper into the skin around its ankles and flanks, I hoped it would break loose, that it would be the one camel to figure it out for all camels—some kind of dromedary prophet that would shake free from the razors and trot away to teach all camels how to do the same.

Just before the last light of that day burned off, Rake flipped his flak helmet off his head, licked his chapped lips and said, "Dumbass animal." He stood, set his weapon into his shoulder, then aimed at the camel and fired. I thought he was shooting at the camel's head. He could have fired one round and ended it, and then we could have both waited in silent mourning for the ground forces to show up. Rake was a good shot. Not the kind of marksman they talk about on television, not like all those assholes who hid outside malls or in towers and shot oblivious civilians. Most of those guys earned marksmen badges because they shot a paper target once or twice a year. Rake was near perfect every time he fired a weapon, on the range and in combat. So when he stood and aimed his weapon, I exhaled in relief. I thanked a god I almost never talked to then and never talk to now for convincing Rake to end the camel's pain. But Rake didn't shoot the camel in the head. He shot the camels' front left leg off at the knee. Then he set his weapon on the ground and said, "That'll get blood flowing in the right direction."

The camel groaned and kicked with its remaining legs and swept its spiny, red-white nub that oozed blood across the sand. I could've taken my weapon over there and shot that animal in the head, but I did nothing except hope the sun would tire of shining down on such an ugly scene and tumble over the horizon so I could pretend a camel wasn't bleeding to death just beyond the fence. And before long, the sun did set, but it only made things worse; the camel didn't die. All night, dull, pain-soaked sounds swirled toward us in the cool desert air. Each gust of wind that sprinkled my face with sand grains carried the moans of that bleeding and trapped animal.

The next morning the camel was wrapped tighter than the day

before—razor wire around its belly, around its throat. A few times it thrashed against its bonds and kicked up dust clouds that hung in the air for a moment or so before the wind shoved them off into the desert. After the third time the camel shuffled, Rake aimed at the camel and fired. He shot it in the belly, and the camel was silent. I hoped it was finally dead because I didn't want to see it that way anymore. With it dead we could just wait out the rest of our time, backs to the tower wall, and then get on with this deployment. Go do whatever it was we'd flown all the way to the desert for, and then go back home and figure out how we'd spend our down time before we'd be sent to another desert, or jungle, or wherever the hell they wanted us to go next.

Heat waves slithered off the sand in the distance, and sweat beads dripped from my thighs, rolled down my shins and calves. My neck and back oozed and Rake and I pounded bottle after bottle of warm water from the case we'd been rationed in the middle of the night. We pissed into the sand on the side of the tower where the sun shone, and breathed in the ammonia-filled air that the sun had baked out of the urine-soaked sand. As the day spun on, we crept with the shadow that wrapped around the tower's base until we were again staring in the direction of the camel. And once the sun had dropped low enough so that our shadows stretched until they were swallowed in the darkness of the swelling night, the camel thrashed again.

"How the fuck is it still alive?" Rake asked.

I said nothing. But I wanted that camel dead. I could've done something a long time before it got to the point it was at that night. We'd sat there, waiting, anxious for the tread heads to arrive, so they could commandeer this airbase, so the Air Force could launch A10s and F16s and whatever else they wanted to send into the desert ahead of us and blast any serious resistance into steel-and-flesh shrapnel. We had no idea how long it would be before they arrived, and it was always hard—the waiting. But we would have been fine if that camel hadn't clopped down the side of a sand dune and stumbled into the razor wire right in front of us.

Night had drowned the world in purple-black when I stood and headed toward the sound of the razor wire, the near-silent jingle as it wobbled in the breeze. I stopped at the fence line but even from that short distance, half the camel's face was all I could see; it had grinded the right side of its face into the sand: one eye set far back on its head, an ear that flapped as if to shake off flies that weren't there, a cleft upper lip, and a blood-caked nostril. It breathed slowly, sucking sand grains into the exposed nostril and blasting them out with each breath. Razor wire had stripped patches of flesh off its rear right leg and had chewed so deep into its flank that the pink-white of still-living ribs shown like some kind of cage that would not let that animal's life escape. The wounded leg and the hole in its belly were caked in sand-filled-blood, and I guess it was the sand that helped form clots and slow the bleeding.

The moon was full, tacked into the sky and shining so bright that stars were hard to see. The camel's bloodshot eye reflected that moon, and I thought about taking tin-snips and clipping enough links so that I could squeeze through the fence and reach down to touch the camel's face, to feel the coarse hairs on its belly near where the round went in. I thought about kneeling there, getting close so that I could feel its hot breath on my face and whisper into its ear that I was sorry for not ending its pain sooner, sorry for razor wire and the necessity of blood, sorry for the possibility of hell, and sorrier still for the possibility of nothing. But when I finally raised my weapon to aim at the camel's head, the crack of gunfire sounded behind me, and the wind of a round swished past my leg and the top of the camel's head burst and scattered across the dark sand farther up the dune. The camel's ribs relaxed then. And there was nothing left for me to do but head back to the tower, sit, and wait for someone to take me away.

ONE NIGHT, A couple years before Rake got so drunk that he broke his back trying to sit on a chair that was no longer beneath him, before he was medically discharged, before his ex-wife found him dead from an O.D. on muscle relaxers, I asked him about that first night in the desert. We'd driven out to the abandoned drive-in to drink and stare at the silhouettes of trees and mountains in the moonlight, to listen to the crickets and to the wind, shaking leaves loose from cold-cracked branches. We didn't talk much because we'd almost run out of things to say by then. There was no unspoken understanding, though. We'd formed no bond that only soldiers can form from living through combat together. So I can't say what it was that made Rake want to spend time with me; I never asked him. But I felt something like comfort sitting near him in the darkness, in a place where I had nothing to fear but my own thoughts and knowing that he'd never try and force them out of me.

I'd fished the last beer from the Styrofoam cooler and Rake had just plopped back onto the tailgate after pissing on one of the yellow, drive-in speaker poles. The shocks squeaked as he settled and when they went silent I said, "Remember that camel that wouldn't die?"

He set his beer between his thighs and said, "Hadn't thought about that in years."

"Sometimes I think about it when I see a dog or deer smashed all over the freeway."

"Out of all the shit we saw, why would you think about that?"

"Don't know," I said. "Maybe I'm in love with camels."

"Maybe." Rake grabbed his beer, sucked the swills from the can, and then crushed it. "You think about any of the guys who got their asses blown off?"

"No," I said. "I hated most of those fuckers."

"Well that was just a camel." Rake tossed the crumpled can over his shoulder, and it clanked against the bed liner. "It shouldn't be hard for you to hate that fucker, too."

IT'S BEEN YEARS since I've been to the desert, and I'm sure the carcass is gone, sun-bleached bones scattered over the sand like the round casings, empty water bottles, and boot prints we left behind. But even though that camel is gone from where I watched it die, there are a lot of nights when I see it headed down that sand dune, toward the razor wire, and I want to crack my skull open so I can crawl inside and tell that camel to turn back. It's funny to me that I've become this man who sits alone on his porch, thinking about screaming sense into an animal that died years ago. Because even in my memory, this thing I can use words to mold into whatever I want it to be, the camel's too goddamned stupid to know I want to help.

It always stumbles, and moans, and bleeds until its head explodes. And it makes no difference if I can make you see the camel thrash against those razor-lined bonds. See its blood drip from the jagged points that smack sun flashes into the sky. See that camel rise and shake free from the shimmering wire that pins it to the desert and then lumber up the dune and melt, one heavy footfall at a time, down into the sand that shifts toward the horizon. See nothing but the glinting razor teeth scattered across the base of that dune where the camel should have suffered long and slow until it bled dry. It makes no difference if you can see that camel's footprints trail off into the desert, because those footprints were never there. They only headed toward the fence; I can't make them go away.

I will say I no more, never again, it is too farcical.
—*The Unnamable*, Samuel Beckett

HIGH DESERT RATS

July 1st, 2000

Derrick wants to go to the recruiter. Let's go. He needs reasons for being and needs things to do; we'll do that. Maybe a couple years of painting ships and stripping barnacles off buoys will help him see that things right now aren't so bad for him. I'm the one who's sweat it out for the last two months inside stripped-down airplane bellies, twisting and binding wires until my hands cramped. He's just sat on his ass, complaining and not *doing* a damn thing to change his situation. I asked Jeff to hire Derrick just like I said I would; that was the best I could do.

Derrick's slumped on the green couch, big shoulders stretching the threads of his blue T-shirt sleeves. He's got a fighter's shoulders, but he's not like the guys Dad tells stories about: big men who knocked noses off faces with sharp backhands. Derrick's just another whiner who wishes something else would be here for him to do because he's so bored with reality. If he saw me the way I wish he did, maybe he wouldn't be so bored. Maybe he'd be enraged. Can't blame anyone for the way he sees me but myself, though. "Let's go," I say.

"Where we going?"

"You said you wanted to sign up for the Coast Guard."

He drags his fingers through his bushy brown hair. "Really?"

"It's what you want." The kitchen's only a few steps from the living room, and I can see him through the square ledge cut-out of the drywall where a plant once stood; it shriveled up so I smashed the ceramic pot on the slab of concrete out back: our "patio." Pot shards and soil are still out there, and they'll stay until someone else cleans it up or the wind blows it away.

I crack open the refrigerator and shove the orange juice carton aside, grab a 22 of Coors Light. "I'm pounding this and we're gone." I twist off the silver cap, but before I can tilt the bottle to my lips, Mom calls my name from her bedroom down the hall. Can't just leave me alone and drift away to nothing. Occasional migraines must be better than constant drooling, but without all her drugs in the medicine cabinet, high school would have been a lot worse on me, would've been worse on all of us.

"Sean. Who's here, honey?"

"You know who's here." I turn the bottle up and chug. It's about half gone when I set it on the countertop.

"Do you have to be such a dick?" Derrick asks. Sounds like he doesn't want her to hear him, or maybe his throat is just getting back into working shape after being quiet for so long. I throw the cap at him, and it bounces off his big forehead. All he does is blink at me. Blink. Reset. Blink. Reset. Like Mom with no excuse.

"She's gonna walk out here naked one day, and you'll wish I'd have been worse."

He clears his throat a couple times and then slides his Vans out from under the coffee table and stuffs his sockless feet in them. He's never skateboarded in his life, but he's always tried to be different in stupid ways. We listen to Floyd and he listens to Meshuggah. We wear polos and he wears T-shirts with Gumby or Bazooka Joe on them. He couldn't avoid the baseball uniform, though: stirrups, hat, jersey, pants. His metal cleats kicked up dirt and sod on the same fields that mine and Liam's did.

"Give her a break," he says.

"Easy to say when she's not your mom."

The rest of the beer goes down smooth and Derrick grabs the baggie of orange hair off the coffee table and packs a bowl. The green one-chamber water pipe stands proudly on the coffee table all day long and Dad hasn't said shit. He took off a few days ago and hasn't been back, but he's been gone for months at a time. Dad's not the kind of person who leaves notes. If he wants to tell me something, he waits until we're in the same room. So maybe my time with him's coming. Mom wouldn't notice the pipe if it was stuck in the back of her throat, and I can't remember the last time she got mad at me or anyone: not for a reason grounded in reality.

Derrick puffs deep a couple times and lets clouds seep out his nostrils. I'd like to punch him in the mouth and make a necklace with the bashed-out teeth. That would be a crime against nature. He never wore braces and has straight teeth. Braces straightened out both mine and Liam's teeth. No amount of straightening could fill in the gap where one of my adult molars never sprouted. A bridge fixed that. Funny that a thing like a tooth can grow for so many people without them ever thinking for a second that there are people whose teeth never come in.

"Sean."

"What, Mom?" The worst thing about talking to her is that it's like she's talking only because it's what she's supposed to do. There's nothing to say: ever. Still she talks on.

"Where's your father?"

"Work!" I walk down the cramped hall and stop in her doorway. Her bare shoulders make me assume she's naked, but the flower-pattern-bedspread covers everything that would make me want to vomit if I was unlucky enough to see it. Her eyes are closed, and I wish she'd just plummet back into dreamland. "You know where he is."

"You working today?" She wipes crusted drool off her thin bottom lip with the back of her hand and then opens her eyes. I want to snip the top off a bottle of Visine and slosh the stuff over her face to wash the red away.

"No."

For a second it looks like she may sit up, but she just shuffles around aimlessly and settles after her black bangs flop over her right eye. "Why aren't you going?"

"Hitting up the recruiter with Derrick and Liam."

"Not the marines, baby." She closes her eyes and rolls onto her left side, facing away from me. The bedspread slips off her waist, and I'm stuck looking at a circular brown birthmark on her right ass cheek. She always wore skirts over her bikini bottoms, and now I know why. The same reason I wore hats all the time to hide my side-parted hair; there are only so many ways you can adjust things before you're forced to accept them or cover them up.

I walk over and yank the bedspread over her. "Not the marines."

"You heard your father," she says. "Never join the marines."

I have no intention of joining anything. I tell her, "Get some sleep." She doesn't respond and that's fine.

Back in the living room Derrick sits forward on the couch and pushes the pipe to the center of the coffee table. I plant the empty bottle beside it and say, "Up and out, man."

He stands and looks down at me with his stupid blue eyes. Some days I wish I could make him cry, but he won't crack. I've tried for years. A moronic progression of mom jokes to pussy jokes and none of them broke him down. Maybe the constant torment helped him become a guy who wouldn't sell me out. I always thought he'd be the one to give me up all those days I went to school floating around on Mom's valium. He didn't, but that doesn't mean he wouldn't have if things had been different. If I'd have been more honest with him, he could have turned on me back then like he's turning, now. Time to make a change, he says. Time to do something that matters. And that means he's leaving me, leaving us, behind.

I want to tell him about Mom rolling over and showing me her ass. Seems like the kind of thing I should joke about, but the thought of laughing at her again makes me sick. It used to be simple to remember things about Mom that wiped away all the stuff this new and unimproved one does. Now all I have are the embarrassing things because they stack higher and higher. The worst thing about her used to be that she was the loudest parent at all the baseball games. I hated that everyone knew my mom was the shrieking bitch on the bleachers. I'm not sure what I'd give to have that mom back, and I'm less sure that it would make things better for very long. I'd be happy with her for a while, but it's stupid for me to pretend she was *better* back then. Her and Dad were together more often. That's all.

I grab a wooden coaster off the coffee table and whip it at the wall. It bounces off and leaves a small dent in the drywall then lands beneath an end table in the corner. "Let's go." Derrick opens the door, heads outside and I follow him into the breath-sucking heat.

The relentless Mojave Desert sun is why we spend so much time in our cars or inside our parents' houses during the day. It's been like this for years, was the same for me and Liam when Derrick moved off to West Virginia last year. It's the same now that Derrick-'s back. This heat makes me wonder why more people haven't gone Manson. Simple—if everyone went Manson, then it wouldn't be

Manson. It would be normal and people wouldn't be able to talk about *Helter Skelter* like it's interesting. And it's not that interesting, but when there's nothing better to talk about, Manson's a good way to get a conversation started. Mostly it's the murders. Some people have this sick need to understand killers' minds, but why they killed doesn't matter to me. Dead bodies have to be carted off and buried whether we understand why they died or not. What's left over doesn't change because of why. You have to clean up the mess. No matter whose fault it is.

Derrick pushes a pair of Pizza Hut *Back to the Future* sunglasses onto his face. They're neon green and shaped like triangles. The long points face away from each other: one angles up and the other down. He says, "It's hot as fuck, Doc," and grins at me.

I say, "Get in the car, jackass."

The Mustang is clean, sparkles in the desert sun, and the bright red paint makes me think of blood, days and years and everything bleeding out on the highway like truck-smacked deer: red becomes brown becomes rotten. I start the engine and am glad that I've had a beer already because this is going to be a long damn day. We're going to talk to a recruiter about joining the Coast Guard, and I'm sure we won't sign anything before we leave. We're wasting their time and ours and that's just how it goes with us.

Derrick's got it in his head that putting on a uniform with rank stitched on the sleeves will make him a different person. Maybe that happens for some people. I doubt it happens for people who don't know who they are, yet. And recruiters aren't stupid. They're in high school lunch rooms with their shiny medals and starched uniforms. Some of them juiced up, biceps stretching the seams on their shirt sleeves. You can be whatever you want to be, they say. And they'll tell you exactly how to do it. They'll help Derrick find himself. They'd like to help us all. But I know exactly who I am, and what I want is for someone to swoop down and shine a little doubt on me. Uncertainty would make posing so much easier.

I PARK ALONGSIDE the curb at Liam's. He's shirtless, lounging in a yellow and green folding chair on his lawn, Mets cap yanked down on his head so far he has to tilt his blocky chin way up just to see us.

He's so skinny it looks like he was born with too many bones. Derrick's the only one of us who looks like he eats. He's not that big: just bigger than us. Size, straight teeth and he didn't have to work for either of them: not that his genetic good fortune got him anywhere better than me or Liam.

The neighbors' sprinklers hiss and water runs along the gutter. Scraps from shrubs and dead branches lie in piles in front of Liam's house waiting for someone to haul them away. His dad must have done the raking because I've never seen Liam do any sort of manual labor, and his mom's too busy hawking houses when she's not fucking Minor League baseball players. Yards in Cal City are so green it's no wonder people in other places die of thirst.

"Get in, Liam," Derrick calls out.

Water burbles into the drain beside the car, and a couple kids click by on bikes, their T-shirts billowing like parachutes. Liam rips his hat off and smacks himself in the face with it a couple times then mashes it back on top of his buzzed head. "Coast guard, huh?" He grabs the white Polo draped over the back of the chair and pulls it over himself, hat and all.

I say, "Beats the Navy."

Derrick laughs and gets out of the car. His shoes splash gutter water around and Liam says, "Sweet of you to hold the door."

"Get the fuck in," Derrick says. Liam squeezes behind the seat, and Derrick shoves him in. Liam can't push back or do much more than sit down with his face mashed against the little rear side-window. Derrick clacks the passenger seat into place and then slides it back as far as it goes. "Is that sweet enough for you?"

"I like it rough," Liam says.

"Game over, idiots," I say. It's easy to tire of their bullshit. "What'd your mom say about you missing your paper route?"

"She's out of town for a couple days, so she won't know that I skipped out," Liam says. "And it's not a paper route. I deliver papers to customers who didn't get them."

Derrick's mouth opens like he's going to say something, but he doesn't. He just shuts his mouth and slaps the door a couple times.

"Were you gonna make fun of his job, Derrick?" I ask.

He stares straight ahead. The hissing sprinklers die out, but the tinny echo of water gurgling into the drain rings on.

"You don't have a comment then?" I say.

"Nope," Derrick replies.

I nod. "Good."

Liam reaches up and knocks Derrick's glasses into his lap.

"Does it look more like the nineties, now?" Liam asks.

Derrick grabs the glasses, cleans the lenses on his shirt and slides them back onto his nose. "Are we ever going to drop the nineties shit? It's two thousand."

"Sure," Liam says. "But no matter what year it is, those glasses look fucking stupid. They were ridiculous before they left the factory."

Derrick says, "Sorry I don't meet your fashion standards."

I say, "If you both don't shut up, I'll turn this car around and we won't even go to the recruiter."

EVERY COUPLE SECONDS I mash the pedal, sometimes with the rhythm of Roger Waters' voice, other times at random. The road is naked today, and it seems like a good idea to drive as fast as I can because someone ought to do that once in a while. It feels good to be so connected to something that knows how fast to go just because of how hard or soft my foot presses the accelerator. Jeff told me to skip out on work today because I was getting popped for a drug test. What he doesn't know is that I'll have to miss a ton of work to clean my system out, unless someone pisses for me, or if I take some Urine Luck and it turns out that Tommy Chong isn't just trying to be funny.

"There's a rabbit in the middle of the road." Derrick's mouth barely moves but the words come out loud. He pulls his seatbelt away from his chest with his thumb and lets it snap back. A jack rabbit sits on its haunches on the solid yellow line at the top of a small hill ahead. If it's sitting in the road, it must want this. I can't help it that I'm the guy driving the car that will smear the rabbit's face across the pavement. It's always someone; today it's me. I stomp on the pedal and close my eyes to drift in flat blackness. Wind rushes past the windows and sunlight fights to burn right through my eyelids. A small bump tells me I've hit the rabbit.

"Nice going, asshole." Derrick shakes his head and stares off into the desert.

Tumbleweeds and Joshua trees stand in the hard-packed sand all around us. That's where the rabbit belonged. Of course out there it would have had to run from coyotes and whatever else chases rabbits. Maybe bigger rabbits. Rabbits in leather jackets smoking Marlboro Reds and cursing their rabbit parents for shitty bunny-hoods. But none of that matters now: not for that rabbit.

Liam reaches up and squeezes Derrick's shoulder. "Maybe you can bring it back to life with a bike pump." He laughs open-mouthed, ready to swallow whatever reply Derrick spits at him. There is no reply, and what good would it do anyway.

Derrick could have grabbed the wheel when I closed my eyes. He could have done something, but he just sat there. He did the same thing that time the guy charged him on the mound junior year. It looked like he would have just stood there and let the kid break his face open, but Liam tossed his catcher's mitt and mask off and grabbed the kid around his neck and pulled him to the ground. The kid never even got to Derrick because of Liam, but the kid never would have charged if Derrick hadn't thrown at him three straight at-bats. It was like he enjoyed hitting batters with fastballs. He did it again and again, and that's why he didn't need to say anything. That damn smile of his said it all. White teeth just visible between his thin lips. His words never meant as much as one of those smiles.

Houses and golf courses spring up from the yellow-gray sand and a stop light dangles from a cable above the intersection. A car with a license plate that reads SASSREA is stopped ahead of me. I ram the stick into park and pop the trunk. In moments like this I amaze myself with how quick I make decisions. It's like muscle-memory, this thing that leads me to the trunk and guides my hand to the bat, the Easton Redline Dad bought me, that rests beside the five-gallon bucket that toppled and spilled baseballs all over. It's not that I don't know what I'm doing; I do. I own my recklessness. Excuses are Derrick's thing. I slam the trunk and smack my palm on the hard-top as I pass Derrick's door. The vibration shivers up my arm, but I don't think about if that hurts or doesn't hurt because Derrick sees me and a bat approaching a random car; that's what matters. The wind isn't blowing much and the clouds are tacked in place and I feel like I could jump up and grab a hold of them. It's like the universe is damming up all the boredom and waiting for the right moment to pour it all over us. I'd rather smash the dam on my own time that way there are no surprises. Let the water sweep me away, and I won't complain as long as I broke the dam myself.

I'm standing in the intersection with my Easton Redline behind a car I've never seen before, and part of me wants to find a reason for this, to explain it to myself. So it's because the guy has a vanity plate. SASSREA is too vain. I golf swing like Canseco and red shards of brake light explode onto the concrete. SASSREA doesn't open his door or shout anything, and if I didn't hear the plastic scraping against the pavement under my shoes, I might not believe I bashed his taillight in.

Moments between what happened and what will happen are the best thing I can squeeze out most days. SASSREA could have a gun, or could be a cop, or could be or do anything, but the odds are always in my favor around here. Something about the color of the sand and the emptiness of the dry lake beds is like a shield: like the purple haze Dad talks about but never could've experienced because he didn't get drafted. Dad and I experienced Vietnam the same way: in movies.

The bat hangs loose in my hand, skips and scrapes across the pavement, and the metal rattles from my fingers to my neck. When the light turns green, SASSREA speeds off, his four cylinder engine whirring like a suped-up weed eater.

I lean in under the roof, toss the bat back to Liam, and then slide into the driver's seat.

Liam presses the bat softly into Derrick's pale left cheek.

Derrick stiff-arms the bat away and says, "What was the point of that?"

"Are you new?" I ask.

"He probably got our plate number." Derrick grabs fistfuls of his tan corduroy shorts and squeezes.

"He's more worried about getting chased than turning us in," I tell him. "Don't be a pussy."

He sucks big breaths through his mouth, and it makes the hairs on my neck spike to see him work so hard to hold his anger in. If he'd hit me, that'd be good. We could trade punch after punch until our faces melted into the shapes they deserve to be in. Two men as ugly outside as they are within.

He almost hit me once. We were in the locker room after losing a game, and I called him a faggot. He threw his glove into his locker and the clang of thin metal rang out. The closest thing to the smell of hate I've ever known rolled off him, burning through the musty odor of feet and sweat stiffened jockstraps. But Dad stepped between us and shoved so hard that we both fell, cleats scratching like rakes dragged across cold concrete. "You're friends, you assholes," Dad said. I can't even remember what I called Derrick *that* for in that moment, but I remember his eyes, so wide and blue that I believed that one word was more than a word to him. I thought I understood why.

Derrick leans his head back onto the headrest and says, "Can we get on to the recruiter with less idiocy?"

"No," I say. "Opportunities are opportunities." I reach into the glove box and pull out the near-empty cellophane bag of orange hair and pass it back to Liam. He takes it from me, and I roll the windows up so he can pack his glass bowl without the wind blowing bud flakes all over the back seat.

"I don't want to get arrested on my way to the recruiter," Derrick says.

Weed-smoke roils into the front. "I don't care what you want." Liam hands the bowl forward. I snatch it and dangle it below Derrick's nose; his thin lips tighten, stretch tight over his teeth. A sweat bead glistens on his blond mustache, and he licks it off.

"I'm not into this right now," he says.

"You look like an idiot with those glasses on." I take a hit and blow smoke in his face. "I could kiss you for being such a fuck-up."

"Now the gay shit again." He wipes his forehead with his palm and dries his hand on his shorts.

I shake my head and pass the bowl back to Liam. "It would only be gay if I kissed you."

Liam grabs both headrests and rattles them. "I don't want to wait around for a cop to crack our faces open on the pavement. If we go to jail, no one will give a fuck if we're gay or not."

"No one is going to jail," I say. "Don't let Derrick get inside your head." I drop the shifter into first and stomp on the gas.

MOST OF THE time I don't tell anyone where I'm going because I hate explaining the why to them. If I'd have told Derrick where we were headed now, and what for, he'd have whined the whole time. There are detours; this is one.

I park beside a couple apartments with gray and bald shingles. Tan walls are cracked in places, look like they're covered in spider webs spun from shadows. Dark, wet patches of sand beneath spigots to the left of each front porch make the air smell like sex.

"What the hell are we doing here?" Derrick asks.

"I'll be right back." I get out and head to the apartment on the far right: number fifty-four. This is where Jeff said I could pick up some crack. *Stop smoking bud because it'll never be out of your system in time for you to pass a drug test.* Yes, sir. I'll smoke crack instead. What the hell did I have to lose?

I knock once on the red door and hear shuffling and whispering. More people scared to death when there's no reason to be scared at all. Life's not a cop drama. No one is coming to get you. If they were, you'd be got already. Same bullshit with those sign-pumping apocalypse people: we aren't important enough for God to end it now. If there is a God, he's waiting on a better crop of. The end is not near; we aren't that lucky.

"Who's there?"

"Jeff sent me over." A bird claw sticks out of the wet sand beneath the spigot, and a water droplet falls onto the sand.

After a slight pause the voice asks, "Jeff in Mojave?"

"Yeah," I say. "Big Jeff from Mojave."

Locks rattle and chains beat against the inside of the door and it swings in. An unfamiliar face says, "Hey." His blond hair's greasy, and his pink tongue pushes against his fat bottom lip while he breathes through his mouth. Another dirty white man living the high life in the high desert. We breed like rats.

"How you know Jeff?"

"I work for him," I say. These interrogations are more irritating every time, and I'm sure the thing that will make me stop using will be these absurd introductions.

He nods. "Jeff come out with you?"

"No," I say. "Just me and a couple of my boys in the car."

He runs his tar-stained fingers down the bridge of his nose and mashes his nostrils. "Little bag or big bag?"

I say, "Little bag." I'm always feeling big bag, but I don't want to drop that kind of cash this early in the week. I might be unemployed soon, and with Derrick leeching off me, money dries up a lot faster than it should. He hasn't even tried to find a job for a month: not that he'd have a way to get to it if he had found one; I'd have to drive him. And it's nice to know he'll be on the couch when I get home every day. Sure it pisses me off that I'm beating the hell out of myself and spending twice the money I would spend if he was gone, but he's here, and every day he stays is one more I get with him before he's gone for good.

"I'll have to roll to Palmdale with you. Come back tonight."

"What time?"

He leaves the door open and disappears into the apartment. Overstuffed black trash bags sit on the scuffed kitchen linoleum and ripped pieces of butcher paper cover the counter. The microwave door is open and a green bowl sits inside; my guess is ramen or mac and cheese. A toilet flushes, and then bedsprings creak from the weight of a body flopping onto them. I kick at sand around the bird claw and unearth a dirt-caked blackbird corpse.

He comes back and hands me a post-it with his name and number on it. "Call around eight. I'm not going anywhere until the sun's down." A dog I can't see shakes and the tags on its collar rattle. "I can't breathe in this heat." He looks down at the corpse, clears his throat and then spits a yellow wad of phlegm onto the sand beside it.

His name is on the post-it. It's Steve, but he forgot the "T".

The door shuts in my face, and locks scratch their way closed from the bottom up. I crunch my way back across the sand to the car and hear deep barks seeping from the house. They die out just before I see Derrick's sun-glassed face peep over the door.

He says, "What did you need from this shit hole?"

I get in and shut my door. "Put this in the glove box." I hand him the post-it, and he stares at it.

"Who the hell is *Seve?*"

"I'm gonna ride with him to Palmdale later."

"For what?" Derrick stuffs the post-it in the glove box and slams it shut.

In front of an apartment a short ways from us, a young girl in a tank top and too-tight, too-short jeans stands beside a Joshua tree trying to swing a peppermint-striped hula-hoop around her neck. It falls to the sand after one wobbly revolution. She squats, picks it up and tries again.

"Crack," I say.

"You kidding?"

I shake my head. "It's out of your system in like two days."

"And it makes you forget how to spell your own name."

"Not everyone can just sit on my parents' couch all day. I have to work, and I have to take drug tests."

Derrick squeezes his fists so tight the knuckles pop. "I only moved out here because you said you could get me a job. Where are you at on that?"

The hula hoop falls around the little girl's feet again and she kicks the Joshua tree.

"I don't own the company," I say.

Derrick shakes his head. "Roll with that guy on your own. I have to say no to some shit."

Liam laughs. "You said, 'No,' to working at Shakey's Pizza."

"Wise decision," I say. "Because you're way overqualified."

Sun beams through the windshield. Wetness spreads over my armpits and my nose clogs. I suck air through my mouth and turn the car on. Warm air blasts out the vents. The girl squashes the hoop, bends it into an oval and then lets it spring back.

Derrick spits out the window, sets his arm on the console. "I hope the recruiter has a spot for me to leave today."

"I'm sure that's how it works." Liam snorts. "You walk in, they toss a uniform on you and you're steering a boat in half an hour."

"None of us are going anywhere," I say. "Not today."

"This is stupid," Derrick says. His forearm slips off the console leaving a glistening sweat trail. A vein in his neck swells up thick as an extension cord. He scratches his head and then rubs his palm over his hair. "It's stupid to fuck around with shit like that."

"Is it?" He doesn't look at me or answer. "You didn't complain when I dished out the Klonopin the other day."

"No," he says. "But I sure as hell wish I knew where that day went. And you told me it was Valium. It's tough to make an educated decision when the educator fucks the facts up."

Liam slaps me on the shoulder. "You guys were drooling all over the place like sloths." He leans forward and lets a clear string of spit hang from his bottom lip. It dangles for a moment before snapping loose and smacking onto the black plastic console.

"Wipe that off," I say.

"Baby Ruth?" Liam asks. Then he disappears into the back seat.

"I can't take you anywhere." I rub the spit off the console with my elbow. "If you get bored enough, Derrick, you'll be right there with us."

The little girl beside the Joshua tree tries again to spin the red-and-white striped hoop around her throat. She drops it, picks it up to try again. Her pink shirt has a deep red circle on her lower back where the sweat has soaked through.

"We need to get moving," Derrick says, almost too quiet to hear over the roaring vents.

"Yeah," I say. "And the only way to do that is join the Coast Guard."

"This is serious," Derrick says. "If you don't want to go, I'll get there on my own. I'll walk if I have to."

I crank the fan control to low and it whirs almost silently.

"Do you need to say bye to Janine?" Liam asks.

Derrick stares straight ahead and the vents blast his hair, make the brown curls flap about his forehead. I don't want to drive him out to see Janine because it's pointless. She's just like all the other girls Derrick messed around with in high school. But if there's the smallest chance that he actually cares about her, or, if for some idiotic reason, she cares about him, I don't want to be the person who stood in the way of an honest goodbye. "You want to stop in Studio City so you can say bye to Janine."

Derrick says, "I guess."

The little girl's gone, and the hula-hoop is slung over one of the Joshua tree's L-bent limbs, swaying gently when the breeze catches it. A rabbit pops up just beyond the farthest apartment; it smoothes its ears with its paws and then bounds off into the desert.

Derrick *guesses*. That's all it should take to convince me. I could say no. Just drive on to the recruiter and Derrick would get over not telling her goodbye as soon as he met another girl he thinks is beautiful and who is dumb enough to think that there's something interesting going on inside his stupid exterior. I won't keep him from this, but he's got to say he wants to go first. "Say you want to go, fucker."

"Why?" he asks.

"Because if you're not sure, I'm not driving over there. If you just want a blow job, it wouldn't be that hard to run some skank down."

Derrick says. "I want to say goodbye to her." He stares out the window.

"Was that so hard?" I ask.

"I hate asking for favors I can't repay," he says.

"Shut up" I say. "No one wants payment. You want to say goodbye. I'll take you."

"Thanks." Derrick hangs his head.

He did the same thing after he pitched his first no-hitter junior year. Coach Silva told him: "This is something no one can ever take away from you." No one else I've ever met has pitched a no-hitter, and it's not something to be ashamed of. Me and Liam were there with him. Liam was behind the plate calling spots, and I backhanded a ground ball on the third base line and gunned down the runner at first for the final out of the game. We did that as a team, and he hung his head when Coach Silva congratulated him.

Liam says, "You ought to get her a ring, man. You could do twenty years in the Coast Guard and she can follow you from base to base getting fatter and more depressed every year. It worked for all our dads."

Derrick sinks into the seat. "Can we go please?"

Cooler air streams out the vents.

"How can you let a girl with a nose that big suck your dick?" Liam asks. "She looks like a crane."

"I'm not fucking her nose."

Liam shrugs. "You could."

"If there was anything up here to hit you with," Derrick says, "I would rocket it at your face."

Liam sticks the bat handle into the front seat and says, "Go for it." Derrick doesn't grab the handle, so Liam lets the bat fall. It thumps against the carpeted floor.

I back the car away from the apartment complex and then jerk the stick into drive, mash the gas pedal and the tires spit sand and dust all over a rusty green F-150 parked in the shade of a leafless tree. The air coming from the vents is cool enough to close the windows now. "Move your arm, Derrick." I say.

He pulls his arm inside and grabs the oh-shit bar. I roll the windows up and notice his bicep twitch. Who's he flexing for?

"There's a party later," Liam says. "Don't wear yourself out."

"Who says she's gonna blow me, anyway?" Derrick reaches back over the headrest, and Liam hands him the bowl.

Derrick grabs a blue Bic from the cup holder and sparks the near-cashed insides.

"Better smoke up," I say. "Wouldn't want to deal with a rejection on a clear head."

The engine hums and the tires and shocks and everything that push against the pavement fill me. Desert, houses, cars and people flit by headed in the opposite direction, and that seems perfect. Right now Derrick is fine, hitting the bowl, riding. It makes me remember gunning baseballs at each other as hard as we could because no one wanted anything more from us, how we broke things because they were there to be broken, and did as much of everything that we could get our hands on. He smiles right now, and no words spill out of his stupid mouth to complain about boredom or fear or whatever else might be swimming around in that muddy head. This Derrick is the one I'd hoped I'd get back when he showed up two months ago. I'll take him to say goodbye to a girl he tells himself he cares about, and then we'll head on to the recruiter. These two things are enough to help him feel like he's going somewhere that matters. We'll ride on down this road together while he's smiling, letting everything be just what it is. I'll pretend this will last forever for as long as I can make myself believe it.

STUDIO CITY YOGURT'S parking garage is underground, so while Derrick does his thing, at least we can smoke and not worry about anyone bothering us. The concrete pillars are so thick that if God grew a foot and started stomping on everything above us, we could sit here undisturbed.

Derrick goes upstairs by himself because Liam and I don't want anything to do with that yogurt. Janine has given Derrick so many blow jobs in the back room it's hard to say how many of his loads have made their way into the vat of cookies and cream.

Once we saw Ben Stiller down here, and Derrick flipped him off. It's not much of a story, but that's the kind of thing people want to hear about: stories with celebrities in them. It's funnier when they can picture the person: even if they've never actually met them. And I like thinking about it. *Fuck you, Ben Stiller.* For once the guy we flipped off had a name.

"Two dudes holding hands," Liam says.

A bald man slams the door to a yellow Lamborghini and walks away holding hands with a dark-haired man. They're both in pin-striped suits and wearing aviators.

I say, "Yep." Because who gives a shit. I'm not holding one of those guys' hands so it shouldn't matter.

"That's funny to me." Liam's teeth are out, full-on smile. He's not lying, and I don't really care that much. He can't help the way he feels; who can? Mostly he's just looking for something to laugh at while we wait on Derrick. If it had been a guy and a girl holding hands, he'd have laughed at that instead. Liam was laughing because the guys were together, and I don't think it's funny, but I understand how the idea of togetherness might make someone laugh.

"Funny thing about those two dudes is the Lamborghini." I point to the yellow ass-end of it, and Liam cocks an eyebrow.

"Why's that funny?"

"People who want attention drive cars like that, but they come to an underground parking garage to hold hands. They're probably married to women, have big families, and they do this on their lunch break."

Liam mashes weed into the bowl with his thumb and then sparks it up. He takes a big hit, exhales and says, "If I knew where their wives were, I bet we could talk them into making a movie or two." He hands me the bowl.

"Right-o," I say.

"Nice car, douche," Liam yells.

The two men turn and look back. The bald one takes a step toward us and the dark-haired guy tugs at the bald man's suit-jacket to keep him from walking over. "Your boyfriend's not going to let you do anything is he?" I ask. Because it's easy to talk shit to guys who would never mess with me. They see me and Liam in this car, smoking weed. A couple fuck ups. We'll shrivel and fall off the earth like all the other rottenness. Me and Liam will remember this a lot longer than those two will. They have things to live for, things that will help them forget that vermin like me and Liam exist.

They turn and walk on toward the elevator. The dark-haired guy rubs his hand on the middle of the bald guy's back and leans in and kisses him on the cheek. Things like this remind me of Melissa, how she always calmed me down when I was millimeters from exploding because of shit at home. She was great until she told me she fucked Derrick. Melissa knew just how to save me and how to rip me apart.

Liam says, "Go on upstairs and into the light." He reaches behind the seat and pulls Derrick's book of CDs into the front. He unzips the black leather case and lets it unfold on his lap, flips a couple pages and asks, "Wanna listen to Bach?"

I snort and so does he.

"What the fuck's this here for?" Liam throws the CD out the window. It skids along the pavement and lands face-up on a drain cover in the driving lane.

"Probably from a classical music class during his failed year of college," I say.

Liam flips page after page and shakes his head intermittently. "It was Bach or face-breaking music. Now it's just face-breaking music. Meshuggah. Chaosphere? Where does he find this shit?"

A few cars pass by, and we smoke a bowl listening to tires squeak and the thick hum of engines that drown the garage because the sound has no way to escape. This has been my life for the last two months: cart Derrick here and cart Derrick there. He never would have asked to come here if it wasn't for Liam's suggestion. Now I wait, thinking about him sitting up on a stainless steel countertop while Janine sucks his dick. At least in my imagination all I see is the back of her head. He's probably still wearing those goddamn triangle glasses. That's exactly the kind of thing he would do just so he could say he'd done it, as if anyone cared what he wore when he got a blowjob from a woman he'd never see again.

Liam clears his throat and sniffs as a couple women click their way to the elevator in heels and short dresses. Their heels smack the pavement. Click. Echo. Click. Echo. It's like the things are designed to announce an entrance.

"Did you see those tits?" Liam grabs the bowl from me.
I nod, but that's not worth thinking about. Anytime of day I can look at a woman and think about her tits and know I won't touch them unless I have no choice. Right now I want Derrick to get down here so we can get on. He doesn't deserve a blowjob from Janine, doesn't *deserve* anything. Any day he could just call his mommy, and she'd fly him back home so he could try college over again. That's what Janine sees: a boy who drifts through life with no worries and complains about being bored. She probably thinks he's smart. He's not. He's an idiot like the rest of us.

It doesn't make a fuck because Derrick will never see her again anyway. He's just making a final deposit before heading off to make a real difference. She's probably practicing on him so she'll be able to latch onto someone worthwhile once she gets a nose job.

"You seriously want to join the Coast Guard?" Liam blows out a cloud of smoke that curls around the rear-view mirror and then he sets the bowl in the cup holder.

"Why would I want to join the least respected branch of the military?" I grab the bowl and tap the ashes out on the side-view mirror. The white glass has browned from all the smoking. "Most people don't even mention it when they list the branches."

"Then what the hell are we doing?" he asks.

"As soon as they see how high and fucked up we are, we're out the door. Derrick thinks they'll take anybody. When there's no fighting to be done, people have to fight to get into the military."

Liam tosses the CDs over his shoulder, and they plop onto the back seat.

"And I want to see if Derrick's full of shit."

"Let's be gung-ho about it, then,' Liam says. "Whatever the dumbest job they have is, we say we want to do that. If there's a job where you test out explosives on your own balls, we say we want that job."

I drop the empty baggie outside the car and say, "I'm in."

"I bet he calls us stupid for choosing a job where we might get hurt," Liam smiles. "Why would you put yourself in danger on purpose, guys?"

We both laugh and watch a couple cars circle the lot for spots. A door slams and an engine roars. I close my eyes to let those sounds be the way I feel for a little while, and the echoes in the garage make me think of caves and tunnels and all the stories my dad told me about Vietnam before I found out that he didn't go. Tunnel rats and dead babies and everything else were too exciting for me to ignore. Why would I question him? Then I grew up and found out he's an aircraft mechanic. Didn't even go to Desert Storm. He was just as amazed by the heroes in his stories as I was because they did things he'd never do. Aircraft mechanics aren't glamorous. Sure, they need those guys in the Air Force; planes break down. But a guy cranking a wrench doesn't have the same gravitas as a guy up in the air, pulling a trigger designed to set the world on fire.

Liam's humming some irritating tune that buzzes through the calmness so I say, "What's this party you were talking about?"

"A couple girls I know across the street," he says, leans his head into the headrest and shuts his eyes.

Couple makes me know I'm not invited, and it doesn't matter. I'll figure it out on my own like I always do. Part of me wants to hate both of them for getting laid while I go get the drugs and the booze and go to work. But I'd be doing the same thing if I was either of them. There's nothing special about me; this is my path of least resistance. I'm lucky our paths ever cross at all.

We see Derrick headed our way so Liam hops over the console and gets into the back. Why he always gives Derrick shotgun, I'll never know. Derrick gets in and slams the door. His thin-lipped smile is even more obnoxious with those idiotic glasses on. Triangles. It's not worth asking why people who design movie costumes think certain things look futuristic: cocaine and incestuous filmmakers.

"Got your goodbye blowjob?" Liam asks.

Derrick laughs and his cheeks shift the glasses up. It's funny to him and no one else. "She said a bunch of stuff about missing me and how honorable the military is." He grabs the cashed bowl from the cup holder, smirks at it, and then sets it back down. "Everything always has to be like a movie with her. Guess that's what you get for growing up in Studio City."

Liam sticks the bat into Derrick's face. "Did she swallow?"

Derrick shakes his head and pushes the bat away. "She says she won't do that until she's married."

I turn the car on. "How would anyone know if she'd swallowed before unless it was on camera?" That's the kind of bullshit Melissa pulled on me when we were dating. Everything with her was a negotiation. "Like a guy's gonna want a girl to swallow so bad that he'd marry her." Some things can't be negotiated.

There is a large wet spot near the bottom of Derrick's shirt. "What's on your shirt?"

Derrick laughs. "When she backed away, my shirt fell down and I blew all over it."

"Were you just gonna wait to see how long it took someone to notice?" I ask.

"I don't care that much." He shrugs. "I'll grab another shirt from your place."

"I'm not driving all the way back just so you can change your shirt," I say.

"I can't wear this to the recruiter."

I put the car in drive and roll toward the garage exit. "You're about to."

"Maybe if you worked at Shakey's you could afford a new one," Liam says.

Derrick drapes his right arm over the door and says, "It's not something to be embarrassed about anyway. You guys should be embarrassed because you don't have come on your shirts."

Liam says, "How hard would it be for me to do that?"

"Only you know the answer to that question," Derrick says.

"Just don't be loud about it," I say. "I don't want to hear you squishing your micro pud while I'm driving."

I pull out of the garage and onto the road. Only a short way left to Hollywood. There's where the opportunity waits: the Coast Guard. Derrick pops a CD into the stereo and says, "*Animals* sounds about right." But it's as wrong as it gets for me because I don't want to be here. It's too close to beginning a lie I'll never be able to run from.

WE'RE SITTING IN the office. There are three blue chairs in a row and a pot-bellied recruiter with a bushy mustache stands in front of us with his hands on his hips talking about some stupid video he wants us to watch. Propaganda on water skis. Derrick's the only one really listening to the guy, and that's fine because I'm busy flipping through this pamphlet that lists the jobs. There's some environmental stuff, some boring stuff, more boring stuff, and then I see what I'm looking for: Gunners Mate.

I bump Liam with my shoulder and point to it.

He says, "Sweet."

The recruiter stops talking and says, "What's got you excited there, Liam."

We did introductions and now the guy knows our names because he's good at his job. I already forgot his name and don't care to look at the name tag on his chest to be reminded. "Gunners Mate."

I glance at Derrick to see if he makes a face. He shakes his head and stares out the window. A man, painted silver, robotically struts down the sidewalk and people pass him by: some cover their mouths and laugh, others shake their heads in disgust. See, Derrick? Paint yourself silver and stitch a coin slot in your Speedos and you won't have to starve. That guy's got a robo-gut, so he must not be that hungry. Build up enough immunity to jeers and sneers and it won't matter what you do for a living.

"That a job you boys think you can handle?" the recruiter asks.

Liam says. "If anyone is suited to blow shit up, it's me."

I nod as the silver man walks past the painted SEMPER PARA-TUS on the window and then on out of sight. "Seen him blow all kinds of shit up."

"I want nothing to do with that," Derrick says. "I want marine science tech: guaranteed."

The recruiter nods at Derrick and then turns to me. "Why do you boys want to be Gunners Mates?"

"To shoot shit," I say. It comes out naturally, and that's because it's true. I wouldn't mind blowing stuff up for a living. Of course, there are better places to do that than in the Coast Guard, and if there's any reason at all to join the military, it's to fire weapons. Marine science tech sounds like the most boring shit on the list next to food services. I'm not cooking eggs in a chow hall, and I'm not going to spend the rest of my life doing Ph level checks.

The recruiter folds his bottom lip under his mustache and makes a popping sound with his mouth. "It's a serious job."

"We're serious about doing it." Liam stands and stuffs his hands in his pockets. After a couple seconds, he removes them, holding a chewed-up blue pen in his right hand. "Where do I sign up to shoot stuff?"

The recruiter walks over to his cherry-wood desk and sits in the roller chair behind it. Pictures of a couple fat boys and a short-haired wife are framed and arranged on the desk: one of the trio hugging and smiling under a red, white and blue beach umbrella that's stabbed into the sand; another one of them pointing fingers at a caged elephant's ass; and the last one shows them sitting on a bench beneath a weeping willow, boys in light-blue suits with frilled shirts, the wife in an olive green pants suit. The recruiter isn't in any of the pictures: guess he snapped them all.

He leans forward in his squeaky chair, fingers locked and hands placed on the desk in front of him. "This isn't a joke."

"We know," I tell him. I stand and walk to the desk.

Liam scratches the pen on his forearm until deep black scribbles show up. "How often do you get guys who come in here and throw themselves at a job like that?"

The recruiter leans back and runs his right hand along his hairless chin. "Not often."

"So you're testing us right now," Liam says. "One of those ask and be denied things?"

I try again. "Sir, we'd like to be Gunners Mates."

He shakes his head. "Really, guys." He grabs a three-inch-stack of paper, pulls out a desk drawer and drops the paper inside. "If you aren't high right now, you were pretty recently."

"Not true," I say. "And what difference would it make?"

"I can't have you sign paperwork like this or choose jobs in the state you're in."

"I told you, motherfuckers." Derrick pushes up from the chair and shoulders his way out the door. Through the window I can see him slide his dumb glasses onto his face and kick over a trash bin. Wax paper with congealed cheese and grease, napkins, banana peels and all sorts of filth spills onto the sidewalk, and then Derrick crosses the street and heads toward the car.

The recruiter shuts the drawer and pulls a silver business card holder from his pants pocket. LOVE is etched on it. He flips the holder open, snatches a card and hands it to me.

"That thing from your wife?" I stuff the card in my back pocket to be sure I sit on it.

"Yes," he says. "A present for my last promotion."

I want to laugh, but Liam does it for me.

"Listen," the recruiter says. He clasps the cardholder shut, sets it on the desk and leans back in his chair. "As much as I want to sign you up, I just can't. I'm going to be honest with you. I need all three of you. You boys will put me on top of the list for this month. That's the kind of thing I need for another promotion."

I don't know why I'm still here having this conversation. Derrick's gone, and Liam and I already agreed this was a joke. But we're still listening to this guy deny us something we don't even want.

He shakes his head. "I'm not going to be the guy who wins recruiting awards for selling kids down river when they aren't committed with a clear head."

"What if we came back tomorrow?" Liam asks.

"Too soon," he says.

"A week?"

The recruiter nods. "That's a start." He stands, grabs a couple glossy pamphlets from a wooden rack and hands them to me. "You aren't the first kids to do this."

The pamphlets dangle in my hand.

"I don't have the time to do all the paperwork and get you all signed up only to have to deal with the bullshit that would come down the pipeline when you failed the drug test at basic." He laughs. "If you ever made it to basic."

"We're not fucking with you," Liam says. He plants his hands on the desk and leans forward like he wants the recruiter to catch the words before they turn into lies. The ink on his forearm looks like a fuzzy atom in motion.

"I know." The recruiter sits down again and kicks his feet up on top of the desk. His black shoes reflect light; scratches and folds are cut into the patent leather like veins in a leaf. "That's why I'm giving you time to get the crap out of your system. That's why you're taking my card. If you really want to make a change," he looks into my eyes, "you've got to prove it."

Through the window I can see a glossy pamphlet on the sidewalk flutter in the wind; a man with a thick gray beard steps on it. He hoists the trash bin up, wipes his hands off on his beard and then walks away. The pamphlet and all the trash that spilled out before remains on the sidewalk. The backwards slogan and the trash would make a great recruiting photo.

"You all need to think about this," the recruiter says. "Making commitments when you're fucked up is no way to go through life. It's like giving yourself a bullshit out." He glances at the picture frames on his desk but looks back at me quickly.

"Fine," I say. "We'll be back."

Liam backs off the desk and says, "This is fucked. We *want* to join. Understand?"

"Call me when you sober up, boys," the recruiter says. He grabs the black phone on his desk and starts to dial. "I'll remember you. Liam, Sean and Derrick."

We walk onto the street and head for the car. My hands don't let go of the pamphlets, but I keep thinking about dropping them onto the sidewalk so they can blow down the street and wind up flat against some building in an alley or in a fire or anywhere other than in my hand where I could open them and look at the dumbass pictures and read the bullshit on every page.

"Give me one of them," Liam says.

I hand him one and fold the other and stuff it in my back pocket.

Liam stuffs the pamphlet down the front of his pants and then spins his Mets hat around backwards. His face is just a sharp nose and gritted teeth holding up a dome.

Up the street a few yards a lady pushes a stroller toward us. She's smiling and the breeze has puffed her blond hair up like loose cotton candy. Liam squats, grabs hold of a cannon that isn't there, and fires imaginary rounds into the distance. The woman walks closer. A pink-bonneted baby riding in the stroller nucks at a red pacifier and Liam growls, "Gunners Mate for life." Spittle flies from his lips as he makes chugging machine gun sounds and the woman pushes the stroller right past us, never looks at us for a second. It's not like she's ignoring us on purpose; she doesn't have to try. But the baby stared at Liam as he made those sounds, didn't take her little eyes off him until the stroller passed us by, until we were out of sight.

Liam does a deep knee bend, hops up and slaps me on the back. It makes a dull thud, and the sting sticks around long enough to make me want to hit him back. "Gunners Mates," he says.

I punch him in the chest and say it back.

Derrick's on the hood of the Mustang across the street facing away from us, so I belt out, "Gunners mates." The stinging in my back slips away some, and Liam echoes me, and I echo him and the sting dies more.

We get to the car and pile in. Once it's moving, Liam and I scream on. We keep it up as long as we can, but Derrick never joins us. As loud as I scream, as often as Liam screams, as much as I jerk the steering wheel toward oncoming traffic, trucks, cars and trailers, Derrick just stares ahead with his dumbass glasses on. And it doesn't bother me that he's silent. I knew he wouldn't scream with us, that he'd never scream with me. Even if the right words rattled out of my throat so loud that the world shook, he'd never hear the words I wanted him to hear. I can't even scream those words loud enough to really hear them myself.

CHAPTER 2

The green Astrovan in the driveway means Dad's home. I wouldn't care, but I dropped Derrick and Liam off at their party, so I'm alone. I lean on the Mustang's hard top and stare at the house's tan stucco walls. There's nothing waiting in there except words I don't want to hear. If I'm lucky, Dad will have already climbed into bed with Mom, and I'll be able to just watch TV for a few hours. I'm not lucky, though: never have been. And Dad boots the screen door open to remind me of how unlucky I am. I consider hopping back in the Mustang and driving over to Steve-without-a-T's place and then on to Palmdale to buy some rocks. Dad wouldn't chase me, but I saw him three days ago, and I figure something's up because normally he's gone a lot longer than this.

He retired from the Air Force two years ago, and it's still strange not seeing him in a brown T-shirt and BDU bottoms. Now he always wears washed-out jeans and T-shirts with frayed collars; somehow that makes him seem less human.

"The recruiter?" The words blast out from under his bushy, brown handlebar mustache.

"Yeah," I say. "Derrick wanted to join the Coast Guard."

He puts a big hand on his stomach and laughs. "What the hell would he want to do that for?" The screen rattles shut behind him as he steps onto the driveway. "A rabbit's caught in your bumper."

I turn and see the blood-caked ears and buck teeth. The little tongue hangs out the side of its mouth, and the only thing that would make it look more comical would be little Xs on its eyes. "That's the new style. All the cool kids are doing it."

Dad walks over and tugs it free. "Take this out into the desert. Don't want coyotes digging through our trash."

The mangled thing dangles from his fist, eyes open, like it's looking right at me. I snatch it by the ears, and Dad lets go and wipes his hand on the front of his jeans. "You gave him your real name, dumbass."

"What?"

He slides his short-clipped fingernails over the gray-specked stubble on his neck. The sound is rough teeth grinding over cement.

He says, "Petty Officer Tiller left a message."

"Good." I head off toward the edge of our yard where the yellow grass meets sand and cracked pieces of foundations that shattered before they ever had a chance to support anything.

"After all the shit I told you," he calls out. "You still have to see for yourself."

"Yep," I say and keep moving.

The horizon is purple and orange, but there's not enough light to illuminate much more than humps of sand and red rocks. It'll all be silhouettes soon, and then I'll be stuck in the house with Dad unless I get in the car and drive somewhere. But there's nowhere to go. Derrick and Liam get play, and I'm tossing a dead rabbit into the desert. The ears are slick from my palm sweat, and the floppy body raps against my thigh with every step. I kneel and set it beneath the first Joshua tree I come to: branches reached up like it's celebrating some kind of victory. *To the victors go the dead rabbits.* I drop the corpse by the trunk and head back home.

DAD'S ON THE couch, steel-toed Doc's propped up on the coffee-table, glass of Wild Turkey in his right hand. That whiskey's the only thing we don't touch, and I wonder how long that'll last. Derrick drinks anything, and the longer he's here, the less he'll hold back. Not that it matters. Dad used to give Derrick whiskey whenever he came over, liked to watch him cringe when the fire lit up his throat. It was funny the first few times, but Dad hit that same note over and over until it sounded hollow. Maybe I expect too much from him. He entertains himself; that's the best that most of us can hope for.

"Sit down," he says. The TV flashes lights over his face. Green and red and white highlight the wrinkles in his forehead; they look like deep black trenches.

"Gotta head out," I say. "Just wanted to say bye to Mom."

"She's out for the night." He pats the couch. "Hang for a few, boy. It's been a while since we really talked."

"Is that my fault?"

"No." He turns the tumbler to his lips and ice cubes clank against the glass. He presses his shoulders back into the couch like he's puffing up to impress me. Talks with him are like bad sex-ed movies. The title says it's going to explain things, but afterward you're more confused and disgusted than if you'd just made it up yourself. "What?" I sit on the couch, throw my arm over the armrest and the wood frame beneath the worn fabric presses into my ribs.

A baseball game's on. The pitcher snatches the rosin bag from the foot of the mound, tosses it up and catches it. White powder dusts his green uniform and hangs in the air around his head like mist for a moment and then disappears as he drops the bag beside the rubber and adjusts his cap. A couple white fingerprints stick to the brim like bleached bones.

"Joining's not always a bad thing." He takes a drink and sniffs, rattles cubes against the glass. "A lot of guys join for good reasons." He sets the glass on the end table. "But you need to understand where guys like me were coming from."

"You felt like a pussy because you missed out on Vietnam." I expect to get backhanded, but only because I always expect that. The last time he hit me, I was eleven and had left my bike behind the van in the driveway. He backed over the bike and bent the tires. I deserved to get hit for doing something so stupid, but Mom gave him hell. He bought me a new bike the next day and never hit me again: threatened to plenty of times but never followed through. Derrick was the one who always showed up to school with bruises, at least until his Dad died. Talks about Derrick's problems at home never got very far, though. He'd deflect the subject, make it seem like no big deal.

"I was lucky I missed out, moron." Dad pulls his feet off the table and leans forward. "I didn't storm the beach at Normandy, and I'm not ashamed of that either."

The pitcher shakes off a sign then hangs a curveball high and tight. The lanky batter turns on his heel and sends the ball over the fence in right center. Derrick shook signs off all the time. Hit so many guys on purpose that guys he wasn't trying to hit would fall down in the box when he threw curve balls. Liam bitched about Derrick shaking him off so much, but what can you do when the pitcher's right? This fool on TV is too confident. That ball in the bleachers should help him remember he's not special. More special than me; he's on TV. I'm just watching. He gets the chance to give up big hits, and I'll never even get to do that. Good for him.

Dad says, "Where's Derrick?"

"With Liam."

"He's moving in with them?"

"No," I say. "They'll be back later."

Dad stares at the TV. "I'm not going to keep paying for him to stay here. It's bad enough I don't charge you rent. You've been out of school for a damn year already."

"What the fuck do you pay for? He's not flushing the toilet twenty-four hours a day or irrigating the desert. I pay for the food we eat. The A.C. wasn't even on until you came home."

Dad scratches his chin. "Who pays the mortgage?"

"I have a job," I say. "Sign the house over. You're never around, anyway."

Dad slides his feet off the table, leans forward and grabs the bong. "How much longer do you think you're gonna have a job while this shit's around. He's not keeping you straight."

"You always think it's someone else," I say.

He smirks at the bong, spins it around like if he turns it enough it'll morph into something he wants it to be: a bottle of whiskey, a more interesting life, a son who admires him. "I just don't understand how you could go for this kind of shit."

All I can think about when he starts to lecture me are stories of him blazing at Floyd concerts, Hendrix concerts, and Iron Butterfly concerts. He's told me these stories since I was eight. His whole life was smoking, drinking, and listening to music, and he can't believe that saying things like, "It was the best night of my life," would interest me. You can't erase that with, "Don't do as I do." Jimmy Hendrix on stage with lights and explosions, a deep voice growling, "I am the Fire God": things like that get seared into a kid's head. Thank God he never bought me a guitar or a drum kit. Then I might be really fucked up. It's bad enough I thought I was going to play baseball for a living. I was just another third baseman who couldn't knock the ball over the fence. Why the hell I believed being part of a winning team had anything to do with my chances of success, I'll never know. There'd be no stars without teams. But without stars no one would give a shit about the game. No one wants to watch average players compete. I've watched middle-age men play softball. It's no mystery why they drink during those games and why there's rarely anyone in the bleachers.

"I should have been harder on you," he says. "Your mom couldn't stand to see you punished. But I should have done more. My old man would have beat my ass if I'd have talked to him the way you talk to me."

"Your old man was probably around enough to beat you." I say, "If you want to beat me now, it would round out the day. You can make up for lost time and see how much I improve between now and the next time I see you. Next year or whenever you feel the need to drop by and let me know I'm a piece of shit. My birthday would be good. We could have cake after the beating."

He laughs out his nose, sets the bong on the table and picks up his glass of whiskey. "You want a shot or a glass?"

I shake my head. "Neither. It tastes like ass." He thinks this is bonding. If Derrick and Liam were here, Dad would be asking about baseball games. *Remember that no-hitter in Trona, boys?* He loves to talk about the way I made that backhanded grab on the third base line and threw off my back foot to get the runner at first; Dad was so proud of it because it was one of the only games he ever saw me play. Derrick was near un-hittable that day, but if I had missed that grounder, it would have ruined it for him. Some days I wish I'd have let it hop by. Not that it would have made a difference. That no-hitter didn't get Derrick into college. But it's something no one can ever take away from him.

Dad pushes himself off the couch and goes to the kitchen for another drink.

"Listen," he calls. Ice cubes plink into the glass and the bottle cap squeaks as he twists it off. "Your grandpa never told me anything about our history." He walks around the corner and sits back on the couch. "I just wanted you to know where you came from."

I say, "Let's not make this a cheese fest."

He sighs and takes another drink. "I told you why I joined."

"Join the military or go to jail is what you said. Or was that like one of your Nam stories where you left out the part where you were never there."

He sets the glass down, grabs the remote and turns off the TV.

"I never lied about Vietnam," he says. "You heard what you wanted to hear."

"Sure," I say. "We jumped out of helicopters into the water. You meant the royal *we*, of course. As in we are America. We did it together. We didn't win in Vietnam, but at least we lost as a team."

He rolls his eyes. "Don't act so fucking smart."

I squeeze the loose fabric on the couch arm and roll my head back. "So you never lied about Vietnam. It was all in my head."

"What do I have to hide? I'm not ashamed of what I do."

"You shouldn't be ashamed of your job." I lean forward, stare at a picture hung above the TV stand. Mom's sitting on Santa's lap. Dad's dark mustache peeks through the false white beard. She's got a leg kicked up, her head's thrown back and she's laughing. Not a mom I remember. "You've got too many other things to be embarrassed about."

"Are you finished?" he asks. "I wanted to explain something to you." He taps his index finger on the tumbler a couple times. "You gonna listen or should we just sit here and watch the ball game?"

"Let's hear the revelation." I want to leave, want to be with Derrick and Liam, be doing anything besides sitting here and listening to some half-drunk sentimental explanation for why he is and I am and we are and all of that. *Here's our new history, son.* It's all a goddamn lie. *We* are nothing.

Dad nods. "I used to beat this kid's ass on the way to school every morning: Charlie Morgan. He just took it, but if he would have fought back, I'd have moved on."

"He was smaller than you I bet."

"He was, but that wasn't why I hit him. Weakness." He pokes me in the shoulder. "That was the reason." Dad takes another drink, sets the half-empty glass on the coffee table. "I had a friend: Brick? I've told you about him. Used to go to bars and tear beers out of guys' hands, chug them in the guys' faces and then smash the empty bottles over their heads."

These guys always have names like Brick or Dent. It's impossible for me to buy any of it, but stopping him's not worth it. "Yeah," I say. "You told me about him."

Dad tugs at his mustache. The taut hairs yank his upper lip away from his teeth. He lets it snap back. "So," he says. "We went to Charlie's house a year after we graduated. Brick's girlfriend was there. She was fucking Charlie, and Brick knew it. I didn't know where I was going at the time, just got in the car and went. It was the thing to do. Work at the lumber yard all day and then drive around drinking beers to pass the time until you woke up to do it all over again."

"Sounds manly," I say.

He nods and clears his throat. "It was. Not like the pussy-footing around you little shits do. We got to Charlie's house, and the door was unlocked. Brick walked in like he was invited, so I followed him inside, and Charlie was on top of Daphne on the couch. His jeans were around his knees, and Brick grabbed Charlie by the collar and dragged him into the kitchen. Daphne didn't even have time to scream, or if she did, I never heard her. She'd probably seen Brick do worse, so I guess maybe I was more shocked than she was."

I tap my fingers against my knees and take a deep a breath. Mildew and dust mix with the smell of Dad's armpits. He likes to be on stage and can sense my attention slipping. He'll just make the story more and more ridiculous until I'm locked back in.

"Charlie was bare-assed on the linoleum kicking his socked feet around, and Brick pulled the refrigerator over on Charlie." His Adam's apple jumps up and down as he swallows. "You need to hear this."

"I'm sure I do."

"I don't even know why I try with you anymore," he says.

As much as I want to take this away from him, I can't. Where am I supposed to run off to? If he would only be honest with me about everything, it wouldn't be so hard to get on board with this kind of thing once in a while. But I'm not even sure I want to hear the truth. He's gone for weeks at a time, but he only works half an hour away. Do I need to know where he stays or who he stays with? He's not here with Mom, and that's all I need to know. "Go on."

He squeezes his fists to crack the knuckles, being dramatic, building suspense. *Make him want the story. Hold it from him so he has to beg.*

"I really do want to hear it," I say. "Come on."

"All right," he says. "Shut up and listen."

"I'm listening."

"Brick pulled Daphne outside by her hair, and I ran out there and shoved him in the back even though I knew he'd fuck me up. His forearms were big as my calves, big as your thighs probably. All that I thought at the time was that Charlie was under the refrigerator, and there was nothing I could do to make that *un*-happen, but I could keep Brick from doing whatever he was about to do to Daphne if I made him focus on me. I stepped out on the porch and said, 'Let her be, man.' Brick turned and looked at me like I must have been some kind of monster, like I was crazy. And while he stared at me, Daphne took off up the street."

And once again he becomes a hero. "So what happened?"

"Brick got in his car and left me there. I pulled the refrigerator off Charlie. He was fine as far as I knew. Just like pulling a fatass lineman off the quarterback, I guess. But Charlie stared up at me, and I didn't know what to say or do. There was this kid I'd punched in the face and kicked in the head and all kinds of terrible shit for years flat on the floor, wheezing with his pants around his knees. The only thing I could think was that he might say I did this to him. He could have, and maybe Daphne wouldn't have vouched for me or God knows what. But Charlie just said, 'Thanks,' so I called the cops, and they came, and I told them everything. They hunted Brick down after that, and I have no idea what happened to him after that." He stares at me, eyebrows raised slightly, like he's waiting to hear me say, Wow, or fall onto the floor and praise him.

"So where's the part about jail or the military?"

Dad's mouth hangs open, tongue pressed against his bottom teeth. Ugly brown hair clings to his sweaty forehead and he's breathing heavy. It's disgusting to see him this way, heaving like a salted slug.

"If I didn't join the military, there'd have been another Brick. Or when Brick got out he'd have come at me so hard there'd have been no way to get around him unless I put him down for good."

"You fucker." Never in my life have I called him this, but being here alone while Derrick is out there with Liam, with those girls, is more than I can take. "You have a disease." I want to punch some thing: anything, but there's nothing to punch except for Dad, and even if he's full of shit he doesn't deserve that. "As much as I would have hated this to be a bonding experience, at least that would have been honest. It isn't, though. It's just another excuse for your life."

He smirks and the creases in his forehead cut deeper, become darker. "I can't make you see it my way."

"What was the point?"

"What?"

"Your reason to join was better than mine. Is that it?"

"If I had to guess."

"Don't guess! You made out like you were going to tell me why it was okay for you to join the military. Instead you tell me this story about how your life was exciting, and I can see how boring your life is, now. That's why you disappear for weeks at a time. You can't handle coming home to a woman who's in bed all day. To a son you don't even know."

"I have to travel for work, boy. Some of us don't have the luxury of choices."

I shake my head. "You made choices. You were too afraid to stay home and face your friend after you sold him out. Now you're too scared to come home and see what you did to Mom."

"Don't say anything about your mother."

"Don't start acting like you care. It's too late." I push up from the couch, kick the screen door open and walk onto the crackly lawn. Wind that carries the faint odor of grilling meat rushes over my face. Not a hundred yards away some family is making dinner and having a good time. Could've had a good night here, too, but that fucker is nothing but stories and bullshit. Maybe he can't help it, but I can't sit around and listen to him run his mouth anymore. All the stories that spill from him when he wants to pretend he's not a terrible father, a terrible person who lets his wife get drugged up and splash around in a pool of her own drool and sweat for weeks at a time. That's fine. He can continue to run away and touch base here whenever his conscience eats him up so much that the booze and whatever else distracts him can't compete. He won't entertain himself with me, though. That's over. I don't owe him anything, and I don't want a damn thing from him either.

Derrick and Liam are probably having a blast with those girls, watching some dumbass movie while they all rub each other and pretend the night will never end, that they care there are actual people inside each other's bodies, that they aren't just puzzle pieces. I bet the girls are so fucking pretty, and they think Derrick and Liam are super cute. It's so easy for them because tomorrow they'll all wake up and get fed. If they kept this up for forty years it would go on the same way because everyone who matters understands how hard it is for them. All that potential and nowhere to apply it. Such a shame they didn't make it in sports. They just need a little time to unwind and get their heads straight. It's so hard to give it all up and become a different person overnight.

Rust has eaten through the chipped scoop of the shovel that's leaned against the garage door, and the white of the garage peeks through the orange-ringed holes. I'll bury your rabbit, Derrick. Don't worry. Everything will be just fine like it always is because I'm here to clean up after you just like your mommy. The shovel's rough handle feels like it's shriveling in my hand, and maybe in a hundred years or so the shovel will twist itself into a billion splinters, and who'd care? More shovels are being hammered out every minute of the day, and that won't stop until long after some bastard's dug the last hole and slung the last scoop of shit on top of the pile. Then the pile of shit will topple so that the next generation won't be without something to occupy their time.

Out past the yard, where the rabbit carcass rests, the silhouette of that triumphant Joshua tree sprawls like a tentacled beast. Too bad it's just a tree that won't uproot itself and raise some kind of hell no one is prepared for. When I'm right next to it, I see how the bark slides over itself like plate armor. That's something Derrick would say: an armored tree. Him and his obsession with knights and bullshit. If it hadn't been for me, that kid would have just been another loser drowning in a sea of fantasy. Games with dice and paper to pass his free time when there's a world outside. He could never get in trouble for hurting anyone in that game. It's only out here where we can get locked up for doing things. He'd never have been caught stealing gas from unlocked garages in the summer if I'd let him sit at home scribbling in his notebook about wizards and whatever the fuck else was in that thing.

I wanted him around, though. Had to have him there to breathe in the night air and beat his chest in the moonlight with the rest of us, break windows and stomp on rooftops because immediate danger was the strongest drug we could get. It was always stronger when Derrick was with me; it is stronger, and I hate myself for having so much trouble letting that feeling go. I want to hate him for being able to let go of all that and let go of us so easily.

The little rabbit corpse is facedown and raggedy. I stab the shovel into the sand and toss the grains aside, jab again and mash my foot onto the blade over and over. Sweat drips off my forehead and soaks my armpits and back. This hole's a waste of time. If something wants to eat this dead rabbit, it'll paw away at the loose sand sprinkled over the carcass and snatch the dusty body away. But even if it's pointless, it feels good to be digging now, and that's better than anything else I've had in a long while.

The hole comes up about a foot on the handle and that seems deep enough. I nudge the rabbit with my shoe and the body flops in; the head tumbles down after it. Maybe I could have done it more respectfully, but what difference would it make. I'm the asshole. It's my fault because my foot was on the pedal; my hands were on the wheel. It was all because I wanted Derrick to stop me. And he wouldn't. Why the hell should he be the one to stop me from doing anything? I don't need help with stopping, anyway.

The hole's filled the best it's gonna be, so I head back to the house, sling the shovel onto the yard and sit on the Mustang's hood. Soon Derrick's going to leave; I'm going to lose this car; I'm going to get fired. I believe these things are true, but that doesn't make them any easier to accept. This or that. Good or bad. Derrick thinks that way because he thinks there is good, doesn't understand that it's all bad for people like us, and that we just have to choose less bad. If he did, things would be fine between us even if he did fuck Melissa behind my back. It's not even because he fucked her. She fucked *him*. Melissa knew exactly how to hurt me when I was most vulnerable, and if I'd said it all, came right out and told her everything, she'd have figured out a way to hurt me worse.

The screen creaks open. Dad leans his big right shoulder against it, another full glass of whiskey in his hand. "Have you calmed down?"

Sweat rolls off my upper lip, and when I lick it off, the saltiness bursts onto my tongue. Clumped hair around my ears is thick with wet, my back is sore. I'm tired and it feels good. Soreness and calm help me sink into my shoulders and melt into the metal of the hood for a minute. In this silence, between gusts of wind and words, it almost feels like resting.

CHAPTER 3

Derrick and Liam never called, and it was too late to get up with Steve about the crack. So when Dad went to bed, I called Melissa and told her I needed to talk. She said, "Fine," and I drove to Jovo's in Palmdale and met her on the concrete patio out back.

She sets a bottle of beer on the wrought-iron patio table. Pale light bleeds through the branches of the thin pines that loom along the fence line. Most of the light cast down on us is from the near-full moon; the rest comes from the buzzing lamppost on the street corner. I can't read the beer label, but it's warm out, so I'm glad she gave me something cold to drink regardless of what it is.

"Thanks," I tell her.

She says, "Sure."

Her hair's a lot shorter than it was the last time I saw her a couple months ago. The day after Derrick got back, we all loafed around F-Area park, smoked and talked about old times: sneaking out of our houses to low-crawl through the tumble-weed-covered desert; stealing cheap bottles of vodka off our parents; breaking light bulbs on car windshields at dusk and disappearing into the desert like angry ghosts. All that felt like fun, but she was a hell of an actress. Derrick had only been here two days when she called and broke up with me. Before tonight, I hadn't talked to her since.

She pulls a chair from beneath the table and the metal legs screech into the darkness. Crickets go silent. Her blond ponytail had dangled between her shoulder blades while we dated, and now her hair doesn't look like it would hang below her chin if she let it fall out of the tight knot it's pulled into.

"Shouldn't we turn a light on?" I ask.

She waves off the suggestion. The nails on her left hand are painted red. She never used to paint her nails, bit them all the time. I liked them much better when they were jagged and too short and sometimes dotted with flecks of dried blood.

"Won't Jovo be weirded out that we're sitting in the dark?"

"He knows he has nothing to worry about."

The crickets start singing again. "Must be a good feeling."

"Drink the beer, Sean."

Traffic whooshing down the street is an odd sound to hear so loudly at this hour. I've never lived in the city. Unlike North Edwards, someone's always going somewhere in Palmdale. Headlights flash through the fence links and cast net-like shadows over the wooden swing set in the yard. I imagine her and Jovo standing at the bottom of the plastic yellow slide waiting for their chubby baby to shoot into their open arms.

"That swing set for the baby?" I ask.

"Jovo's sister has two girls."

She always said she wanted to finish college first; she never even enrolled. Wouldn't have made much difference: this is where she was going to end up anyway. Now she doesn't have to feel bad about not using her degree.

Excited screams burst in the distance and a car rolls by; a thumping bass line trails behind and shakes softer and softer until it dies. "When's the baby due?" I set the beer down and lean my head back, let the hard rail of the chair press into my neck. The metal's cold now, but in the daylight it would be hot enough to burn any naked skin that lingered on it.

"You didn't come here for this," she says.

"I can't ask about the baby? I can't care about what's going on in your life?"

"You could have asked me this stuff over the phone." She rubs her eyes with her knuckles. "If this wasn't important, you could have waited until tomorrow."

"You're right." There are so few stars visible tonight that even if I knew anything about constellations I doubt I'd have a clue what I was looking at. That's how it must have all started out: some guy with a piece of rotten hide that he'd scratched star after star into until he had a map he could trace shapes on; the original constellations were surely dicks, tits, and vaginas. That's where it all starts, and what it all comes down to. Symbols are the only things that ever change. "I came to say I'm sorry."

"For what?"

"I lied to you." It feels forced. Like I said it for myself and not for her, and that's because I don't even feel like I'm here. If she'd wrap her arms around me, it might be different, but that won't happen. I'm doomed to float here with nothing more than the cold, hard rail of the chair to remind me I'm awake. The longer my neck rests here, the warmer the rail will become, until the coolness fades completely and all that's left to remind me that something is propping me up is pressure.

"Lies are things you say," she says. "Not things you are."

Melissa never used to talk like a camera was rolling, or maybe she did, and I just didn't notice because the camera was on me too. We were together for months while she was fucking Jovo, and I might never have known if she hadn't told me. Maybe she would have done it forever if she hadn't gotten pregnant; that would have been impossible to hide eventually. But how can I be mad at her for not telling me the truth when I was never honest with her? If it was logical, then I wouldn't have to care. "Is it stupid for me to be mad at you?"

"You weren't attracted to me." She laughs. "How is that my fault?"

"Just because I wasn't trying to climb on top of you every five minutes doesn't mean I wasn't attracted to you." A sick feeling swirls in my stomach when I say it, but I can't stop myself. All those moments were real: holding hands, bending her over the hood of my car and fucking her, swimming naked in the base pool under a new moon. I was with her no matter where I was inside my head. No matter who I had wished she was in those moments, she was her and no one else. It was more than acting. It felt good while I was doing it. It felt good when it was over. But when I look at her now, her big, hard nipples trying to poke through her tank top, the soft cheeks and hair, there's nothing about her that I can point to and tell myself, *That is why she's beautiful; that is why you love her.*

"It's more than that." She crosses her arms over her chest, hides her nipples.

"What more is there?"

"We didn't talk," she says. "We didn't do anything except sit around with Derrick and Liam."

"We did all kinds of shit together," I say.

"Smoking weed and shooting beer cans in the middle of the

desert every weekend stops being fun after a while. We have nothing in common. We weren't friends, and you stopped fucking me. It was like you'd never wanted me at all."

"That's bullshit," I say. "I wanted you."

"If all you want to do is argue, I can go inside. You wanted to see me. If you'd say whatever the fuck is on your mind I wouldn't have to do all the talking. You know what? Fuck it. Good night."

"No." I reach for her arm, the soft hairs and freckles I used to stare at when I fell asleep with her, the stomach that cushioned my head on what seems like a million nights are both just inches away, but she pulls back, and her short hair falls in front of her face; a few strands stick to her upper lip, and she blows them away.

"Don't touch me."

"Sorry."

She brushes the wild hairs behind her ears and rubs her squat nose with the back of her hand and sniffs. "Talk already."

"This was never a problem before."

"It was always a problem."

I can't believe that's true. When things started it was just us. Derrick, Liam, me and Mel drank and shot guns and did whatever the hell we wanted to do together because we wanted to be around one another. It was the closest thing to a family Mel and I ever had. Her parents were more fucked than mine. Her dad hit her mom, and her mom hit her dad, and she had a front row seat to the flying fists her whole life. The only thing they hated more than each other was me. Their little girl was too good for some desert rat. "You'll be lucky if he learns a *trade*," her mom had said the night I showed up to take Mel to our senior prom. I was standing right there, and her mother wouldn't even look at me; she never looked at me: must have thought that if she didn't see me then I wasn't really there. Her dad always left the room when I showed up.

"I'm joining the Coast Guard."

She laughs.

"What's so funny?"

"The Coast Guard. That's not funny to you?" She scoots away from the table and grips the chair arms to push herself up.

"What the hell did I say?"

"You can't disappear for two months and then come over here and tell me you're going to join the Coast Guard and expect me to care." She stands and her yellow tank top slopes over her belly. The curve isn't big, and I never thought she'd be the kind of woman to swell up with pregnancy, whatever kind of woman that would be: every woman, I guess. She folds her arms and tilts her head almost onto her right shoulder. Such an actress. She played Mrs. Claus in *Santa Sings the Blues:* the dumbest thing I've ever seen. But she sang all her songs like she believed they mattered and even though I hated the whole play, when I thought about why, I knew it wasn't because of the writing or because it was about Santa; I hated the characters. I hated them all, and I don't think that would've been possible if Melissa hadn't done a good job. How the hell she ended up like this, a girl having a baby and living in a house with people she barely knows I doubt I'll ever understand. It's probably love, and I want it to be love because then I don't have to understand. Love just *is* whether it destroys everything it touches or not.

"You're the only person I can talk to, Melissa." The words sound wrong when they're out, and I wish I could suck them back in, suck myself inside my lungs to hide until everyone is gone, and then exhale myself, start over without watching them leave.

"Really?" She nods fast. "What about Derrick?"

"He's joining too. I didn't want to at first, but when I got in the office and saw the uniforms and talked to the recruiter and everything, it seemed like it wasn't such a terrible idea." The words gush out, talking about the Coast Guard like it makes a fuck to either one of us, like somehow saying this shit to her will help me to turn this into a solid thing that I can set on a wood block to carve it into something useful or smash it into a million pieces.

Melissa's face softens and she licks her lips. "You'll find a way out of it."

"I have the flier in my car."

"That's nothing."

"We're all joining together."

"No." She shakes her head. "You shouldn't have told Derrick you could get him a job out here. You should have just let him stay in West Virginia. He's better off without you."

"You shouldn't have fucked him."

She doesn't walk away, and that surprises me. I'd always thought those words would hurt her, but they just disintegrate into the shadows and the sounds of tires pressing against pavement. "Are you done?" she asks.

"Why did you have to fuck Derrick? Why not run to Jovo first?"

She sighs and shakes her head. "I just told you I fucked Derrick to piss you off, Sean. I was trying to make you jealous."

"You're walking around with Jovo's baby in your guts, and it's been there since before we broke up. But I'm supposed to believe that you and Derrick was a lie."

"I like sex. A lot." She throws her hands up. "If the person I'm with doesn't like it as much as me, there are going to be problems."

"Did you really fuck Derrick?"

She mashes her face with her palms and groans. "He was gone for good. It shouldn't even matter anymore."

A light beams out the kitchen window, and I feel the urge to run. It must be the way cockroaches feel: hide in the shadows until the lights go out and then skitter on toward your goal. So many traps to avoid it's impossible to win. Just breed on and hope a few babies run fast enough to make it somewhere safe.

"Jovo won't like it if we're fighting," she says. "He'll come out here if we keep this up."

A moth flitters its way up the kitchen window, batting its wings so fast that they're a gray blur. The tiny body crashes into the window over and over, each time making a small thump.

"I guess I should leave."

"Great," she says. "Thanks for coming over and drinking one of Jovo's beers *and* pissing me off. This is just the kind of closure I'd always hoped for."

"This wasn't my plan, Mel."

She holds her hand up and closes her eyes. "Don't do that."

"What?"

"Don't call me that." She opens her eyes and slips her thumb through a belt loop on her jeans. "I really do feel sorry for you. And Derrick and Liam," she says. "It doesn't matter because you're all too stupid to admit that you're causing your own problems. No one did any of this to you."

I grab the beer and chug it. "That thing growing in your stomach is making a future for you, and I'm stuck in a place that rots more and more every minute." I stand and shove the bottle at her. She grabs it. "Tell Jovo thanks for the beer. Derrick's over at my place if you want to drop by and fuck him before he leaves."

She smirks and her left ear shifts up the way it did the time she told me about her and Derrick fucking in the locker room. "You did this to Derrick and to yourself. Don't *you* ever come back here. You're poison, Sean. For everybody. It would be hilarious if it wasn't so depressing."

I want to say something to rip her apart inside, but I can't think of anything better than meaningless bullshit that isn't true. I just say, "I won't," and walk away. Past the yellow plastic swing that sways in the wind as if a kid were sitting in it, grasping the chains and waiting for a shove. I walk through the gap in the chain link fence and on past the Mustang because if I drive right now, I'll do something stupid. No one needs to get hurt because of the way I feel. Why I care about that now, I'm not sure. A million other times in my life, I would have just got in the car and peeled out, spun the tires as long as I could to leave behind a melted-rubber haze, a lingering reminder of my anger. But I'm not leaving, yet. I have nowhere else to go tonight except home. and there's nothing there that I want to see. Melissa was impossible to please. And it wasn't because of her. It was because of me. She cheated because I didn't fuck her every time her parents were out of the house, because I'm not manly enough for her. These are things I swallow. I will never be what Melissa needs, and she'll never be what I need. And in between us both is Derrick. The only difference is that she had him the way she needed him for a little while, and I'll never have him the way I need him for a second.

A couple blocks down the street a pawnshop's yellow sign glows. There's got to be a liquor store nearby. Derrick and Liam might be back at my place when I get home. I may as well bring some vodka back, to make sure Derrick and Liam and I are all on the same page. It'll be a celebration. We'll drink and dance on the rabbit's grave while that Joshua tree shakes its angry limbs at the purple-black sky. We'll drink as much as we can and pass out and wake to do it again until there is no liquor left, until there is no time left, until I'm alone on my couch, gripping an empty bottle.

CHAPTER 4

July 2nd, 2000

I wake to Derrick and Liam ringing the doorbell; the wall clock that's been an hour behind for two months lies and says it's seven o'clock. I open the door; they're all smiles and laughs, so I leave them in the living room while I check on Mom.

On Mom's nightstand, the answering machine's red light flashes. I press the play button. *Hello, Sean. This is Chief Petty Officer Tiller calling to let you know I'd like to meet with you again next week to discuss what we went over at our last meeting. Please give me a call back at the number on the card I gave you. If you don't have the card, my number is—*

I mash stop. Delete the message. His card's in my pocket, but I'm not calling him. Tiller: ancestors tilled the soil. Petty Officer Tiller. How can a man with petty in his title feel good about himself and what he does?

Mom doesn't make a sound, but the flower-pattern bedspread rises with her breaths. Some day she'll stop breathing, and home won't be much different than it is now. I've had hour-long conversations with her, and the next day she didn't remember a word I said; some of those words took me years to say, and now I wonder if I'll ever say them again.

Watching her sleep instead of shamble around like a zombie is an improvement. Before she was drugged up and sleeping all the time, she'd stumble around the living room while my friends were over, trying to ask normal questions like nothing was going on, *How's your mom? How's your dad? Have them call me.* And Dad, when he was around, would throw an arm around her shoulders and guide her back to the bedroom and stay with her while everyone in the living room tried to erase what they'd seen so that the rest of the night didn't get weird. It still got weird every time; people didn't expect to see a mother act that way: not my friends anyway. Their parents have problems of their own: Mom's is just a problem that's hard to hide in plain sight.

Liam's mom fucks around on his dad, and his dad knows but does nothing about it. Derrick's parents are like puppet masters who both think they're in control, but neither of them really is; they work too much to know their son. Both Liam and Derrick have families that most people would be happy to be a part of: based on what's visible on the surface. My family is the one that looks fucked up to the rest of the world: inside and out. And it is. I stopped denying that a long time ago.

There was only the message from Tiller, so that means Jeff still hasn't called. I don't think he'd fire me over the phone, though. Something about giving a person bad news face to face seems more honest, and he's always been honest with me. It's been three days since I was stuffed inside the guts of an airplane, and I thought I'd feel better by now. I don't. The heat was hard to deal with before Jeff handed out salt pills and Gatorade. "Eat a banana every morning," he said. "You won't cramp up and you'll shit more regular." I never ate a single banana. There's never been fruit at home, and I wasn't about to go to the grocery store to pick some up. Bananas would just sit on the counter and rot while I drank beer and watched them change colors: green, yellow, brown. It's hard enough to keep flies and gnats out of the house.

Twelve or sixteen hours a day of scooting along my back and feeding cables through guide holes, biting electrical tape off of spools and wrapping it around the wires I'd stripped and spliced. Money was good and Jeff never called to say don't come in; things are slow. Things were never slow, and I figured they never would be. It was a good job even if some nights I had to massage my right hand for an hour or more to work the cramps loose. I'd drink a few beers and pass out while Derrick and Liam drank and did whatever they could to put themselves to sleep each night. I didn't care that I was taking care of Derrick, feeding him, giving him a place to stay. It was good to see him there every night and to watch him laugh at the stupid shit we'd talk about, to see his jaw tighten up when I fucked with him about not washing his pubes off the bar of soap or whatever other silly fodder I could find.

"Baby," Mom says.

"Yeah."

"Can you get me a glass of water?"

I go to her bathroom and snap one of the flower-print Dixie cups from the wall mount dispenser. She'll probably just spill it all over herself. I fill it and bring it to her. "Here."

She opens her moist, bloodshot eyes, takes the cup, puts it to her lips and swallows the water in a single drink. "Thank you."

I reach my hand out to take the cup, but she crushes it and rolls onto her side, the cup clenched in her clasped fists. There's a picture on the wall above her empty shoe rack. Dad and Mom and me are holding hands. Mt. Rushmore is in the background. I can't remember going to Mt. Rushmore. Seeing how big those faces are and how high they are, just in this picture, is enough to make me wonder what kind of person it took to carve them. And what if those faces weren't even close to what the men actually looked like? Forever people would see these gigantic faces carved out of a mountain as the real faces of men who are long dead and unable to tell anyone that they never looked like that at all. I guess if the faces on that mountain look better than the real faces it's an honor. But an ugly face blown up to that size might scare the whole world off. I'm not even tall as Dad's knee in that picture. My arms are outstretched so far that it looks like they're tearing me in half. Who took the picture? I'd ask Mom, but she probably wouldn't believe that it's a picture of us. Doesn't look like her anyway. The woman in the picture is smiling, big white-framed sunglasses on. Her hair's parted down the middle, drapes over her shoulders and curves around her breasts. Dad doesn't smile. His shoulders are pressed back; he's wide as ever, arms filling the sleeves of his green polo; chest hair sprouts out the unbuttoned collar. And there I am, arms yanked taut like a clothesline, a curtain rod for them to hang a little Notre Dame football jersey and jean shorts on.

We haven't gone anywhere together in three years. Our last trip was a two-day snore-fest at Lake Havasu. We loafed around at the beach and watched boats and jet skis spray by. Mom and Dad fought the whole time, and both nights Dad left Mom and I in the hotel room where we played hearts. She kicked my ass almost every game. Even though she won, she didn't seem to enjoy it any more than I did. Each hand I lost was one hand closer to being back with Derrick and Liam, and maybe Mom saw each hand as one hand closer to being trapped at home.

I never wanted to go on that trip. There weren't a lot of days that Derrick, me, and Liam could just do whatever we wanted together after we started high school. Our summers were chopped smaller and smaller every year as baseball became more important. That year, our sophomore year, we had a solid month off, and I hated that I had to bail on those guys even if it was only for two days. They both lost their virginity while I was out of town. I'd slept with Melissa freshman year, before either of them had sex, and once I'd told Derrick about it, he acted like some giant rift separated us. He was goofy around Melissa, barely talked most of the time she was with us, and he found all kinds of bullshit excuses to take off. But after he and Liam fucked those freshman girls, Derrick talked about sex differently. He'd always commented about asses and tits when girls weren't around, and then pretended to be chivalrous when a girl showed up; it pissed me off: how easy it was for him to assume the role of whatever character he had to play in any given situation.

Mom clears her throat, drops the cup, and rolls over. I grab it and head out to the hallway. The wall clock reads nine p.m. A whole day gone. I figure Steve won't give a shit if I show up unannounced today instead of yesterday. He probably forgot what he told me, and I could just say I thought he said today: if he even remembers me. The worst that could happen would be that he'd tell me to come back another time. So what if we buy crack later than we'd planned on it?

Back in the living room Liam and Derrick are watching ESPN. "The Mets crushed the Braves yesterday," Liam says.

"The Mets?" I ask.

"This is their year," Liam says.

"They got tromped ten to two today," Derrick says.

"Get on board or get left behind," Liam says.

"Speaking of on board," I say. "Let's grab Steve, and see if we can get a couple rocks. You in, Derrick?"

"Most definitely not in," Derrick says.

"You're just going to sit here?"

"Yep," he says.

"You've been here all day not doing anything. And now you can go with us to do something, but you say no?" I ask.

"Have a great time." He grabs the remote and flips through a few channels, finds some World War Two documentary and drops the remote on the cushion beside him.

Liam stands and slaps himself in the face a couple times. "This is going to be a journey to remember for all eternity, Derrick. Come on."

Derrick swigs from his beer. "Nah. I want to see who wins the war this time. Looks like it's gonna be a close one. And the war is in color now. So it's better."

"Fuck you then," I say. "I want to get back before midnight. I have to go into work tomorrow and tell Jeff I quit."

Derrick yawns and stretches his arms over his head. "Finally decided to join?"

"No." I throw the crumpled cup. It bounces off his chest and lands in his lap. "I'm going to quit before Jeff fires me."

Derrick flicks the cup onto the coffee table. It bounces once and stops beside the bong. "You're out of a job either way. What difference does it make?"

"One's my choice."

A bomb plummeting from a plane screeches, then there's a deep thud and a gray-white plume of smoke roils up from what was a building. Derrick grins. "What about your car?"

"They'll come get it."

"Then how are you going to get around?" he asks.

Machine gun fire and narration fill the silence. The boys are on the march to Berlin. Hitler: the best villain since Satan. "Why are you so concerned about my car all of a sudden? Are you worried that once I lose my job I won't be able to cart you around anymore?" I walk into the kitchen and open the fridge. The case is empty, but there's an open Coors Light. I'd drink some of the vodka I'd bought, but I don't want to get caught driving drunk on my way to or from a crack buy. The can's half-empty, and the flat beer sloshes around the aluminum as I turn it up. Something bumps my lip, and I spit beer onto the linoleum.

Liam laughs. "Did you pull off that open beer?"

I look into the mouth hole and see a soggy cigarette butt floating inside. "Motherfucker, why'd you put it in the fridge?"

"I knew some jackass would be dumb enough to drink without looking in the can first," Liam says.

I round the corner and throw the can at him. It hits him in the chest and falls to the carpet. He snags it and says, "Still some left." He swigs and drops the empty can to the floor, starts chewing. "Butt-filtered goodness."

"Get moving," I tell him.

Derrick says, "Hold up." He heads into the kitchen. Silverware rattles as he opens drawers, and when the clanking stops he walks into the room holding a wooden-handled steak knife. "You can't go without any protection."

"A steak knife?" I ask.

"You have a better knife? A gun?" He starts to take the knife back to the kitchen.

We had guns before Dad sold them all after he retired: a Smith and Wesson M&P 9, a .22, an AR-15. Not that I'd have been interested in carrying one of those with me. "Give it up," I say. He stops walking away. More machine gun bursts. "You know my dad sold all the guns."

"Then this is all you've got," Derrick says.

"If you came, it'd be less likely that they'd fuck with us. You look intimidating even if you are just a little bitch."

Derrick shakes his head. "If you want this so bad, you've got to go alone. But I don't want you rolling in there so confident that you look stupid." He holds the knife out for me.

"You realize how stupid I'm going to look if I pull this out?"

"Would you rather look stupid in a time of crisis or be defenseless?"

Liam walks over and says, "Give it here. A knife's a knife."

"Fine," I say. "We'll take the knife. You giant pussy."

Derrick slumps back onto the couch. "He's going to try and fuck you over. Two white boys with money; that's what you look like. No one can see past the Mustang and the Jordan's. If you rolled in to the dealer's place with shredded clothes covered in pig shit, you'd get a better deal." Derrick watches tanks rumble over trees, barbed wire, and crackedbricks. Black blood spills from soldiers' mouths. When will they let that war end?

I say, "Have a good time jacking off in the shower or whatever it is you do all day."

Liam opens the door and Derrick says, "I'll write an elegy for you. Two idiots set off on a quest to kill themselves, but they died before they reached their destination."

"What the fuck is an elegy?" Liam asks.

"Does it matter?" I push Liam out the door, and then pull it shut behind us.

A STEAK KNIFE isn't going to be much help if the dealer has a gun, but Derrick is right about what me and Liam look like: stupid white boys with money, the kind who should carry something to make sure what they say is taken seriously. So here we are parked outside the two-storied building Steve directed us to, and it's just the kind of place I figured it would be: a deserted building in a neighborhood of deserted buildings. A green Lancas 13 tag on the wall is crossed out with red and surrounded by a bunch of letters blocked off old English style. These claims mean something up here in Palmdale. Down in L.A. though, the gangs that spray-painted this shit would get hacked apart by MS13 or the Mexican Mafia.

I gave Steve the cash what seems like a long time ago, but the car's off, and I don't want to turn the key to see what time it is because each time the clock would tick, I'd be one minute madder. The green and red door he disappeared into is the only door I can see from here, and I have to wonder if it wouldn't be smarter for Steve's dealer to set up in a house on the West side, closer to the living part of the city. Once we have what we rode out here for, I'll have no reason to care about any of this. And what the fuck do I know about business, legal or not, anyway?

Liam's in the passenger seat tapping some off-time beat on his thighs. The erratic slaps make me think of a room filled with a hundred babies clacking spoons against pots, and that's more than I can take. "Cut the drumming."

He says, "Sorry," grabs his Mets hat from the dashboard and pulls it onto his head. "I was trying to liven this place up."

The street light behind us buzzes and kicks on, and then the one at the intersection down the street flickers and shines onto a black truck with chrome rims that rolls through the stop sign and rumbles off into the night.

"He's been in there a while," Liam says. "No reason for that unless he's smoking."

"Maybe so." I didn't like carting Steve along, but sometimes you've got to roll with a scare-billy if you want to get your hands on the stuff you're looking for. The problem with that is strangers can say they'll do anything for you, and until you get them where they're headed, there's no way to know if the shit that comes out of their mouths is worth more than the air it's made up of. I was pretty sure Steve was broke and feening, so odds were Liam was right. Steve was probably in there smoking some of the rocks he'd bought with my money, taking us for dumbasses.

"Let's just go in." Liam pops his door open and leans out. "Even if he's not smoking, then at least we can get back to North Edwards sooner. I'm tired of loitering on Rape Boulevard."

I say, "Fine." And we get out of the Mustang and head over to the building.

A single dandelion stands in the dirt where a corner piece of the sidewalk cracked off and shattered. Three petal-tufts extend from the drooping head. Liam stomps on the weed as he walks to the door; it slowly rises, like it's been stepped on a thousand times before, like some weed God that will rise again and again regardless of how many feet mash it into the earth from which it grows.

From across the street, the door Steve entered had looked like it was half red and half green, but up close, the center line's wavy. Specks of green dot the red and specks of red dot the green. Of course the paint job on an abandoned building's door is bad. Why the door is even painted is a mystery. "Got the knife?" I ask.

Liam lifts his loose Polo and pulls the knife halfway out of his front pocket, his thumb and index finger on the blade.

"Hold the handle, idiot."

He flips it over and drops it back into his pocket. It'll be a miracle if it doesn't cut him before we get out of here.

I raise my fist to knock. "Did Steve knock a certain number of times?"

Liam leans over straight-legged, grabs a rock, and then flings it down the street. It skips and plinks against a light pole. The sound rings out, and a bark from some place unseen echoes in reply. "Wasn't paying attention."

It's stupid to think these people would have some kind of knocking code. It's just as stupid to think someone will answer the door. I knock three times anyway.

Liam molds his hat brim with both hands. "Is it unlocked?"

I turn the silver knob. "Yeah."

"Get in there then." He pushes the door open and is swallowed in the darkness.

I expect to see a light bulb swaying from a chain, to smell piss and old sweat, a bunch of guys with AK's and a piranha tank full of human skeletons. There's no light in this room though, except what leaks in from a broken window and the doorway we just passed through. Ripped clear-plastic tarps are flopped all over the place, and the tile floor is covered in dust. If not for all the shoe prints, I'd have guessed no one had been here in a long time.

Liam points to the other side of the room. "Stairs over there."

Each step creaks under Liam's weight and then again under mine as we ascend.

The handrail's missing supports every few feet, so it shudders, and when we make it to the top, I can see it isn't anchored to anything.

Down the hallway, light shines out from beneath a door, and a large hump sits just beyond that. At this distance, whatever makes up the hump seems to be nothing more than shadows piled on top of shadows.

"Remember The Great Trash Heap?" he says.

"What?"

"She had two rats and glasses on a stick."

"Are you serious right now?"

He laughs. "Forget it."

"Stand over there." I point to the left side of the door. "I'll stand here and knock."

"What if they come at us?" Liam asks. He looks at his pocket and then up at me.

"We run, man."

"What?"

"Don't even think about pulling the knife."

Liam raises his brow like he can't believe I suggested something so cowardly. But I know as well as he does that we aren't the kind of guys who pull knives on drug dealers.

I knock once on the door, and a deep voice calls out from inside, "Who's there?" Something smashes and then there's laughter.

I could just turn around, walk back outside and drive away, let Steve figure the rest out on his own, but Liam nods at me like this is all okay, so I clear my throat and belt out, "Sean."

For a couple seconds it's silent, and then there are the sounds of mine and Liam's breathing that are broken up only when muffled speech leaks out from behind the door and when the floor creaks beneath our shifting feet. I hate this, my heart thumping so hard I feel it in my wrists and head, the sound of air as it's sucked through my half-clogged nostrils. It's like standing in the batters' box while the pitcher shakes off signs and twists the ball around in his glove. Just throw it. I don't care if it comes at my head. At least if he throws it at me, I have to get out of the way or get hit. The worst thing that ever happens is when the pitcher steps off the rubber, and it all starts over again, all the previous worry for no reason at all.

It feels like a long time passes where Liam and me are just breathing in the hallway, but eventually heavy footsteps slap their way to the door, and when it swings open, Steve's there shaking two pink plastic baggies by his bony, scruffy cheeks. "Alvaro's all business."

Liam and I step around Steve so we can see into the room. A guy, who must be Alvaro, and a woman sit on a holey black leather couch. Alvaro nods at me with his shaved head and the woman smirks; her eye shadow and lipstick, if not black, couldn't get any closer to it.

"New boys again," the woman says. "Cute."

Steve says, "Jeff always sends em runnin' when the chips are down."

She laughs and rubs Alvaro's chest. "Working too hard on those airplanes. Poor babies." She fake pouts, pushes her bottom lip out so far that I can see how pink it is where the lipstick ends. Alvaro's other hand hangs over the couch arm, fingers wrapped around a black handgun. The barrel glints in the dim light that shines from a cream colored fixture dangling from the middle of the ceiling. Part of me wants to ask them how they got electricity here, but that's probably the kind of dumbass question they expect from guys like us, and it's the kind of thing Derrick would definitely ask. Like you need money to connect wires that the power company already ran. The power's there if you know how to take it.

"We're good to go," Steve shoves the baggies in the left pocket of his red windbreaker. "Appreciate it, man."

Alvaro waves us over with the gun. "Stay a minute."

His woman leans back on the couch, slides her hand slowly up and down the crease of his tan Dickie's, and when I look up, Alvaro smiles at me. He has a black tattoo on his neck the shape of which I can't make out because of the shadow his chin casts over his throat.

"We should probably roll," Liam says.

The woman sighs and something about the way her cheeks sink makes me think she's a lot older than she appears. Her fingers are long and capped with black nails that she scratches along Alvaro's neck. She says, "Aren't they young, baby?"

Alvaro laughs. "Look at the baseball hat and the wide eyes. You boys play baseball?"

"Not anymore," Liam says.

"I played basketball," Alvaro says. "Shooting guard." He taps the gun lightly on the couch arm, and his big shoulders shake while he laughs silently. Liam clears his throat. "Did you play around here?"

Alvaro thumbs the safety off and on with two quick clicks. Steve raises his blonde eyebrows and stuffs his hands far into the pockets of his windbreaker.

The woman says, "You boys still live at home, huh?"

I nod reflexively but doubt it matters. This woman seems to have known me before I showed up.

"Alvaro," she says. "You're selling to little baby boys."

He stops tapping the gun on the couch arm and sets it on his thigh. I recognize the model; it's a Smith and Wesson M&P 9 millimeter like the one Dad sold, like the one Liam, Derrick, Melissa and me had fired at an abandoned car out in the Mojave Desert a couple years ago. She pulls her hand away from him and fingers some of the torn leather on the couch, flicks at a triangle flap without ever looking away from me.

"Steve," she says. "Have you shown them your teeth?" She rips a small square of leather free and then rolls it up in her thumb and forefinger. "His smile's so pretty."

"No." He looks down when he says this and presses his hands deep into his pockets like something's in there he must put pressure on to keep his body from crumbling, and I'm reminded of picking teams on the playground in grade school, of all the kids picked last or not at all.

"Alvaro," she says. "Make him play." The woman tosses the balled up scrap of leather toward us, and it lands between me and Liam.

Liam gently bumps me with his elbow. His fingers are barely inside his pockets, holding them open, and I'm sure it's because he doesn't want Alvaro to know about the knife. Steve's in front of me, and I figure, if it came to it, I could shove him onto Alvaro, and Liam and I could break the hell out of here. We'd be short our bag and the money, but I can get more money if I go back to work. I can get another bag. And there are a million Steves to lead us to places like this if we absolutely have to find another one.

Alvaro clicks the safety off and on a couple times and says, "Don't be coy."

Steve sighs, turns around and opens his mouth. There's nothing but gums on the top right side, and his right canine is black as the woman's lipstick; the rest of his teeth are gray. The woman and Alvaro laugh, and I'm sure it's because of the face I've made in reaction to Steve's oral hygiene.

She looks right at me and says, "You're so pretty, Stevie."

Alvaro stands and points the gun at the woman. "You boys into her?" He taps his cheek with the barrel and lifts his chin at me.

"What?" I ask.

She leans back on the couch and presses her spread fingers into the cushions. Her face is calm.

"You. Like. Her." Alvaro opens his eyes wide and shifts his thin eyebrows up.

She's batting her huge eyelashes, smacking her lips together, and I wish he was asking Liam or Steve or anyone else.

"I don't want to answer that while you're holding a gun," I say.

Alvaro smiles. Now that he's closer, I can see the tattoo is a tail that crawls out of his collar and coils around the back of his neck. The end looks like a scorpion's stinger ready to strike his throat. "Not so stupid." He walks over, throws an arm around me, and his garlic breath makes my eyes water. He laughs and shows me the bottom of the gun: no clip. Then he squeezes me around the neck and leans hard onto my shoulders. The weight goes all the way to my spine, and I have to lean into him to keep my balance. "Now answer."

"No," I say.

He stares at me with his brown eyes, his nose almost touching mine, leans harder onto my shoulder so I have to slide one foot out to keep from stumbling. "No clip, kiddo."

"What about the chamber?" I ask.

Alvaro lets me go and shakes his head.

The woman stands. She's almost as tall as I am, looks like she could tear my face off with her fingernails. "Let the babies go home." Her boots, just like Alvaro's, are black with black laces, and her loose sweatshirt hangs off her left shoulder revealing a red bra strap.

Alvaro turns and walks slowly toward a wooden table near the broken window that lets some of the pale light from the street lamp shine into the room. A clip sits on the table along with an open box of baggies and a white digital scale. The woman looks over to the table, bites her lip then blinks and cocks her head at me. I don't wait to see if that means anything. I head for the door and Liam and Steve follow.

As soon as my feet are in the hallway, I'm sprinting. The loose handrail wobbles as all three of us stomp down the stairs, and when I break into the cool, windless night, I wonder why I'm running. But I don't stop. None of us do.

Once we're in the car and driving away as fast as I can take us, I ask Steve, "Why are there two baggies?"

Steve rubs his right eye with a knuckle and shakes his head at me from the passenger seat.

He's slouched like he's had a long day. "I bought a dub, too."

Liam leans into the front seat and holds the knife in front of Steve's face, "How much is in each bag?"

Steve pushes the knife away with his palm and laughs. "I'm not gonna hold out on you."

Liam says. "What did this fucker's place look like inside?"

Holes in the drywall, slashed bags of trash, dirty microwave. "He had some nice shit."

A street light flickers as we pass through an intersection. Buildings go from deserted and wrecked to just deserted the nearer we get to the freeway, and all the chain link fences look like great nets dredging the world for trash: newspapers, plastic bottles and cans stacked two feet high in almost every corner.

Liam says, "We could take both bags and leave him in the desert."

"What?" Steve throws his hands up. "Jeff sent you to me. I know him. I wouldn't try and get over on Jeff's friends."

"Shut up," I say. "Both of you."

"You want to get fucked over by some stupid snap?" Liam asks.

"I'm not fucking you guys over," Steve says. "I bought this bag. I *know* Jeff."

I slam my fist on the dashboard. "Shut up."

Liam shakes his head, yanks his hat off and sits back.

"Relax. Alvaro always fucks with the new guys." Steve nods over and over like if he does it enough I'll start nodding, too.

"You're right," I say. "We do need to relax."

Steve's fingers shift beneath the red fabric of his jacket, and he rests his head and closes his eyes, but his eyelids crack open every few seconds, and I'm sure he's watching me.

The overpass next to the 14 has pooled water beneath it from the rain this afternoon, and an overturned shopping cart stands in the center, looks like it's standing on black glass. I stop the Mustang and shift out of gear.

"We can't smoke out here." Steve opens his eyes and blinks, fakes a yawn like he's supposed to have been asleep or something.

I stare at his pock-marked and scraggly-bearded face, his chapped and cracked lips, and think about what would have happened if Alvaro hadn't had a gun. I would've shoved Alvaro out that window. I would've taken everything and sold it myself. Then that woman would've scratched my back, rubbed my chest and made Steve perform for me. But one day she would've wanted more than I could give her. She'd fuck Liam or Steve or Derrick, and I'd be right where I am now, staring at some idiot just like this one, a man who's going to end up toothless and spend the rest of his days gumming a crack pipe: nothing more than a joke to everyone who sees him.

"Do you think I'm stupid, Steve?" I ask.

"No." He backs away like my question seemed so crazy that he had to dodge it physically. "Why would I think that?"

I yank his hand out of his jacket pocket, reach in, grab the baggies and fling them into the back seat. Steve swings at me, but I throw my elbow up, and his fist hits the headrest. The next punch lands on my stomach and knocks the air out of me. Liam reaches around and opens the passenger door a little, and I grunt and spin so that my back's against my door. I kick the passenger door all the way open and backhand Steve's face and chest as he unbuckles and tries to crawl into the back seat.

"Don't fuck me over!" Steve says.

Liam holds the steak knife to Steve's stomach. "Get out."

"I bought that other bag," Steve says. "It's mine."

The tightness in my side makes me cough a couple times, but I've been hurt worse from grounders that took bad hops. I mash the side of Steve's face with my shoe and say, "Get the fuck out." My foot slips up on his cheek and exposes a few of the gray and black teeth he has left, and I can see that woman with her black lipstick and hair, laughing. I pull my foot away and it leaves little red circles of shoe print on his cheek.

"I took you there," he says. "I'm not trying to steal on you."

Liam pushes the knife closer to Steve's stomach. "Listen to how fake you sound."

Steve's eyes are full of tears as he backs away from the knife, and I stick my foot on his chest and kick him out onto the pavement. He rolls over and water splashes, drips off his jacket and stringy hair. "Don't take my bag, guys." He reaches one dripping arm toward the car but drops it to the ground and hangs his head.

I say, "Don't say shit to Jeff," and then stomp on the gas. The momentum shuts the door, and in the rearview, I see Steve sit on his heels for a second and then lie back and stretch out like a dead man floating on an inch of water. Too bad it's not deep enough for him to sink and disappear because when he gets up the only thing that'll be any different is that he'll be wet, and it won't take long after the desert sun rises for him to dry off completely.

Liam crawls over the seat and shakes both baggies beside my cheek. "Fuck him. Fuck Alvaro, and fuck that crazy bitch." On his jeans, the side where he'd kept the knife, there's a red oval the size of a quarter. It'll probably take a while for him to notice that he cut himself, but I'm not saying a word.

I pull onto the freeway and mash the pedal. The vibrations of the wheel rattle up my aching hands and die out in my forearms. I say, "Fuck em all." But I don't care about any of them. Leaving Steve behind in that shallow water only helps me to see why Derrick will move on, why he will be the one who gets away, able to point and laugh at his friends' failing bodies and minds and tell us he told us so even though he'd never told us anything we didn't already know. He'll look like the one who learned something, the one who'd trudged through all this shit and managed to come out clean. We are the ones he's running from, and he's right to run as fast and as far as he can.

CHAPTER 5

July 3rd, 2000

Dad's still gone when we wake the next evening, but the radio's on. The Moody Blues are playing; Mom used to listen to them all the time in the car, and that makes seeing her standing in the kitchen less of a shock. Her black hair's pulled back from her face in a loose knot, and she sways back and forth to the rhythm, controlled, sober, alive.

She says, "You boys want some spaghetti?'

The fact that she's wearing something other than pajamas makes me wonder if I'm hallucinating. Her red button down shirt hangs past her waistline, and the white jeans fit her well. A pair of black flats on her feet is an improvement over the pale, blue-veined toes normally on display. "What?" I ask.

She pulls a box of noodles from the cabinet and shakes it in my face. "Spaghetti? Is that too much Italian for you?" Her lips stay open long enough so that I can see the small spaces between her canines and her upper incisors. We had full dental coverage when Dad was still in, and I wore braces for three years, had my wisdom teeth yanked, a bridge wedged into the gap where that tooth never grew. Maybe Mom is scared of dentists or thought she was too old for braces, would've been embarrassed to talk to other parents with metal in her mouth even though the way her teeth look now embarrassed me for her. Maybe she just missed the appointments because she was too fucked up.

"Sure." I grab the big pot from beneath the sink and fill it with water. Mom reaches over, shakes salt into the water, and then cranks a burner to high.

"Set it there when it's half full."

I heft the half-filled pot onto the stove, set it on the red eye. Water on the pot's underside sizzles and white smoke swirls up. The crust of whatever was last cooked burns off into nothing, smells like burnt toast. Mom twists open a jar of Ragu and sloshes the red sauce into a pan, sets it on another eye, and then twists the dial to medium.

"You gonna make some garlic bread?" I ask.

She licks her lips and squeezes her chin like she's thinking hard on it. "I think I can take care of that."

"All right," I say. "Let me know when it's done."

I head back to my room. Liam and Derrick sit on the foot of my bed, mashing buttons on Super Nintendo controllers while cartoon fighters bash each other's faces with oversized fists.

"We're having spaghetti," I say. It sounds odd, like it started to come out of my mouth a hundred years ago and just now made it past my lips.

Liam presses buttons furiously, but his character is hit again and again: head then gut, head then gut, until the life meter is fully red and his character floats in slow motion and crashes to the ground, flimsy and defeated. Liam says, "That high low strategy is bullshit," before throwing his controller onto the floor and leaving the room.

Derrick calls after him, "You're terrible, dude. You knew it was coming and you still couldn't stop it."

I follow Liam out to the living room and sit on the couch beside him. A baseball game's on. He's sitting on the couch edge like he needs to be ready to sprint onto the field at any second. It's a shame none of us made it. We'd have taken everyone else along with us because that's what good friends do: help each other out of the desert. Liam was a terrible hitter, though. He'd smash someone's face in with the bat in a second if they stepped up at any of us, but he couldn't hit a curve ball. He wasn't scared to take a hit from a ball that didn't break. I just don't think his brain bends enough to hit something that comes at him crooked.

"Your mom's cooking," he says. "It'll be nice to eat an actual meal for once."

"Yeah," I say.

"Your dad coming home later or something?"

"Maybe." Every time Dad leaves I figure it'll be the time he doesn't come back, and last time he was here I made it clear how much I hated him, so maybe he really will stay gone this time. I scratch my head and stare at the bong. All that shit I said to Dad was more than I should have. It's hard for him to live like this too. No. Dad doesn't need my help. He can make his own excuses.

Years of leaving Mom in bed drugged-up are just the newest development. There were years that he was gone, and Mom was stuck in the desert while he worked. No one around to talk to but me, and that has to be hard on anybody. If she'd had an affair, then maybe that would've helped her feel alive. What stopped her from fucking around on Dad back then, I'll never know; I'm sure it had something to do with opportunity. If she'd had the chance, I want to believe she'd have taken it.

A commercial comes on and Liam says, "Remember that time we drove out on the lakebed in Derrick's truck? It started raining, and we kicked his little brother out where that fake shark fin stands in the sand all year. He had to walk half a mile through a quarter inch of sandy water."

"Yeah," I say. "What about it?"

"His Nikes were caked with grime, and he had blisters from the sand rubbing against his ankles. Why'd we do that?"

"Why do we do any of the shit we do?"

The smell of garlic drifts into the living room, and I close my eyes to picture Mom and Dad at the table together, back when we held hands and said grace before meals. We'd make spaghetti sandwiches and talk about the mundane shit that happened in our days, spelling tests, math tests, stupid pictures of animals standing in fields with spaceships flying over the sun. The more I think about that, the easier it is for me to understand why Mom gets fucked up. If the most interesting thing I had to talk about every day was a little kid's homework, I'd have a lot of headaches, too. I did grow up, though. And other parents manage to make it through the mundanity of discussions with their children just fine, they seem to *enjoy* it even. So what the hell was wrong with my parents?

How can Mom suddenly float around this way, dropping fistfuls of cracked noodles in the pot, shaking spices into the saucepan, stirring and smiling as if everything has been just fine for the last ten years. Tomorrow things will be exactly the way they were yesterday. If she makes it all the way through dinner, I'll be surprised.

"Almost done." Mom peeks around the corner and smiles. All the tiny gaps in her teeth seem wider than before, make me think of Steve and that dark-haired woman.

I stand up from the couch and walk out into the warm night. Feels like the sun went black and still burns, heating the planet without illuminating anything. Not much else I can do but get in the car and drive. Maybe just get on the freeway and hit it, go as far as I can go from here with the money I've got left. Start over in some place where no one knows the me everyone here knows. But then I'd be no better than Dad or Derrick. I twist the front porch light out of its socket, and then head over and get in the Mustang. When I start the engine, Liam opens the passenger door and says, "Beer run?"

"Something like that," I say.

He gets in. "Let's do it."

But before I can peel out, Derrick steps through the front door, and Liam says, "Damn it." He crawls into the back seat, and then Derrick opens the passenger door and gets in.

"I'm not staying there alone," he says.

"Must be nice to have a choice," I say. And then I gun the engine and drive off into the night.

I DROVE US to a hill outside Edwards Air Force Base that overlooks a bunch of rusted-out school buses to smoke the only crack rocks I've ever bought. The buses form a huge square, bumper to bumper. Their empty wheel wells are stabbed into the sand, and I'd ask where all the wheels rolled off to, but anything capable of leaving this place would be stupid to stay: inanimate or not.

The three of us stand in front of the Mustang; its red paint covered in dust and dirt-crusted bird shit. Some bastards will show up and cart it away soon or else I'd clean it. I could barely afford the payments while I was doing electrical work, and even if I were able to get work at a grocery store or something, it wouldn't pay enough to keep the car. Dealing's the only thing I could do around here without wheels, and I don't have the connections.

Liam pokes me in the chest and says, "Who run Bartertown?"

I shove him and his Mets hat falls off his head. He bends down, grabs it with his long fingers and pulls it on backwards: so low that it hides his thick eyebrows.

Derrick pulls one of the bottles of Absolut I bought at the liquor store from a paper bag and then kicks at a pair of pink baby shoes half-buried in sand. "Anybody seen the baby that goes with these shoes?"

"There's nobody out here," I say. "This is where people ditch shit they don't want."

"We haven't seen anyone," Liam says. "That doesn't mean that half the Manson family isn't inside those buses plotting a Sharon Tate rerun."

"They'd have to dig her up first." I hand Liam the light bulb that I grabbed from the front porch so he can make a pipe, and he sets to work. An engineer of convenience. "Don't bust that."

He nods. "Have faith."

No clouds slip across the sky, and the full moon's sickly blue light shines down on the flittering pages of a faded book. Tumble-weeds and Joshua trees surround this place, and it looks and feels like the perfect place for everything to end. "This is where the final battle will go down," I say.

Derrick laughs. "A zombie battle or a religious war?" He picks at a patch of flaky skin on his elbow. "Guess it could be both."

Liam hands me the bulb bowl and says, "People will become amphibi-men. It's the only way we'll survive all the changes."

"What changes?" Derrick asks.

Liam shrugs. "The climate?" He pulls both pink baggies from his front pocket, and we all sit on the Mustang's hood. Derrick twists the cap off the vodka and turns it up. He'll drink it one gulp at a time until it's gone and pass out in a pool of his own vomit. He won't smoke crack with us, though. A man's gotta have principles.

"El lighter-o, please." My hand is out, waiting for Liam to drop the lighter into my palm.

Liam says, "Did you bring one?"

I pat my pockets. "Negatron."

Liam opens the passenger door and crawls into the back seat. The car rocks and squeaks as he searches. "Unbelievable."

"Get out here and drink." I slap the pink baggies on the hood and sling the bulb into the darkness. It shatters but the sound is muffled by Liam's footsteps, and when the passenger door slams shut, a light beams out of one of the bus windows.

Derrick takes a drink, swallows, and then says, "Shit."

Liam walks around to us and says, "There's no lighter."

The light glides from the back of the bus toward the door. "Someone's in there."

Derrick says, "Maybe we should bail."

A bus door squeaks open and then the sound of shoes scratching over sand fill the air: a low hiss that rises with each step. The light shines toward us, hits me in the eyes, and I turn my head.

"Maybe this cat's got some fire," Liam says.

It's hard to see the full shape of the person headed toward us, but the long hair and swaying hips make me think it's not a man.

"Hey," a woman's scratchy voice calls. "What are you guys doing out here?"

"What are you doing out here?" I ask back.

She stops, shines the light onto the ground and clicks it off, becomes a silhouette like the hills and Joshua trees that surround us. "I live here."

Liam laughs. "Did you move out here because you wanted to increase your chances of being raped and murdered?"

"It's free and no one bothers me," she says. "Not before tonight, anyway."

"You got a lighter?" Liam asks.

She shoves her right hand in her front pocket then cocks her head to the side. "What for?" A silver earring flashes when it catches the moonlight.

"Came out here for an eye opener," Liam says. "But left our lighters at home."

She walks closer. Pretty and smells like raw onions. Flat and cute nose like Melissa's, and her dark hair hangs past her shoulders in tight braids. She sits on the hood, pulls one knee up to her chest and says. "An eye opener? I'm not giving you my lighter so you can smoke crack."

"What difference does it make?" Liam asks.

"It's stupid." She unzips her hooded sweatshirt enough so that her orange bra and cleavage shows. Derrick glances at her chest and sets the bottle on his thigh.

"We've located the anti-drug oracle." Liam snatches the bottle from Derrick and drinks.

"Trevor will be back soon," she says. "You guys should leave before long."

"Is he your pimp?" Liam asks.

She swipes the bottle from him. "That's the only thing you could think of? I live in the middle of the desert, and I'm dirty, so I must be a whore."

"I never said you were a whore," Derrick says.

She looks at his crotch. "The bulge in your shorts says different."

I laugh. "That kid's got a hard-on all the time. Don't take it as an insult. But it's no compliment."

She turns the bottle up and chugs.

"Who's Trevor?" I ask.

She hands the bottle to Derrick, coughs a little and says, "My big brother."

"Is it just me," Liam says, "or do ninety-five percent of murders start this way?"

"If I don't fuck for a living, I must kill for it." She scratches her scalp with her index finger and says, "Maybe I'm a senator. Or a judge."

"Stop me if I'm wrong, but this shit's not run-o-the-mill," Liam says. "You're the only person I've ever met who lived in the middle of the desert: bus or not."

Derrick passes me the bottle, and I drink while he stares at her dirty jeans. Why would he want to fuck this girl? Because she must be easy, because he can fuck her and never have to see her again?

"The only thing not normal about any of this is that you guys are here. It's been weeks since I got to sit around and talk with anyone other than Trevor. I saw your headlights and heard you guys talking and figured it was now or never. So here I am."

"What's your name?" Derrick asks without looking up from her chest.

"Simone."

"Bullshit," Liam says.

"Why would I lie to you?" She tosses a few dark braids over her right shoulder. Even though I'll never be attracted to her, I can see what Derrick might like, how all the dirt on the outside can just be washed off. If there's something pretty about her when she's filthy, then who can say how beautiful she is beneath the dirt. There's no way to wash the me off of me.

"You ever read *The Butcher Boy*?" she asks us.

We all shake our heads.

"Too bad," she says. "There's a copy in the bus."

"Fuck you," Liam says. "We follow you into the bus and a bunch of masked dudes hop out and rape us. Or tear out our kidneys."

She groans and then laughs. "I'll go get it. I'm not a trap-door spider."

"What's the book about?" Derrick asks.

"That's not a very good question."

"What the hell else is he supposed to ask?" Liam grabs a sand clod and rockets it at the nearest Joshua tree. The clod explodes against an *L*-bent limb and dust sprinkles the ground.

"I don't read books for about. Maybe it's a good question for someone else. Just not a good question for me; that's all."

"Okay," Derrick says. "What's a good question?"

"That's a good question," she says.

"You're like a hippy Yoda." Liam rubs his palms on his jeans.

She smiles. "What's your name, backwards hat guy?"

"Liam," he says. "Please write it on my chest so the police can identify my body after you dismember my corpse."

Her jaw drops. "How did you know my M.O.?"

Derrick laughs and adjusts his crotch, shifts his dick up and under the waist of his shorts to strangle the erection. He's done that for years; that's *his* M.O.

She puts her hand on Derrick's thigh and says, "What's your name?"

"Derrick." He clears his throat.

"Well, Derrick. A good question might be what is one good thing about the book."

"Okay," he says. "What's a good thing about it?"

"It makes me cry," she says. "Only two books ever made me cry. *The Butcher Boy* and *Slaughterhouse Five*."

"See," Liam says. "Butchers and slaughterhouses."

"Shut up," I say. "I read *Slaughterhouse Five*. It was better than any of that crap my dad made up." If Derrick had read that he might not be dumb enough to think he's going to make a difference by joining the military. Derrick says they need good people. What he doesn't understand is that we aren't good people, and the military doesn't need us. It was fighting before we were born. It'll fight after we're gone.

"You read?" Liam says.

"It was assigned in English class," I say.

Liam says, "That book was so small I figured it couldn't be any good."

"Size doesn't always matter." Simone rubs her hand up and down Derrick's thigh, nail-bitten fingers sliding over his tan corduroy shorts. She leans close to him, smiles, and then pulls away.

"You two aren't fucking on my car," I say. I don't care how well she knows books or how much of a pain in the stride Derrick's dick has become.

"What the hell?" Derrick scowls at me.

Simone squeezes Derrick's thigh and says, "Are you his mom?"

"Basically," I say.

"What does that mean?" Derrick grabs her wrist and sets her hand on the hood.

"I pay for everything while you sit on the couch all day. Isn't that what a mom does?"

"I'm leaving soon, asshole."

"Not soon enough," Liam says. "Sick of you talking about making a difference."

The dead air feels like lead aprons stacked on my chest. I glance at Simone and smirk. She bites the corner of her lower lip and says, "I'm gonna grab that book." Then she clicks on her flashlight, hops off the hood, and jogs down to her bus.

When she's little more than a shadow, I say, "Whenever the next big STD shows up, I guarantee they trace it back to her pussy and your dick."

"She's nice," Derrick says.

"Does she have a choice?" Liam asks. "She lives in a school bus:

in the desert."

"She likes me," Derrick says.

I say, "So do I."

Derrick shakes his head and bounces his heel against the bumper. "Don't be a fag, Sean."

I take a drink, spit out the bitter saliva that coats my tongue, and then hand the bottle to Liam. The flashlight floats through the bus and stops at the back.

Liam says, "We should jet before she comes back with chloroform and a hacksaw."

"She's harmless," Derrick says. "And besides. I want that book."

"You want that box." Liam offers the bottle to Derrick.

Derrick pushes it away and says, "Fuck you guys." He hops off the hood and jogs into the darkness after her, a broad-shouldered shadow that fades into a backdrop of purple and black and then disappears. Soon all that's left behind is the slap of his big shoes on the bus steps. I don't want to think about what will happen in there, but Melissa told me how Derrick fucked her, and I can't get it out of my head. His arms locked out so he could stare down at her face while he pounded away, sweat dripping off his nose and onto her little tits. How she raked her nails across his lower back and drew blood. She showed him the red on her fingers and he kept on anyway.

Liam says, "If he screams, we know he's getting killed. If he doesn't scream, it might be because they told him not to."

The flashlight moves from the back of the bus and stops in the middle. After a few seconds, the light goes out. Maybe he's in there talking about novels, trying to get to know her better through literature. And maybe the repo men will track me all the way out here and yank the Mustang from under my ass.

Liam takes a drink and then hands me the bottle.

"This is the perfect one-night stand," he says. "Unless she fixes up one of these buses, she could never come tell him if she got pregnant. She wouldn't know where to drive anyway."

No squeaks or moans have traveled up here. I don't need to hear them, though. Derrick gets scared when he's got to take control, but

Simone wasn't subtle. Neither was Melissa. She grabbed his hand and led him into that locker room. He never would have asked her. Not because he didn't want to, but because he was scared she'd say no.

"Headlights." Liam points to a couple lights in the distance.

I say, "We better go get him."

Liam says, "He's bailing. This will give him a head start on independence."

"We may never see him again."

"He's fucking a drifter, man. He's not up here reminiscing about the good old days."

These are the good old days. No reason to reminisce about things that never change. "I'm not letting him get fucked up."

"He ditched us for pussy, and soon he'll ditch us for good. He deserves whatever he gets." The headlights glow brighter and the shocks squeak as the vehicle rumbles closer. Liam taps the half-empty bottle on the hood.

"Once he takes off, I won't be able to do anything," I say. "But he's here right now."

Liam stands. "You're lucky I don't have anything better to do." He takes a drink. "'Cause I'd be doing it."

We hop in the car and roll down the short hill to the buses. Liam steps out and knocks on the bus door. Trevor, if that's who those lights belong to, isn't far away. Staticky voices and guitars swell as the lights near.

"Push the door open," I say.

Liam shoves the door in and stomps up the steps. He shouts, "Come on, Derrick." Tires crushing tumbleweed shards and loose sand make a cage of sound around me. Headlights illuminate the rust-pocked yellow bus, and through the window I can see Liam's backwards hat, Simone's braids, and Derrick's face stretching the threads of his red T-shirt as he pulls it over his bushy head.

The truck stops hard and slides a few inches on the sand. High beams burst on, and the engine gurgles, idling loud and erratic. A deep voice says, "Who the fuck's in there, Simone?" The truck door opens and a man steps down, a double-barreled shotgun gripped in his left hand. His tan boots and jeans with holes in the knees make me wish Derrick hadn't run dick first into this.

The man says, "Whoever's in the bus better get out now."

I shout, "Come on," and see both Liam and Derrick hop down the steps. Liam turns and sees the gun then says, "Fuck," and dives into the back seat. Derrick's pulling his shorts up, balls of corduroy in his fists as he stumbles toward the car.

Trevor doesn't raise the gun, and the only reason I can think of that keeps him from doing it is shock. *How did these boys find my sister out here in the middle of the desert?* You can't go anywhere and escape this. This is us, and we are everywhere. Desert to forest to sea. Generation after generation and all the way down to each individual and pathetic finale.

Derrick flops onto the seat, buttons, and zips up. A warbling steel guitar pierces the static, and Simone hops off the bus and sprints toward Trevor wearing only her jeans and an orange bra that glows against her pale skin. Her dark braids bounce between her shoulder blades, and she says, "He didn't hurt me. They didn't hurt me." He raises the gun and Simone drives her naked shoulder into his stomach.

Liam says, "Hit the gas, you fucking idiot."

I drop the gearshift into reverse, and Trevor shouts, "She's fifteen years old."

Derrick ducks, and I mash the pedal, throwing sand and dust all over Trevor and Simone, and once I've got enough clearance, I slam it into first and tear across the sand. Gunshots echo and a series of clanks sound off from the trunk.

"Are you all right?" Derrick asks. The thrumming engine is the only response, so he says, "Liam. Are you all right?"

"Yes, fucker."

The tires hit the pavement and catch. I slam the shifter into third, rev hard until I drop it into fourth. Let Simone and Trevor alone. They're running from something. There's no other reason to live out there.

"He shot the car," Liam says.

"Thanks for the verification," I say. "I was worried that no one would say anything and then the damage would get confused and fix itself."

Derrick leans back into the seat and drops a raggedy book on the dashboard. "All that for a book." A scent wave of vodka burns my nostrils, and I see the bottle on its side next to Derrick's shoes. "That shit spilled all over the floor." He picks up the empty bottle, rolls down his window and drops it onto the freeway.

Liam says, "You fucked a fifteen-year-old."

Derrick grabs the book from the dashboard and peels it open. "No. I didn't." It's too dark in the car for him to read, so he shuts it. The front right corner of the cover looks gnawed off. He sets the book on his bulging crotch and holds it there. Can't even scare the hard-ons out of him.

"Where's the crack?" Liam asks.

"Shit," I say.

Liam says, "I knew that bitch was a head."

"She's not a head," Derrick says.

"Stop defending your girlfriend, pedophile."

I say, "The baggie was on the hood. It must have blown off."

"We have to go back," Liam says.

I'll drop you here, and you can walk back there and get shot on your own."

Liam groans. "No drugs. No pussy. Not even any booze. What are we going to do?"

"Enjoy each other's company," I say.

Liam says, "Bullshit."

I doubt Trevor will try to chase us down, but if he does, I'd rather be in a place with a lot of people. The car skids a bit as I whip into the turnaround in the median, and the tires grip the pavement and we speed away.

"Where are we going?" Derrick asks.

"Not back home," I say. "Dad'll flip out if he sees the bullet holes." But if he never comes home, he'll never have any reason to be upset. And he'll never come home again. I wouldn't.

"Does insurance cover that?" Liam asks.

"Yeah," Derrick says. "It's included in the event of a shooting during a botched attempt to smoke crack clause."

"I'm going to sleep," Liam says. "When I wake up, it'll be like you were never here."

The needle bounces near E, and I want to see how bad the

damage is. If it's not too bad then it might look like some kind of stupid mistake, a hunting accident maybe. Once I've seen it, it'll be easier to make up a story. A guy who hasn't got out of the car to look at the bullet holes in the trunk probably seems a lot more like a guy who's running from something than one who can say, "Yes, sir. I am aware and I'm going to have it taken care of as soon as possible."

I pull off at a Chevron and park at the pump. The station's open twenty-four hours, and the clerk doesn't do anything more than give a quick glance in our direction before he gets back to reading the magazine in his hands. I get out and head into the store.

"Twenty on pump three," I say.

He doesn't look up, just extends an open hand. His fingernails are long, and he has a tattoo of Gazoo from *The Flintstones* on his left forearm. "Anything else?" he asks.

"Nah," I say. And then drop a twenty in his hand.

Back outside I walk around the front of the car. Don't want to stop at the trunk before I start to gas up. If he looks out here and sees me staring at something he might get suspicious. Derrick has the book opened, and Liam is knocked out in the back. I shove the nozzle into the tank and then head around to the bumper to see the damage. Three holes. The taillights are good, and he didn't fuck up the spoiler. One hole's near the trunk keyhole, and the other two are just above the bumper. The spread seems strange, but I must have been far enough away that most of the grains had spread out so much that they floated off into the darkness without doing any damage.

The pump clicks off. I yank the nozzle out, shove it back on the rack, and then twist the gas cap on.

"Hey." The clerk's leaned against the entrance door. "What happened to your car?"

I didn't think he could see anything from inside. "What do you mean?"

"Those holes," he says. "I'm more of 'vette man, but it's terrible to see a car like that all beat up."

I say, "Not much to do after it's done."

He nods and sips from a glass Coke bottle. "I know a guy who does body work. He could have that fixed up in a couple days, probably." The clerk heads over and the door hydraulics hiss as he walks around the rear. "Got his card here." He pulls out his wallet, un-Velcroes it, snags the card, then offers it to me with two fingers.

I take it and say, "Thanks."

"The whole damn world's a war zone these days," he says. "There's a good man's number on that card, and that's harder to find than you might think."

He takes a final look at the holes, lets out a wet whistle, and then heads back into the store. I get in, shut the door, and pull out slow.

"What did that jackass want?" Derrick asks. He drops the book on his lap.

"To help," I say.

Derrick taps his fingers on the book cover a few times and says, "Help."

"He gave me some guy's card," I tell him. "Says he does body work."

"They're just going to repo the car. What difference does it make?"

"It doesn't make a difference."

All that matters is that the tank is full right now, and I'll drive until it's not, all over this desert until it's time to drop Derrick off at LAX. He's right next to me, but he's already gone, has never been here with me at all. I told him how I felt but it was nothing more than a joke that got swallowed up in tepid bursts of wind and dust. Swallowed up like our friendship, like Melissa and me, like Trevor and Simone. All of us, inside and out, sun-bleached bones scattered over the red and brown sand of lifetimes spent doing nothing in nowhere. Some people say it doesn't have to be this way, that you can be whatever you want and whoever you want. But this is who I am now and who I will be for however many miles I choose to travel on or until someone stronger comes along to shut off the ride. And as much as I want to just tear down the interstate, drive us as far away from all of this as I can, instinct guides me right back home.

CHAPTER 6

THERE'S A BIG blue rip in the sky, and I wish I could say it was because of drugs, but I never did hallucinogens so I don't even know if this is the kind of thing you might see if you were on a drug that could make you see things. I pretend the blue glow is there to tell us, *Here comes the war that will make all your lives matter. Now it's time for you to live.* If I believed in God or angels, then I might believe I was lucky enough to be witnessing the start of an existence that wasn't just a place-holder in some thing's grand scheme. I can feel in my bones that there's a logical explanation for this, though. Trucks still rip down the freeway in the distance, and we're the only people in my neighborhood outside. No one else seems to notice or care. It's possible that the whole world would be oblivious at first, but it seems impossible that *I* would be the first person to notice the apocalypse considering how many people there are in the world looking for the end days without blinking.

"Was there anything on the news about this?" Derrick's staring up at the thing, the last bottle of Absolut hangs loosely in his right hand.

"Which one of us do you think watched the news?" I ask.

Derrick drinks, and the porch light makes the vodka sparkle as it sloshes around the bottle. "No one." He rubs his lips dry with the back of his left hand.

The front door swings open and Mom struts out, naked, clutching a pink and white travel bag to her chest.

"Um," Derrick says.

"Should we go?" Liam asks.

I say, "Jesus, Mom. Where are you going?" I can't remember seeing her vagina before, but there it is. The hole that was stupid enough to release me into the world is covered in a thick black bush. "Please go inside."

"Your father needs me." Her eyes are bloodshot, half-closed, and I'm surprised she's able to stand.

"No he doesn't." I pull my shirt off, and then hold it up to cover her from the waist down. "You need to go back to bed."

"He's lonely," she says.

There is no embarrassment in this. Liam sits on the lawn, facing away from us, and Derrick's drinking vodka and staring at that blue cloud that slowly drifts apart, becoming less blue with each passing moment. All of this is happening at once, but it's not all happening to them. That hole in the sky won't go anywhere. I have to get Mom into bed.

"What do you think that is?" Derrick asks.

Liam says, "Missile defense test maybe? I think they do that in Vandenburg. I didn't realize it would tear a hole in the sky."

Their voices trail off into mumbles as I guide Mom through the front door. Her hands are cold and wet, and all the hate I have for her, all the stuff that makes me wish she was someone else oozes out of me. This is Dad's fault. "Let's get you in bed, Mom."

"You have to tell him that I tried," she says. There's no struggle in her voice. "I did the best I could. You have to tell him."

"I will." It doesn't matter if I tell the truth or lie. Tomorrow this will not have happened. She'll never remember this. I'm the one who's stuck with the memory. In the bedroom, I take the bag from her and set it on the floor, help her crawl under the sheets. Yellow streaks on the sheets let me know it's been forever since they've been washed. I could at least do that. I'll wash the damn sheets from now on. It doesn't take long. Rip them off and toss them in the washer. Go do something else while it runs. No sweat. That's what a good son would do. I can be a good son. That's one thing I can control.

"He said he'd bring home steaks for the barbecue this weekend." She closes her eyes, and I pull the sheet and bedspread over her pale chest, up to her throat. All those wrinkles on her face. She's a thousand years older than she should be.

"He'll bring the steaks." I can manage that. Not that we have a grill to cook them on. I'll have to fry them in a pan. I could broil them if I had any idea how the hell to do that. If she remembers any of this, I'll take care of it. I have a hundred dollars left, and I can get back on with Jeff. He'll understand. This was just a stupid vacation; dumbass kids like me do this all the time.

"I'm so glad you're home, honey," she says. "It's so nice to have you here."

"Glad to be here, Mom." The picture on the wall beside the bathroom door of me and Mom stretched out on beach towels seems impossible. Neither of us were ever the people in that picture: the smiles, the zinc on our noses, that straw hat that casts a shadow over her face.

She shivers and groans the way she did the night when I told her how I felt about Derrick. Did she not ever mention it to me because she wanted to believe she'd never heard it? I said it to her, flat out. *This is who I am, Mom.* "I'm sorry, baby," she'd said. She was sorry, and now she's glad I'm here because we never had the conversation that made her sorry for me. None of the painful things ever happened. Just like that goddamned picture on the wall doesn't show the blisters I got because Mom and Dad were too drunk to put suntan lotion on me. All over my body the skin felt like it was peeling itself away from my bones. An eight-year-old kid who'd been burnt so bad that the pain he felt from shifting his shoulders or legs made him vomit. And for what? So my parents could drink until they passed out and leave me there on the beach while the tide rose and the waves shattered the sand castles I'd built. That's all it's ever been for them: excuses. "Married your mom because she was pregnant," Dad said. "We didn't want you to grow up without two parents." *We* didn't want. That's all there is to it: them and what they wanted. That's why I'm where I am now. Because I'm not what they wanted, and they didn't want each other, and all that's left over is this disgusting house in the middle of the desert that I want to burn to the ground.

I pull my shirt back on and stomp outside.

Derrick's sitting next to Liam on the lawn. He turns and says, "She okay?"

"Did she look okay?"

"Sorry I care more about your mom than you do."

"You should be."

Liam says, "Looks like a huge blue pussy in the sky."

Derrick laughs.

"For real," Liam says. "Maybe a giant baby will ooze out of that thing? Think how many jobs a baby the size of Texas would generate. Or maybe it'll just start raining regular sized babies, and then we'll all be so busy that we won't have time to think about how boring our lives are."

Liam half smiles at me. I get it. He wants to distract me, but his stupid jokes aren't going to be enough. "No more sitting around talking about giant pussies in the sky. No more Mom or Coast Guard talk."

"All right, then," Liam says. "Let's fuck something up."

I walk over to the Mustang and get inside, start it up. Liam squeezes into the back seat, and then Derrick walks over and gets in too. Mom can lie in there for the next million years. She can do whatever she wants while I'm not around to see it. All I've seen so far won't go away. I can't change that, but I don't have to watch her kill herself. I don't have to stay here and wait for Dad to show up, hoping that when he does he'll finally care, that he'll actually stay behind and take care of the things he's responsible for.

"Bye-bye, blue vagina," Liam says.

Derrick leans against his door, right leg mashed against the door-handle. He slides his sunglasses on and rests his head on the window. If I told him that there was no one in the world I'd rather be with than him, what would he do? Kiss me. I laugh out loud and can't believe I've done it.

"What's so funny?" Liam asks.

"Nothing yet." And it's true. It hurts because it's not funny. It's less funny than any of this shit we've been through. Mom, Dad, sunburns and Melissa fucking around on me. All of that is funny because it is what it is on its face. The ache in my stomach that can't be stomped out when I'm around Derrick isn't real to anyone but me. I will kill it, though. I will make it bleed and die.

WE DROVE AROUND on base for a couple hours: until I was too tired to drive anymore. I parked at F-Area park, and we slept until the sun rose. We ate breakfast at Burger King, and then walked around the high school, trying to remember all the things we'd done that were worth remembering. Most of the memories weren't even funny.

Liam brought a porn into school one day in Mr. Arhets' Spanish class, and then he shoved it into the VCR. Someone else in the class had a universal remote and turned the TV on and played the porn. It was only playing long enough for a man to say, "May I lick your asshole please," Mr. Arhets yanked the TV's power plug, and then shouted, "You can either live in the gutter, like animals, or you can help animals out of the gutter. It's your choice."

"Remember," Liam says. "I thought he was gonna explode."

"I do," I say. "But I don't remember much Spanish."

Most of the day passes this way, memories that fill me with regret after regret until finally we decide to play home run derby on the minor league field where Derrick had broken Kelly's nose junior year.

Kelly had punched Derrick's little brother in the face and Derrick never asked Kelly or his brother, Nathan, why. Derrick knew Nathan was an asshole, knew it was probably, at least partly, Nathan's fault. But Derrick punched Kelly in the face and then kicked him in the ribs five times while he rolled on the ground holding his bleeding nose. We had to pull Derrick off Kelly before things got out of hand.

The next time I saw Derrick was at baseball practice. We were changing into our practice jerseys. He slipped his T-shirt off, and I saw purple and yellow bruises on his ribs. Kelly didn't do that to him, so I asked Derrick what happened, and he said he was on his roof and had tried to jump onto his garage but slipped. He mashed his ribs on the side of the garage roof. Nothing about the way he said it would have made anyone in the world think it was a lie except for how elaborate the story was. I knew it, though. Derrick wasn't the kind of guy who does stupid shit like try and jump from his roof to his garage for fun.

Kelly's dad was an officer: a major. So Derrick had beat up a major's son and then Derrick's dad beat the shit out of Derrick. And three days later, Kelly grabbed Nathan in a headlock on the football field after school; Kelly choked Nathan until he passed out. And when Derrick saw Kelly again, he was walking just outside the right field fence to the varsity baseball field. Derrick was warming up on the first base line, getting ready to throw batting practice. Liam said,

"There's major douchebag." Derrick caught the ball that Liam had tossed back to him and then walked toward the fence. He said, "Hey, Kelly. Come here a second." But Kelly wasn't stupid. He turned and ran. Kelly's neon green wind breaker and loose black sweatpants billowed in the wind gusts that he struggled to run against. Derrick sprinted to get closer and then crow-hopped and gunned the ball as hard as he could. It slammed into Kelly's back, and Kelly fell face first onto the dirt. Derrick came back and threw batting practice. Our coach didn't say anything. Derrick didn't come to school the next day, though. And when he did come back to school, he couldn't stand up straight. He said he had a kidney stone. We let him believe that we didn't think his story was bullshit.

It's strange to see Derrick on the mound again, a plastic bucket of baseballs poured out around his feet. The last time he pitched, he struck out ten batters in five innings and only gave up two hits. It wasn't the best game I'd seen him pitch, but it was about as bad as he ever did. There were real hitters at times who'd sit on a curve ball and make Derrick try harder, but even the ones who sent a ball over the fence on their first at-bat never homered twice. Derrick remembered the pitches guys liked to chase, and if he couldn't out-pitch a hitter, he'd throw at the batter's head until the batter was scared enough that he'd swing awkward. If the batter never got rattled by the fastballs that zipped past his chin, Derrick would walk him. He never cared about statistics or winning the game; he just liked beating batters.

Derrick lobs a ball to Liam and Liam turns on his heel and sends it over the left field fence. The aluminum pang echoes and a dust cloud bursts where the ball lands out near the road, just another hundred feet and the ball would've smashed into the train car across the road that houses a Baskin Robbins and Anthony's Pizza. The fence here is only two-hundred and fifty feet at center, and even though the ball sailed well over the chain-links, it would have been nothing more than a low fly ball on any field where guys our age should play.

"That's one," Liam says. He knocks the bat on his shoes and spits on home plate. "I could hit it five times farther if you weren't floating them in here."

Derrick laughs. "Whatever." He snatches a ball with his glove, winds up and lobs it to Liam.

Liam turns on his heel again, swings hard but misses and falls on his ass.

"Calm down, roid rage," Derrick says.

Liam rolls onto his knees and then pushes himself to his feet. He steps into the batters' box and cocks the bat back.

Derrick whips his leg up and then pushes off hard with his back foot before lobbing the ball again. He follows through, bends forward, rakes the dirt with his fingertips.

Liam waits on this one and connects solidly, sends the ball down the first base line.

"How can you swing so late on a pitch that's coming forty miles an hour?" I ask.

"You can't hit something late," Liam says. "It gets hit when you hit it. If it stays in play, that's all that matters." He smacks home plate with the bat and says, "Gimme another."

Derrick grabs a ball from the bucket and flips it up, bounces it off his knuckles and catches it in the same hand. "You think philosophical excuses make it okay that you swung late?"

"Throw the ball, Sergeant Assfuck."

Derrick kicks his knee to his chest and then whips the ball toward the plate. Liam drops into his stance and swings. He misses and lets the bat fly down the third base line. The ball thumps against the black-rubber backstop. Derrick laughs and Liam stands up and jogs to the mound. Derrick backs up a couple steps and throws his glove at Liam. Liam swats the glove away and catches Derrick around the neck and drags him down to the infield.

I walk down to third base, grab the bat, and then head to the mound. They wrestle around like a couple morons, and I toss balls up and knock them over the fence. I don't know why this is the way it's going to end for us, but now that we're here, it seems like it was inevitable. We should move on. Derrick's leaving. I should too, but I don't know where to go. I know that wherever I end up, I want Derrick to be there, and that's one thing I will not get.

Watching them roll around on the short-clipped grass makes me see that this can't be the way we end what might be our final day; it isn't enough. I want Derrick to come with me down one last road so he has something exciting to remember, so that maybe one day when he's old and done looking for greener grass he'll think about one thing we did together and smile. Derrick sits on Liam's chest, knees pinning his arms at his sides. He slaps Liam's face a couple times and then stands.

Liam stands. "When we're Gunners Mates I'm gonna blast you in the face while you're cleaning my cannon."

"Blatant homosexuality," Derrick says.

"Shut up about gayness," I say.

Derrick says, "What's your deal?"

"We need to get out of here and do something for real."

"Like?" Derrick asks.

Liam says, "Give me the bat."

I hand it to him, and he jogs over to the green light-control-box and smashes the bat into it a couple times. It's not as loud as I expected it would be, but it's loud enough so that if anyone else is around they'll notice for sure.

"Port-o-potties," I say.

"What?" Derrick asks.

"Get in the car."

"What about all the balls?" Derrick asks.

"Leave them and get in the damn car."

Liam stops smashing the box, and we load up and drive off. We haven't done anything like this in so long that I can't even remember how it feels. The windows are down and "Have a Cigar" is loud and roiling from the speakers. We're headed toward destruction because it's the best way for us to spend the rest of our time, the best way to finish up these last hours before I never get to see Derrick again, before it becomes me and Liam, until Liam bails because he's decided he needs more than the desert can give him, more than I can give him too.

Signs are tacked to the C-Area houses that have been draped in plastic: ASBESTO. Giant plastic condoms keep asbestos from drifting on the wind and filling the lungs of spouses, airmen, and children at school. I don't care about that, though. What I'm interested in is that workers need bathrooms. Blue and green and red port-o-potties stand all over the place, and I pull up beside a red one and pop the trunk. "There's a nylon rope in the trunk. Tie it to the chain on the back of that shitter."

Derrick says, "This is not a good idea."

"Then you do it, Liam."

"I'll have to ride shotgun."

"Fine," Derrick says. "I'll do it." He hops out and snatches the red rope, slams the trunk and kneels by the bumper. After a few seconds, he pulls the opposite end of the rope over to the port-o-potty and slips the end through a chain link. He ties a thick red knot, runs over, hops into the car, and then says, "Go."

I stomp on the gas and spin tires on the pavement. Burnt rubber fumes waft over us, and I feel the rope strain from the weight of the shithouse. The back of Liam's head and the port-o-potty are clear in the rearview. Someone shouts, "Stop," and, Liam says, "Fuck yes." The potty tumbles onto its side and skids behind us. Sparks hop off the pavement from the clanking chain links, and the Mustang pulls forward with no trouble at all. A group of kids walking on the sidewalk, tossing sticks and pop cans at one another, cheer at us as we drag by sparking and hissing like a chimera bound by frayed duct-tape.

"Where are we taking this?" Derrick asks.

"Out the gate, " I say.

"Don't do that," he says. "They'll catch us at the gate."

"I can't slow down and dump it somewhere now. Whoever yelled for us to stop is going to call it in. We have to drive it off base or turn ourselves into the SPs."

Liam says, "I love you idiots."

If we get to the gate and they try to stop us, I'll just hammer it down and gun right past or turn into the desert and slip over the sand until I find a way off base and back into reality where something this stupid will only make people laugh. So what if we get caught? Then I won't be able to sit around and bitch about Derrick leaving. I won't have to think at all because it will be do or don't, black and white, the way Derrick sees the world.

"You better get on it," Liam says. "We can't outrun the radio. If the SPs get to the gate before we do, we're fucked."

"They won't beat us to the gate," I say. We'll get off base and this spark-slinging shit house will make it as far as I want to take it before we set it free.

"This is so fucking stupid." Derrick slips his sunglasses on and his mouth is stretched tight, like he wants to smile but won't. He won't let me know he enjoys this as much as I do, as much as Liam does. The grinding metal-and-plastic box careens as I round a gentle curve and pull onto the final stretch between us and the gate. The housing areas are long gone, and there is nothing but the low light of dusk, red-orange clouds that drift by on wind that blows too far above us to cool the night. We've been out into the desert here before. A week before Derrick left last year, he and I drove out to the base of a tall hill with a few beers and his dad's Ruger. We shot up the beer cans and then drove back to civilization. It felt good to do that then and this feels good right now. All the weight behind us can be severed whenever we want. We won't do that on base, though. We're gonna see how fast this shit can travel.

The guard shack stands alone a mile ahead of us. Not too many people come in the North Gate this time of day. The guard's probably just sitting on his ass with his gun on top of his radio, the safety on. He's scratching his nuts, thinking about what he'll do as soon as he gets off. Even if someone has called this in, he's not going to risk his life to stop us. Dad always said the last thing anyone should ever do is be an SP. *Everyone in the Air Force gets treated like shit, but SPs get the worst of it.*

A car headed the opposite way passes us, and the port-o-potty skates to the right, plows into the sand, and kicks up a brown cloud that trails the car. I cut the wheel right, and the port-o-potty tumbles over and crashes onto the pavement. The red door flaps open and snaps closed, then opens again. The grinding sounds like a monster groaning in agony.

"Don't hit the gate shack," Derrick says.

The most beautiful thing about North Gate in this moment is that there is no gate arm; it's just the shack. If there's no blockade, and they haven't dropped tire tacks, we'll zip right past and out into the real world. Cops have more important things to do than chase some kids who stole a port-o-potty, but if the thing slams into the shack, things will be different. Destruction of government property is no joke, and this needs to remain as harmless as possible.

Only a few more seconds to get the cargo back into my lane, so

I cut left and send the port-o-potty back to the right. It rolls a couple times, grinds hard in the sand and then scratches into the shallow ditch that lines the road. The box hops off the sand like a ship's bow catching air after bashing through a thick wave. A guard stands just outside the shack with his hands on his hips. His beret is cocked back on his head, and when we're right by the shack, I can see he's smiling. I stomp the gas and gun it past the shack, stick my arm out the window and flip off the guard. In the rearview I see him pop a half-assed salute. He's got a story now, and we've got one too, but we have to do something with this port-o-potty before it becomes serious. The main problem is that they'll figure out it was me soon because I'm the young asshole with a Mustang who lives close by, the young asshole who can get on base, the young asshole who lived on base and who's father retired from the Air Force not long ago.

Derrick places his glasses on the dash and says, "We should dump this thing now."

Liam says, "Haul it to the ocean. See if it floats."

Derrick shakes his head. "We'll never make it to the ocean."

"That sounds like a challenge." All the way to the beach from the High Desert; that would be a great way to send Derrick off. No way the port-o-potty would hold up that long. "It'll get ate up before we make it." The darker it gets outside, the brighter the sparks that sprinkle the road glow: cinders hopping on the asphalt.

"You think those sparks could catch the shit on fire?" Derrick asks.

"What kind of idiot are you?" Liam says.

"There's methane in there," he says.

"There's gas in this car," I say. "You worried we're gonna blow up?"

Liam leans forward and lightly backhands Derrick on the cheek. "Dump this or we ride it to the beach."

I'd like to take the port-o-potty around the world, grease it up so the road can't grind it down to metal splinters and plastic shards. But soon, if it hasn't already happened, the shit in the container will start to spill out over the road. We'll be arrested for something worse than the actual crime: pollution, biological warfare, fecal terrorism. I slow down and pull onto the shoulder. Sand flips up and plinks against the wheel wells, little rocks smack the undercarriage, and as I brake, the port-o-potty cruises past and stops a few feet in front of us. "Anyone have a knife?"

"Here," Liam hands the steak knife to Derrick, and Derrick kicks his door open, runs around back and starts sawing the rope.

Flashing lights fire up the horizon behind us. "Hurry up."

"This blade is dull as hell. Were you cutting concrete with it?"

The lights are getting brighter. "Just cut it as much as you can, and then get in."

He says, "I just have to stretch it taut. Then it'll cut through."

"Go, man," Liam says.

"No," I say. I'm not leaving him on the side of the rode with the port-o-potty. Even if he is leaving, he's here right now. Derrick saws furiously, grunts, breathes through his mouth. "He'll get it."

Liam says, "I'm not going to jail for him."

Derrick yells, "Mother fuck. It won't cut any more."

The lights spin: white, red, and blue. A siren whispers. "Just get in," I say.

Derrick drops the rope and hops in. I mash the pedal, and we rock onto the road and fly past the toppled port-o-potty. The rope catches and the port-o-potty follows us onto the pavement, chains screaming and sparking, a last-ditch explosion of sound and color that says we did all that we could to make our mark on this day, and that we are all that we can be. The siren's familiar warble gives me goose bumps. "We aren't going to jail today, boys." And the rope snaps. The port-o-potty skates behind us as I gun it, 80, 90, 100. Soon there's no sign of the port-o-potty in the rearview.

The siren fades and Liam shouts, "Holy fuck."

No light is left in the sky except that cast by a little sickle of moon that looks like it's been pasted onto a black construction paper sky. I'm hoping for a cloud to sweep across it, to tuck it in, and help us hide. Take a nap, moon. Don't let anyone see the frayed red rope flapping behind the Mustang like a skinned cat's tail. 120. "What's the governor set to on this thing," Derrick yells. 130. Air blasts in through the window, peels my lips apart, flattens my eyelashes. Headlights coming the other direction leave us behind even faster than the cars I swerve around. Soon we'll reach the exit, and I'll have to slow down, but we won't get caught. Not tonight. Not for this. Tonight we escape together.

CHAPTER 7

July 5th, 2000

The coffee table's littered with the unopened envelopes I pulled from the overfull mailbox: bills and credit card apps for Dad. The VCR's rolling a Pink Floyd documentary that I've started a thousand times but never finished: *Live At Pompeii.*

Derrick comes back from the kitchen, sits on the couch and says, "Playing at a volcano is so badass. It's like daring it to blow."

"Yep," I say back and notice my empty hands. We drank all the beer, and there's nothing left but one bottle of vodka and Dad's whiskey. When those are gone, we'll be hard up for something to drink. But I've got less than a hundred dollars left, and I'll need at least twenty of that to pay for gas to get Derrick to LAX when the time comes, and I'm sure that time is near. He leans forward and rests his face in his hands, breathes deep and lets the breath out through clenched teeth. These are exactly the same motions that he made the time he told me that Melissa had been talking to him about *our* problems. He told me he fucked her right after I told him it was no big deal that they were just talking. I'd been glad they were friends and that she had someone other than me to talk to; I was glad that he was close to her; it kept him close to me.

"I can't do this any more," he says.

"What?"

"Nothing."

"Let me get something to drink." My legs feel weak. It's odd to feel tired even though I've not done much more than stay awake. I don't want to need sleep unless I earn it, and it's frustrating to think that I'm no longer even in control of something as simple as that. The vodka bottle is missing, and I can only assume that Derrick or Liam drank it all. So I grab Dad's bottle of Wild Turkey and a couple shot glasses from the cabinet, and then set it all on the coffee table. "Let's do a few." Whiskey spills out faster than I expect and overflows the glasses; the brown liquid slips down the dusty glasses and soaks the unopened envelopes, turning white paper translucent and fragile.

Derrick grabs his glass and says, "Here's to *doing* something."

I raise my glass and toss the shot into the back of my throat so I don't have to taste it long. We both set our glasses on the table and then Derrick leans back into the couch.

"Remember when we pulled the fire alarms at all the schools?"

I laugh and pour another shot.

Derrick says, "Someone got scared and pulled an alarm early so it screwed everything up."

"Didn't your brother get caught?"

"Yeah."

"He never sold us out, though."

"He would never do that." Derrick clears his throat. "Nathan and his friends were fucking around at the football field, and if the field hadn't been in the center of all the schools then they never would've been there to get caught. He was always in the wrong place at the wrong time."

I take another shot, pour one for him, and then twist the cap on and push the bottle away. "Run faster. Hide better. You can't blame it all on luck."

"Dad beat Nathan for that," Derrick says. "Made me watch it. Dad knew I was the one who'd pulled the alarms, but he beat Nathan anyway. He looked right into my eyes each time he snapped the belt across the back of Nathan's knees."

"Come on, man," I say. "Your dad wouldn't do that."

"He had Nathan bend over a chair and grab his ankles. Sometimes Dad hit us with the buckle. Sometimes--," Derrick takes another shot. "Forget it."

"Whatever," I say. "Your dad wasn't like that."

"I was *there*, you know?" He grabs the bottle, twists off the cap and throws it over his shoulder. "It's not worth arguing about. It's done." He takes another shot and refills both glasses. "You coming with me or what? You can't keep living like this. We could have got really fucked up today."

His face glows. It's too hot in here, but I'm not turning on the AC. Until I see Dad's back to pay all these damn bills, I'm using as little as possible. Money is as good a reason to join the military as any. I'd get paid. Maybe not a lot, but a hell of a lot more than I make with no job. But *The Coast Guard?* "I don't think I could do it," I say. "I don't want to live that way. Not being able to say no to things I don't want to do."

"Look," Derrick says. "I don't want to bail on you guys, but this just can't last."

"Maybe," I say.

"We could've avoided all this wasted time."

"How?"

"If we'd signed up, we could've been gone already. These two months have just been a huge waste. And these last few days have been a total shit show."

I crack my knuckles and tongue the softness beneath my upper lip. "Why do you think there are only two choices all the time?"

"I don't think that *all the time*. Not for everyone. But for us. For me. That's all I've got."

"There are all kinds of jobs. A lot of them suck, but you can drop those when they get to you. Once you join the military, you're stuck. Pick a bad job, and you're doing it for four years. Wash out in tech school and they'll stick you wherever they want to. You'll be that asshole standing in the guard shack watching three idiots dragging a port-o-potty out the gate."

"I won't wash out," he says. "It'll be good."

"It won't be good." It can't be. I know this more than anyone. Mom was up, dancing around, cooking spaghetti and cleaning the house just yesterday. Now she's right back where she always ends up: drugged out of her mind, fighting off a headache that medication may never cure. "This is bullshit," I say. "You want to join the Coast Guard because you think it's going to be the least evil of all the branches. But it's just as bad."

"I know that if we go to war, the Coast Guard is the safest place to be."

"Why is that the safest place to be?"

"Floating on a ship in Lake Superior is a lot safer than doing anything near combat."

"You know all kinds of ships have sunk to the bottom of the Great Lakes, right?"

"Not from torpedoes," he says.

"It doesn't always take a torpedo."

Derrick stands. "I'm not trying to hurt you," he says. "I want us all to do well. We just can't get anywhere by sitting around in the desert and waiting for something to come along and rescue us from ourselves. We're wasting our lives out here." He walks out the front door, and the screen smacks closed behind him. I follow him because I am not letting this stop here, where he wants it to end. He's leaned against the fence post, and the sound of his piss splattering onto the dry lawn is loud. The air is colder than usual in the summer, and a steady breeze sweeps sand and cracked brush and everything else too light to resist the wind down the street and out into the desert.

"We're finishing this," I say. "No more implying things and walking away. Talk to me."

"I'm finished talking," he says. "Talking isn't doing anything more than keeping us from moving on." His belt buckle clangs as he shakes himself off. He tucks his dick back into his pants, and then he turns and says, "I called my parents earlier. They're buying me a plane ticket."

What do I say to this? There's nothing in my hands, there's nothing on the ground to grab hold of and smash into his face. There's just Derrick standing there with his hands in his pockets, staring at the ground. He's not even looking at me, can't look at me because he knows he's being a pussy. "You can't see past this and see what it could be. We did so much for you. I did so much for you. We could have made an all right life here."

He's nodding and kicking dirt around with his shoe like a scolded child.

I grab him by the shirt collar and pull him close, smell his bad breath and stare into his eyes. They're the same light blue they've always been, but for the first time ever in my life I'm so close to him that I can see my own face reflected in his dilated pupils. "Fucking talk to me."

He breathes deep and forces his thick shoulders back. "Mom said this was stupid, that I should have joined before I ever came back out here. But I never listened to Mom and Dad the first time. You always made me feel like I was an idiot for listening to my parents, and look where listening to you got me. I wanted to believe I was different, that we were different than our parents."

I let go of his shirt and push him. He staggers a couple steps and smiles, the same smile he'd flashed the time he'd hit the first batter of a game on the forearm and the kid hopped to first base before sitting on the bag and crying until they gave him a pinch runner. I can't believe he's smiling at me the same way now.

"Hit me," he says. "If you're so pissed at me, and you feel like you're right. Hit me. It's not going to make me change my mind. But if it'll make you feel better, I want you to do it."

"You don't know how bad I want to."

He shrugs and pulls his hands out of his pockets. "If you wanted to bad enough, you would. You just have to do it, Sean. Don't think about it. Close your fist and hit me. Don't *want* to hit me. Hit me."

There has to be a way to hurt him, but I can't think of anything that could hurt him as bad as he's hurting me. Maybe that's all there really is to it; maybe he's always been hurting me, and I was too stupid to see that, too blinded by what I wanted him and me to be to see that he's always been hurting me. He doesn't need me the way I need him. I know that, now. He has a family and they hate him for caring about his friends. Blood, blood, blood, they've told him his whole life, and we even cut our palms and shared that with each other. But I was too young to know that was bullshit. We were blood brothers because we had been bored and had the guts to run a knife over our palms.

"Why did you fuck Melissa?" I ask.

"I don't know."

"That's it?"

"What do you want me to say. She was crying and talking about how fucked up you were to her, how you didn't even look at her. It was like some shit off a soap opera." He spits. "Why the hell do you want to talk about this again? She's gone. You would have done the same thing if you were me."

If he knew how hard it was for me to fuck Melissa, he'd understand. No. He can't understand because it isn't something anyone I know *would* understand. We all act like we're above so many things, like things have changed so much, but the only place they've changed are in classrooms and on TV. When Dad gets home, Mom will be drugged up, and I'll be myself, drunk or high because all I can do is hope that the next drug I do will turn me into someone I can't become on my own. I have to let it go. I have to let him go.

"You're right," I say. "I'd have fucked your girlfriend if she came on to me. That's what good friends do."

"This isn't about Melissa," he says. "If it was about Melissa, we wouldn't be friends any more. What's bothering you?"

Of course this isn't about Melissa, but that doesn't mean we can't fight about Melissa until what this is about disappears and he leaves and I forget about all of this the way I should have forgot about it when he left the first time.

"I'm joining the Air Force," he says.

"What happened to the Coast Guard?"

"Come on," he says. "You read the dumbass pamphlet. They make you do all kinds of horse shit before you even learn a job. I'm not painting ships and stripping barnacles off buoys for two years before I go to tech school. I'm going to learn a job I can do when I get out. Mom says the Air Force will treat me the most like a human out of any of the services."

"So you're going to sit in a chair in an office in camouflage?"

"If that's what the job is, that's what it is. But I'll be out of here. Anything is an improvement over this."

"So you'll join the Air Force so you can grow old and fat and die without ever having done anything? You're going to deal with all the bullshit and stress and never leave the military with a story worth telling. You'll be just like my dad, reliving glory days that were never yours."

"What are we doing now? You had a job, but you hated it. A car you can barely afford. You spend all your time trying to find drugs and booze so you don't go crazy with boredom. You're as unhappy as I am. You're more unhappy than I am. You need to get the fuck out of here and no one is stopping you but yourself. We can leave, man. We can. All you have to do is sign up. The rest will take care of itself."

"You know who you sound like?" I smile. "Your dad."

He scowls at me. "Shut up, Sean."

"All those times you whined about him for being such an asshole, for not seeing how hard it is for you." I laugh. "It's hilarious. He *made* you play baseball: bullshit. You were good, but you liked complaining so much that you wouldn't admit you enjoyed it."

"At least I was good," he says.

"Yeah," I say. "You were. But it got you to the same place as me and Liam. And all those times you came to school with bruises on your neck or when you took your shirt off in the locker room, and I was the only one who saw the yellow and black all over your back and chest. You wanted sympathy. You wanted me to tell people so they'd feel bad for you. But I didn't tell anyone because I was dumb enough to believe you really wanted it all to be a secret. I bet the real reason you were sad your dad died was because him beating you was the only thing about you that was interesting."

Derrick says, "Shut up, Sean."

"All those times you bitched about the things your dad did to you and your brother, about all the things that went on behind the closed doors of your house, you were happy that it was happening to you because it gave you something to complain about. You enjoyed it. Didn't you?"

He shakes his head. "Melissa fucked Liam, too."

"So?" I say. "This isn't about Melissa. This isn't about who she fucked. This is about you. It's always about you, and has always been about you. Admit it."

He snatches the bottle from me, turns it up to suck down the last drink, and then drops it on the lawn. "I fucked Melissa a lot. Every day. It was pretty obvious, and if you weren't so high all the time maybe you'd have noticed. But you're right, Sean. I fucked her because I wanted her. I wanted to take her from you. I didn't think you deserved her, and once she broke it off with you, I didn't want her anymore. I wanted her only because you had her. I wanted to be happy, and taking her from you made me happy." He bites his lip, can't look at me.

"Liar," I say.

"Maybe," he says. "But it doesn't change anything."

"It isn't changing anything because none of it can change," I say. "I want to tell you that you're becoming your dad. But that's a lie. You're already him, and he always hated me and Liam. He hated you, too. You're going to see one day that I'm right. And then you'll remember this, the desert, the empty bottle of whiskey. Pissing on my front lawn. You'll hate yourself."

"My dad didn't hate you guys. He hated watching us go nowhere. He didn't want us to get behind. Didn't want us to struggle the way he did." Derrick grabs the shovel off the lawn and heads toward the open sand where I buried the rabbit. "It doesn't matter. Let's hit some sand clods."

I follow him and we both kick around in the half-hard sand for clumps. He grabs a clod, tosses it up and swings the shovel. The clod clinks and explodes into a thin cloud that sprinkles over his face and T-shirt. "I got sand in my damn eye." He pulls his collar up and rubs it over his face and then blinks hard a few times and hands me the shovel. I toss a clod up and knock it into oblivion. Then I grab another and smash it and another and smash another until Derrick sits on the sand and wraps his arms around his knees. Sand-spray rains over him, but he's closed his eyes.

"What are you going to do?" Derrick stretches one leg out, grinding his heel into the sand and leaving behind a hole for his calf to rest in.

"Find another electrician job, I guess. I'm certified, and it's good money."

He grabs a handful of sand, lets it drain out the bottom of his fist. "Not about jobs, man."

I stab the shovel into the sand and knock my hands clean on my thighs. "About what?"

"Your mom?"

"What can I do about her?"

"There's got to be some place you can take her or someone you can call."

"I'll stuff her in a box and send her back to the factory. What the fuck would you do?"

He shrugs. "Never thought about it."

She's not my responsibility; she's my mom. "Don't worry. I'll do what I have to."

"All right," he says.

"When do you have to leave?"

"Tomorrow," he says. "I fly out of LAX."

"Good. I was getting sick of you anyway."

"You don't mind giving me a ride do you?"

"That never stopped me from doing it before."

"What am I going to do about that girl?"

"What girl?"

"Simone."

"*Do* about her?"

He crushes some hard-packed sand with his fist. "I took that book from her, and she's just out there in the middle of the desert. Alone. I can't leave her there."

"She's with her brother," I say. "She's with her family. It's none of your business."

"I feel bad for her." He hangs his head, pulls his knees into his chest.

"It's because you want to fuck her," I say. "If you thought she was ugly or annoying you'd have dropped this a long time ago. What if she was a guy? You haven't mentioned a word about saving her brother."

He shakes his head. "Don't use that against me. She shared something with me."

"Her pussy."

"For the millionth time, I did not fuck her," he says.

"Fine," I say. "So she gave you a beat up book. Take it, read it, and get on with your life."

"It's stupid," he says. "But I feel like there aren't going to be a lot of times in my life where I've got a chance to help someone. I feel like I could really save her. I'll be making money and--"

"Save her? With what? Are you going to adopt her? This is some real Woody Allen shit, man."

"It's stupid. I know I can't do anything. And there's no way I could get her away from Trevor or anything. But she told me that they ran away from home because their dad molested them. She doesn't trust Trevor either, and she can't get away from him."

"That's a good reason to leave home," I say. "It sucks. What can I say? But how do you know she was telling the truth. Anyone can say they were molested."

"I was--" Derrick says, he closes his eyes. "I was going to. I had my shirt off and had slipped my shorts down. It was dark so I couldn't tell if she was smiling or scared or what."

"I saw you holding your shorts up when you were running to the car."

"I didn't, though. She told me about her dad and I stopped because…. She gave me the book and said, 'Read it.' That was before Trevor showed up and shot at us. I believe her, man. She wasn't making it up."

"How do you know that?"

"I just *know*, all right," he says.

I believe him as much as I've ever believed him before, and it's not because I give a fuck about him and that girl. It's because I hear something in his voice that makes me wonder if there isn't something inside him that makes him pretend to be someone else, that maybe he's been pretending all this time too, something I couldn't see because I was blinded by my own act.

"Remember that time I called you a faggot," I say. "My dad knocked us both on our asses and told us, 'Friends don't do this shit.' We didn't talk for a week after that."

His knuckles pop as he squeezes his fists. "Why?"

"I'm sorry," I say. "I was pissed off about the game."

"I've been over that for a long time." He clears his throat, grabs a clod and tosses it at the Joshua tree beside the rabbit's grave. The mound where the rabbit had been buried is gone. Unless it was a rodent Jesus, that means something dug it up, and carried it away.

"I'm sure," I say. "But I never apologized. I just wanted to before you took off for good."

"Those were just words." He stands. "It's stupid of me to want to go see her again, isn't it? She wouldn't come with me, and I couldn't get her a ticket to West Virginia, anyway. I hate that there's this burning in my stomach that won't tell me if it's my dick talking or my heart. Do you know what it's like to hate yourself because you feel like you've got some kind of sickness gnawing at your insides. I feel like I can't trust myself to know when I have good intentions."

"Blame your dick," I say. "Everyone else does."

"I don't love that girl," he says. "I understand why things are so hard for her. But I can't love her, can I? I don't even know her. It doesn't make sense. She'll be fine without me. And even if she doesn't end up fine, it won't matter because I'll be long gone."

"That's right, man. She'll be fine."

"I'm sure you're right," he says.

"Let's go watch the rest of *Live at Pompeii*."

Back in the house, we sit on the couch, and Derrick passes out with his hands folded over his stomach. I press play and watch his chest rise and fall, a slow rhythm, the rhythm of someone sleeping well. Before long, I shut my eyes, and the last words I hear before I fall asleep are about an albatross, echoes, and labyrinths drowning beneath the waves.

CHAPTER 8

Liam and Derrick arguing in the kitchen wakes me. The TV's hissing to let me know that I've missed the end of *Live at Pompeii* for the millionth time. The clock ticks, and I glance to see it's a little bit after three in the morning.

Derrick says, "I thought we were fucked."

Liam smiles and says, "You would have been if Sean hit the gas the way I told him to."

"Whatever." Derrick walks over to the couch.

"For real," Liam says. "I'd have had no problem ditching you. You're bailing on us. Why shouldn't we bail on you?"

Derrick sits. "Okay, man."

"Think it's no big deal all you want," Liam says. "You think *we're* nothing. That's fucked up."

"I never said you were nothing," Derrick says. "I said I need to get the fuck out of here."

"It's not here that you're leaving," Liam says. "Get it? Who gives a shit that it's here? You're going to go somewhere else and find out that you left us. Here is always here, man. *We* won't be here forever. That's the thing that we've been trying to tell you."

"Jesus Christ." Derrick leans forward. "Are you on your period?"

"Maybe I should ditch *you* both," I say.

"This is retarded." Liam says. "I can't believe you don't agree with me, Sean." He stomps down the hall, and I can hear him say, "Unbelievable," and then the toilet seat clunks.

All I can think about all of this is *good*. I'm still riding high after all that escaping, stolen freedom. No part of me considered leaving Derrick back there, and I can't believe Liam would tell Derrick that he'd tried to talk me into it. I'm not ditching either of them. They have to leave me; that's the only way it'll work.

Derrick says, "That was crazy."

"See what you're gonna be missing out on." I grab the remote and switch the input to TV and then flip over to ESPN. A pitcher whips it high and inside and the batter sends the ball over the left field wall.

The toilet flushes, and then Liam walks down the hall. He leans against the hallway corner and says, "Your mom's passed out in the bathtub, man. I didn't see her in there before I started pissing. I wouldn't have gone in if I knew she was in there. Sorry."

"What?"

"She's sitting in the tub behind the curtain."

"Is she breathing?"

"Why wouldn't she be?"

I drop the remote and stomp past Liam and on into the bathroom. "Mom." I belt it out like it's some kind of order, rip the curtain back to reach her. Drool has hardened into the corners of her mouth; her bluish lips make the hairs on my arms stand. I snatch her by the hair and turn her face toward mine. "Are you all right?" I let go of her head, and her chin bobs down into the softness of her white robe. The robe bottom is soaked in piss and shit. An empty bottle of Absolut lies on its side near her blue feet: the bottle that was gone, one of the bottles I'd bought for Derrick and Liam when I was killing time, trying to calm down before I drove away from Melissa's. I never thought for a second that Mom would take it. The last time she drank was at her and Dad's seventeenth anniversary party two years ago. She had a backless orange dress on, and at ten o'clock she tripped on the living room carpet and scraped her knees. Blood seeped from the tiny cuts and Dad had to drag her into the shower and cool her off because she was bawling. All those people I didn't know stared at me like I was supposed to do something. I told them there was plenty of beer in the fridge, and then I left; that was the last anniversary party my parents ever had.

Her pale forehead is covered in cold, wet sickles of hair. I want to slap her until she wakes, until she screams at me, until she's cooking spaghetti, until Dad comes home to ask what's for dinner.

"Should we call nine-one-one?" Liam yells from the living room.

"Yes," I say.

I grab the empty vodka bottle and stand. Mom's riding this tub into hell or heaven or wherever a doped up depressed woman earns a place, and there isn't anything I can do to stop it now.

A hand squeezes my shoulder; it's Derrick. His blue eyes are opened wide and he says, "What do we do?"

"Nothing," I say. "She's dead. What can we do?"

He says, "Well--"

If there was a better thing to say at a time like this, I don't know why I would expect it to come from Derrick. Mom's stringy hair is filthy, and I feel like a weaker person would flip out and turn on the shower, try and wash her or maybe pick her body up and run out to the desert and bury her where the rabbit's corpse was unearthed. Maybe I should start crying and smashing things. Maybe I'm supposed to shove my face into Derrick's chest and beg him to wrap me in his arms and pat my back and tell me that everything's going to be fine. "It's nothing," I say. "She was dead a long time ago."

"No." Derrick shakes his head. "This is something."

"Let go of me." I knock his arm away. My shoulder feels cold, and I wish he'd put his hand back on me. But I shove him out of my way, head to the living room and crash through the screen door.

The Mustang's paint is dulled from all the dust and dirt it's collected over the past few days, and the only thing I can think to do is throw this empty bottle at the windshield. It feels like someone else is throwing it. That's okay. I want to be someone else right now and forever because, if I was, then I would never have to deal with any of this. I could just stand by and watch it happen: like Derrick and Liam get to watch me and feel awkward because they don't know what to do when something this serious happens. It's not their fault. They're just visiting. I am a local. I always will be, and I can never be someone other than myself.

The bottle crashes into the windshield. Glass spiderwebs and bottle-shards slide into the space between the hood and the windshield, skate over the red metal and trickle to the pavement.

Derrick and Liam stand on the lawn, staring at me. They don't say anything, and I don't expect them to. They stand there, gnashing their teeth with sullen faces like we're at a funeral for a person none of us knew. And this is so goddamned funny to me because it's just the first time I'll have to do this. I dig and dig for feelings for a woman who was dead and gone long before today, but the search for an emotion that suits the moment gets sidetracked by practical questions. How long will it take for the ambulance to get here?

Will they be glad she died in the tub? What will Dad say when he gets home? *I remember when my mom died. She's in a better place.* Or maybe he won't come back at all. Maybe this is his cue to get the fuck out of here and cut his losses. It'll be fine. I can take care of myself the same way I have for so long.

"Should we bail?" Liam asks. "I mean, should we go?"

Of course we shouldn't. We should wait right here for the guys to show up so they can see how pathetic we all are, and then they can blame our pathetic-ness on the corpse in the bathtub. *She was drugged up all the time. It's no wonder he's such a horrible person. It's no wonder his car has a smashed windshield and bullet holes in the trunk. Of course he was dragging a port-o-potty on the freeway. Wouldn't you have done the same thing?*

"Sean," Derrick says. "We've been drinking, and you smashed your windshield. There's those bullet holes in the trunk."

"She did it to herself," I say. "That's that."

"What if they recognize the car?" Liam asks. "The nylon rope is still on the trunk."

"Look, you pussies," I say. "My mom just died. I'm not leaving. Take the car and head off somewhere if you want, but I'm not letting her sit in the bathtub alone so some strangers can come drag her off while I'm away."

"You're right," Derrick says. "If we leave, they'll think we ran because we did something."

"Holy shit," I say. "I'm staying because I belong here. Not because I'm afraid of what they'll think or because of what might happen. Nothing is going to happen that hasn't happened already." There still are no lights or sirens.

Liam says. "What'll we tell them?"

I say, "She's dead. That's all there is to say."

Liam says, "I'm sorry, man. I just don't know what to say right now."

"Shouldn't you call your dad?" Derrick asks.

"No." There's no reason to call my dad because he would handle this worse than we are. It might not bother him at all, and that's the least human way to react; I don't want to listen to him try and pretend to care. He married mom under false pretenses. He told her he was a lot of things and none of what he told her was true. He was just a jackass who needed to get away from a life that was going to break him. Dad had stupid heroes that died young and, for whatever reason, those deaths gave him some kind of inspiration. He dragged mom along to this place in the middle of the desert, and she started getting headaches, because of boredom or because of some real problem, I'll never know. I'm getting a headache right now just thinking about all the people in my family I've never met that might start calling and sending cards and flowers and all kinds of bullshit that I'll throw away because I'm one death away from being my own family. A family that can be good. A family that I will care about. One that might care about me.

"It'll be okay," Derrick says.

Sometime soon after that I hear the sirens. I can almost feel the heat of the lights as they blast through the darkness, one revolution at a time. Here comes the last ride, Mom. "She died in the bath tub," I say to whoever's listening. It makes me laugh. The ambulance pulls up behind the Mustang, and a couple guys hop out. They crack open the back doors, and I close my eyes. Words and sounds, wheels screeching over the pavement, shoes smacking toward the house, doors opening, closing. It won't be long. Soon they'll all be gone, and then everything and everyone will be just fine.

CHAPTER 9

July 6th, 2000

I sit at a paper-littered desk, styrofoam cup of cold coffee in front of me. I don't drink coffee, but I'm sure I look like hell, and the officer across from me was only trying to help when he offered to get the coffee for me. I drank a few sips to make it look like I haven't given up. Men and women are seated at other desks around the room, some crying and some so angry that they slam their fists on desktops and tug at their own hair. The cops that sit across from those men and women have short hair and the bushiness of the men's mustaches seems to exist in direct proportion to the size of their guts. The cop sitting across from me asks me questions and tells me, "Sorry, son." He asks if I'm hungry, and I watch cop faces across the room nod at familiar cop faces and then turn toward me and give me looks of compassion. It's so fake that I want to scream, but I know there's a place for everything, and this isn't a time and place for screaming. This is a place for nothing. So that's what I give them.

"Was your mom an alcoholic?"

"No."

"Was your mom addicted to pain medication?"

"I don't know."

"Where is your father?"

"I don't know."

"She's never overdosed on pills before?"

"Not that I know of," I say.

"Where did she get the pills?"

"From the doctor." As far as I know, that's all that matters. Because she got the medication from a doctor, this is a tragedy. She's not just another drain on the economy like all those fiends that litter the streets, not like Derrick, Liam, and me. That poor, poor woman, they'll say. She never got the help she needed.

"What about her headaches?" The cop with a thick brown mustache leans over his desk, looks up at me and cocks an eyebrow.

"What about them?"

"Your mother had migraines. Was she feeling especially bad lately?"

"No," I say. "She cooked spaghetti a couple nights ago."

He nods and scratches something on a piece of paper. "How often does she cook?"

"It had been a year or so."

"Are you okay?" he asks.

"What?"

"How are you handling this?"

I could tell him that I was fine, that I'd lost her forever ago, or I could tell him that I'd be doing a lot better if I could get the fuck out of here, so that I could take Derrick to the airport later. Tell him that once Derrick's gone, I'll be perfect, won't lose another loved one again until Liam takes off. "I'm just really tired," I say. "It's been a long few days already, and then this happens, and I have to take someone to the airport this afternoon."

"Can't you get someone else to do that?"

"There's no one else."

The cop licks his lips and says, "All right, son. We've kept you here long enough." He stands and extends his hand. "We're still trying to get ahold of your father to let him know what's happened. We called you a cab."

I shake his hand and feel the sweat on his palm. His nostrils flare when he breathes and a couple stray whiskers poke out through the splotchy skin beneath his Adam's apple. He says. "If there's anything we can do to help, please let us know."

I let go of his hand. "I appreciate you saying that." He can't help everyone. Who can? It doesn't matter that Mom is dead and Dad might stay gone forever. It doesn't matter that I'm living a fucking lie, being someone who never existed because I don't want to kill the possibility of a life with Derrick that there's no way I'll ever have. This man's promise is a lie; I am a lie. I want to say that I don't care. I want to say that knowing the truth makes it easier for me to deal with how much it all hurts. I want to say so many things that I don't have the strength to move my tongue.

THE RIDE HOME is long and silent. The cabbie doesn't try to make small talk, and I'd thank him for that if it wouldn't interrupt the silence. I roll my window down and stick my head out, let the wind smack my face hard. Semis and sedans and a few sports cars rumble down the freeway. The sunlight that's spilling over the horizon makes me feel like this is just the beginning for some people, for most people. For me it's late and Derrick and Liam won't be at my house when I get there. I hope Dad won't be there. What would be the point now? I don't want him to come home or to tell me he's sorry about any of it. I want him to stay gone: wherever he's run off to.

When the cab pulls into the driveway, I see Melissa sitting on the concrete step of the shadowy front porch: short hair, white tank top, pregnant belly. Nothing is stopping me from telling the cabbie to back up and drive the hell away from this except that I don't know where else I'd go. The Mustang sits along the curb right where I'd parked it before I walked into the house to find my mom dead. Bullet holes still in the trunk, dusty, bird shit spackled red paint, dents in the hood. It's not pretty anymore, but I can't get Derrick to the airport without it. I can't live out here without it.

Melissa looks up, and the shadows around her eyes are a lot wider than they should be. There's the girl I dated for so long, the girl who fucked around on me when I stopped fucking her, the girl who left me and told me she never wanted to see me again. She's on my front porch with black eyes and a baby inside her, and there's something growing in my stomach that makes me feel sorry for her even though she did it to herself.

I kick the cab door open, hop out, say, "Thanks for the ride," and then slam the door behind me. The cab backs out of the driveway, and I jog over to Melissa. "What happened?" I try to grab her chin, but she looks away.

"I'm not here for sympathy."

"Then what are you here for?"

"I heard about your mom."

I step back from her. "Who told you?"

"My mom," she says.

"Your mom doesn't give a fuck about me or my mom. Thanks

for the condolences, though," I say. "Can you get off my porch, now? I'd like to get inside and go to bed for a couple hours. I need to drive Derrick to the airport later."

"Damn it," she stands and steps aside. "I'm really sorry, Sean. Can you not see that?"

I pull the screen door open, slide my key into the lock and turn it. "Sure," I say. Then I shoulder my way into the living room. "Come in. Unless you're gonna walk back to Palmdale."

There's a half-empty Coors Light on the coffee table, so I grab it and sit on the couch. Melissa sits next to me. The TV holds our reflections; it looks pretty damn perfect: a beat-up pregnant girl and her ex-boyfriend drinking at seven in the morning. I hold the can up to her and say, "Here's to bastard babies."

"Do you take lessons on being an asshole?" She breathes deep. "I'm sorry. I know your mom just died. I'm sorry."

That's funny, makes me smile a little. "So Jovo beat you up?"

"His brother."

"Did he catch you fucking the mailman or some other random guy in a uniform?"

She scratches the back of her neck and some congealed blood behind her ear flakes off. The red-black crust and her blonde hair looks like art, like a painting that eats, sleeps, and breathes.

"He found out Jovo isn't the father."

"How did he figure that out?"

"I'm not sure."

"I don't believe you," I say.

She sighs. "Don't believe me, then. He still beat me up." She points to her eyes, the purple-black swelling beneath them. "This is real no matter what the reason is."

I finish the warm beer and throw the empty can at the TV. "Your life is a soap opera. The only way it can be this bad all the time is if you want it to be this bad all the time." I lean back into the couch. "Who's the father?"

"Derrick," she says. "Please don't hit me."

"Why the fuck would you even say that?"

She shakes her head. "I don't know."

"Just tell me the goddamn story, Melissa."

"I didn't know what to do. Derrick wouldn't have helped me with the baby. He's a baby himself. But Jovo loved me, and it was stupid for me to do it, and I'm sorry that I did it to him, and that I cheated on you. I don't know where else to go."

And there I am. That's my reflection in the TV, laughing. My mouth is opened as wide as it goes, my fists slam onto the couch cushions over and over, and I can't help but feeling that it would make a lot more sense if I was floating over my shoulder, watching all this from a better seat.

She says, "I wish I never cheated."

I say, "I forgive you."

She says, "I wish I never lied."

I say, "I forgive you."

She says, "I'm so sorry about your mother."

I say, "I can deal with that. What's important now is you and the baby. You deserve better than this. I'm so sorry for you that I can barely stand it. But you did this to yourself."

"I don't have anyone else. My mom called me a whore and--"

"Get out."

"Please," she says. Her hand lands on my thigh, and it feels good, just the warmth of a hand, the touch of someone who needs me. It's warm the way I need it, and my neck loosens up. I know if I could, I'd start crying. "Please give me another chance."

We look so ridiculous. She's leaned toward me, really getting into her role. The other side of her face is the good side, the less bruised side, and that's what I see on the screen. This side has the four freckles in the corner of her nostril that so often look like a cluster of pimples from just a short distance away. This side has the breast with a big birth mark beneath the nipple that makes it look deformed. This is the side with all the imperfections, and I've seen them all. I know all the things about her that are wrong, and maybe that's worth more than I ever thought it would be. She can't surprise me anymore, and maybe that's all I need.

"I don't have anything left to give you," I say. "There's nothing I can do to make things easier on you, and I don't want to deal with Jovo and his brothers when they come looking for you later. Maybe if Derrick and Liam were sticking around, it would be different.

Then I'd have friends here to back me up. But I don't. You wanted Jovo and his brothers. That's a world you wanted to get into, and you got into it. You've got to deal with this on your own."

"No." She shakes her head. "Jovo and his brothers won't come here. They just wanted me gone, and I am. I need you to help take care of the baby. I thought Jovo was the best man I'd ever met, and that's why I lied to him." She rests her head on my lap. "But you're a better man. You're better for me. You know you are."

I rake some of the clotted blood out of her hair and pat her head. "You're so bad for me, Melissa." I've never been more sure of anything in my life. "There's nothing about you that's good for me." I run my fingers through her grimy hair, push a few strands over her bloody ear to cover it. "This will never last."

"Derrick's leaving now." She grabs my hand and locks her fingers in mine. "You'll stay. And he'll be gone. It'll be like the way it was supposed to be before he came back. You'll stay. And I'll stay with you, and we'll have a family out here in the middle of the desert away from everyone, and everything will be fine."

"Not for us." I squeeze her hand. "I can't trust you. And I might not even have a job anymore. They're going to take the house, the car."

"They won't take the house," she says. "You won't lose your job. You'll keep the car. It'll all be fine. I promise."

There is nothing more that I could ever want than to just pick up and leave, but I can't get away no matter how hard I try.

Melissa's having Derrick's baby. Why would she tell me it was Derrick's? If she was lying to keep me, wouldn't she say it was mine. That would make more sense. Or is this just another one of her sick games. "Why don't you ask Derrick to raise the baby? It's his kid. He can send for you and the unborn bastard when he gets stationed somewhere. You can both live a nice enlisted life. It'll be like your childhood except you'll be the shitty mother, and he can be the terrible father."

"I can't depend on him." She shakes her head. "He told me to get an abortion."

"You already talked to him about it?"

She nods. "I told him I got the abortion."

"And then you come to me and ask me to help raise the kid. Are you insane?"

"I can't kill a baby," she says. "It feels wrong."

"It *feels* wrong. For fuck's sake," I say. "People kill babies all the time. You wouldn't have to do anything. Go to the clinic. Hand them the money. Problem solved. Then you can go to college. Do something with your life. Anything. You don't need me."

She lets go of my hand and stands, rubs the back of her neck. On the TV her head is cut off. She's just a pregnant belly, cargo pants, ankles, and open toed flats. "I don't want to go to school anymore. I want to be a mother. I can be a good one. But I need help. Your help. This isn't perfect, but we can make this work."

"I don't want to live the rest of my life 'making it work', Mel. I want it to work on its own."

She heads for the door, and I feel everything slipping away from me: Derrick, Melissa, the wall I'd constructed that made me feel invincible is crumbling. Derrick and Melissa smashed through that wall and left me here on the couch, staring at myself as myself stares right back at me. She's right. I'll keep telling myself that. We can make this work. I will make this work.

"Mel," I say. "Stop."

She stops and turns, blackened green eyes full of tears that slide down her puffy cheeks. It's all an act. The tears, the walking away, the slow movements and breathing. But she's making it work. I will too. I stand, float over and grab her, squeeze her around the shoulders, feel the heat of her body, the heat of the baby, the heat of the desert that sweeps in through the open door. This isn't right or wrong; that much I know. I kiss her on the forehead, taste the dirt and sweat of a long day. Her day was as long as mine, and we'd each lived through it alone. No more days will be like that. From now on, on long days like this, we'll be together: at least at the end. It doesn't matter that I'll hate her for the rest of my life, or that I'll hate myself too. This is where I was headed all along. There was never a life with Derrick waiting for me. He's leaving; nothing can change that: not me or my love for him, not my desires, hopes, or hates. He's cutting himself loose from the desert. He won't let anything hold him here: not me, not Melissa, not even his unborn child. So I'll let him go. I'll become this man tied to this woman and a child that isn't mine.

It's not hard to be angry at Derrick for telling Melissa to have an abortion, but I forgive him. I don't want to understand why he wouldn't say anything about the pregnancy or his reasoning for telling Melissa to have an abortion to me, but I understand. He decided, and then it was over, and he kept whatever feelings he had about it to himself; his problems are his own. That was a common lesson all our fathers taught us. But it doesn't matter anymore. He's headed back to West Virginia, and then on to basic training, and then on to wherever the Air Force sends him. I won't have to spend any more time worrying about his bullshit. Our friendship, our life together, is over the minute he walks into the airport.

LAX ISN'T SUCH a long drive, but it feels like forever with Derrick in the passenger seat. He's not saying a word, just chewing gum with his mouth open. I roll the windows down because I can't handle the silence. The bursts of wind help me keep my mind off what's waiting at the end of the drive. I can't keep from talking to him for long, though; this is probably the last time I'll see him. Both lenses of his sunglasses are poked out, and I figure he finally had a real fight with Liam last night. "Take those off," I say. "I'd rather remember you as a guy who didn't try so hard to look like an idiot."

"I like the way these look now. There's something sophisticated about lens-less glasses."

"Did you and Liam get in a fight?"

"Yeah," he says. "He's pissed I'm joining the Air Force. He wanted to join the Coast Guard together."

"Is that why he didn't come out to the car to say goodbye?"

He nods and says, "I busted his nose. His mom's gonna be pissed."

Cars and trucks are backed up pretty deep on the freeway and just ahead of us is a van with JESUS IS ON TIME—EVERY TIME stenciled in white letters on the back glass.

"Is there any reason for a bumper sticker like that?" Derrick kicks his shoe up on the dash board. If this was two months ago, I'd care, but the repo men will probably be by to rip the Mustang off of my driveway tomorrow morning. Scuff marks on the dash are nothing compared to the other scars on this thing. But if I can get back on with Jeff, I can have those things fixed. The engine is fine;

I can make the outside shine the way it did before Derrick came back, and before I drove the car into the ground. All it'll take is soap, Bondo, and a little paint; that and the money to buy it.

"It's a sticker," I say. "The reason for a sticker is so it can be stuck somewhere."

"Yeah," he says, as we lurch forward and then stop again in the rubber band traffic.

"So you and Melissa are getting back together?"

"I guess, " I say. "Jovo's brother kicked the shit out of her. And she's pregnant."

Derrick laughs. "Again? Can she not figure out how to slide a condom over a dick or get on birth control?"

I unlatch the glove box and tear through receipts and pieces of paper, looking for something to smoke or chew: anything. The post-it with Steve's number on it is still inside. I ball it up and toss it out my window.

Derrick scoots over some, like he's afraid I'll touch him. And I should have known that this was as close as we'd ever get again because he could never feel the same way about me as I feel about him. All I've got left is this chance to hold on to the piece of him growing in Melissa's belly and try not to fuck up the way all our parents did. Derrick has to leave, should have stayed gone the first time. I could've just let it happen if I'd only been smart enough to tell myself I didn't care about him over and over until that became the truth.

There are no clouds in the sky and the light blue might go on forever if it wasn't slashed at by jagged mountains on the horizon.

"Guess I smoked it all," I say.

"So Jovo got her pregnant?" Derrick asks.

"That's what she said."

"That's fucked up that he kicked her out then," he says. "No one ever wants to take responsibility for anything."

"Melissa can be a bitch sometimes."

"And you're right there to save the day again." Derrick slides the glasses off and turns to look at me. His right eye's swollen, a small cut in the eyelid is sealed shut by a red-black scab. "If you ask me, it's a fucking mistake. She's gonna hurt you again. There'll always be another Jovo. Tell her to get an abortion and move on."

"I can tell her," I say. "That doesn't mean she'll do it."

"It's a mistake, man."

"I'm sure you think it's a mistake. I can't afford a baby. It's stupid to raise it with a woman who'll probably run off after it's born. But if it is a mistake, at least it's a mistake that I understood when I walked into it. And in case you forgot, you fucked her while she was dating me. So half the reason she cheated on me, at least one time, is you."

"I didn't forget it, man." He looks back at the road.

What would it do to him if I told him the kid was his? Would that keep him here? Maybe he would say fuck it and get some shitty job and try to convince Melissa to let him be a part of the baby's life. Maybe we could all live together in our little house in the desert. I could prove to him how much I cared for him by raising his child and letting Derrick do all the things he needed to do to be happy. But I can't keep him here. I can't make him a prisoner. I laugh and Derrick smiles.

He says. "If any one of us should be a father, it's you. The kid's lucky Jovo booted Melissa out."

"Yeah," I say. "You ever finish the book that girl gave you?"

"I read it."

"Well?"

"What can I say?" He unzips his backpack and rummages through his clothes and then pulls the book out. "I can see why that girl would cry about it. It's sad." He looks at the book and then looks at me. "You want it?"

I shake my head. "I don't."

"Maybe you'll change your mind." He tosses the book into the back seat and zips his bag shut. "Do you ever feel bad about all the shit we've done?"

"Like what?"

"I don't know," he says.

"Leaving that girl in the desert?"

"Yeah," he says.

"I feel bad about a lot things, Derrick. But I'd rather have these memories than none at all."

Derrick smirks. "Too bad nothing that we did worth remembering adds up to something to be proud of."

"Maybe we're not that lucky." Just lucky enough for a life that might be made up of me and Melissa and Derrick's kid. A little Derrick I can play with and watch grow up while Melissa fucks around on me.

"Everything would have been so much easier if we'd played ball in college," Derrick says. "We could have had a chance at avoiding all this bullshit. The military. Wiring airplanes. Getting shot at in the middle of the desert by some drifter."

"Maybe you," I say. "I couldn't hit for shit. You threw those no-hitters."

"I just used what I had going for me. All those hours of throwing a ball against a brick wall in the backyard still didn't get me anywhere. All that time and practice got me was a chance to join the military and follow in my dad's footsteps. I used to tell him that I'd never be like him." He laughs. "And here I go. Couldn't even join a different branch."

"It's different," I say. "You're not like him." But he is becoming his father, and I'm becoming mine. "You'll make it out in four years. Do something you can be proud of." It's easy to hope for that kind of thing. I like imagining him successful somewhere else doing something that makes him happy. One day, when he's relaxed, not worried about anything worse than making it to his kid's game or a PTA meeting, he might look back at some of this and smile because he was here and felt the pain, the fear, and the happiness. He might smile and remember me, this ride, our friendship.

Traffic breaks up, and we whip around some slow-movers; the air rushes over us fast. Neither of us talks the rest of the way to the airport. I leave the CD player off and let the wind sing, blasting rough through the open windows, slapping our faces and hair. Before long we've passed the giant white LAX sign and the advertisement for LIVE! NUDES NUDES! NUDES!, and not even that billboard causes us to break the silence. There's no reason for me to waste time parking. Derrick only has a backpack with some underwear, socks and small shit, so I park at the drive-up for domestic departures, and say, "Next time you get on a plane you'll be headed to basic. And then, who the fuck knows where you'll wind up."

I notice men and women in dress blues hefting bags onto carts and pushing them through the open sliding-glass doors. A woman in a flight suit bounces a curly haired baby on her hip and pinches its nose. The woman's flight cap looks ridiculous. "I bet you can't wait to wear one of those vagina hats."

"Guess I'll always have pussy on the brain, yuck yuck." Derrick slaps his thigh. "I wish you'd come, man. There's nothing here worth sticking around for."

"Maybe not," I tell him. "Try not to get yourself killed. I know you think it'll be all paperwork and riding it out on your ass. But things change."

He laughs. "It's the fucking Chair Force." He slides his broken glasses back onto his nose and throws his backpack over his left shoulder. "There's nothing to be afraid of. I'll keep my head down and won't volunteer for anything. Before I know it, my time will be up. Your dad made it twenty years without going to war. I only have to make it four. I'm not doing some crazy job like my dad did. I'll be fine."

"Good luck anyway. Even if you don't need it."

"Good luck with Melissa." He smiles, turns, and walks away. Becomes nothing but wide shoulders that stretch wider and wider with every step he takes. I close my eyes and try to imagine getting on that plane with him and that we're headed somewhere together. Us going to some place where none of the things that stand between us matter, none of the expectations, or the wants of others. But I can't picture that place because there is no place like that. No matter how I imagine it, it's always wrong because I am not the me I've shown him, and he is not the him I want him to be. We're just two guys who'll never be together the way we might have been if the world was just as I wanted or if the world was just as he wanted. This world that I'm a part of doesn't care what only I want or what only he wants, and that's why now, back home, Melissa sits on my couch growing the last piece of Derrick I'll ever touch.

When my family finally disappears, I'll build a new one, a better one. That's the only choice I have. Melissa will fuck around on me because I won't be able to give her what she needs. But at least I'll have the baby. It will be a reason to try harder, to do something more than all this nothing I've done for so long. There's still a chance that Jeff will take me back on; he never called to tell me I was fired, and all I need to do is show up and tell him I'm sorry that I missed so many days. I'll tell him Melissa and the baby need me. That the house and the Mustang won't pay for themselves. I'll say I'm sorry because I know it's not his fault, that it is my fault because I chose all of this. But no matter who I pretend to be, I can't change the fact that people depend on me now.

I open my eyes, and Derrick is gone. His absence is the best thing I've seen in a long time. There are faces all around me, and all they'll ever know of me is what I show them. That's what matters. Here I am. This is who I'll be for as long as I can manage to make it real: one choice and one day at a time.

The End

More Thanks

Additional gratitude is due to every single person not yet mentioned who has read one of my essays or stories, and, of course, to every one who's bought one of my books. And I would be a terrible person if I didn't specifically thank Nelle Smith for her constant support and promotion on social media and by word of mouth; you're the best sister-in-law a guy could have. Kendra DeStefano, thank you so much for all the help with facebook promotion. You sure didn't have to do that, and I won't forget it. Thank you so much for being so generous without asking for anything in return. I am so blessed to have met such a large number of kind, generous people in my life. I may write the words, but there's much more to being a writer than typing. Getting a book into readers' hands takes a lot of voices; thank you all for caring enough to lend me yours.

To see more of Eric Smallwood's art, or to contact him about cover design, book trailers, and more, please visit:

www.ericsmallwood.com

photo credit: Kristine Jennings

Brandon Davis Jennings is a USAF Operation Iraqi Freedom veteran from West Virginia and the winner of mulitple wrtting awards, including: *The Iron Horse Literary Review* Single Author Chapbook Competition, *Passages North*'s Thomas J. Hrushka Prize for Nonfiction, and both his Kindle Singles (*Waiting for the Enemy* and *Battle Rattle*) are best-selling fiction Kindle Singles. To contact Brandon or to learn more about him and his work, please visit: www.brandondavisjennings.com

You can read and write reviews of Brandon's work on Amazon.com or Goodreads. Follow him on amazon.com and @brandonsbass on Twitter.

www.ingramcontent.com/pod-product-compliance
Lightning Source LLC
Chambersburg PA
CBHW060918250626
47159CB00008B/3056

* 9 7 8 0 6 9 2 7 1 7 1 0 3 *